Talcott Parsons and the social image of man

International Library of Sociology

Founded by Karl Mannheim

Editor: John Rex, University of Warwick

Arbor Scientiae
Arbor Vitae

A catalogue of the books available in the **International Library of Sociology**, and new books in preparation for the Library, will be found at the end of this volume.

Talcott Parsons and the social image of man

Ken Menzies
Department of Sociology and Anthropology,
University of Guelph

Routledge & Kegan Paul
London, Henley and Boston

First published in 1976
by Routledge & Kegan Paul Ltd
39 Store Street,
London WC1E 7DD;
Broadway House,
Newtown Road,
Henley-on-Thames,
Oxon RG9 1EN and
9 Park Street,
Boston, Mass. 02108, USA
Manuscript typed by Betty R Ozzard
Printed and bound in Great Britain by
Morrison & Gibb Ltd, London and Edinburgh

ISBN 0 7100 8369 6

Contents

Acknowledgments

First, I must thank the Canada Council which supported me for four years while doing research on Talcott Parsons (LSE, 1968-9; Essex, 1969-72). My largest intellectual debt is to Allan Bitz who has read and criticized in depth draft after draft. Derek Wilkinson and Jan Maher have provided major and helpful critiques of several chapters. Herminio Martins, now a Fellow of St Antony's, Oxford, was my PhD supervisor at Essex. I have had the benefit of his wide knowledge and perceptive suggestions then and since. John Rex, the editor of this series, was my external examiner for the PhD and his comments then have proved valuable. Other people have read drafts of various chapters, and Roy Enfield, Ernest Gellner, Martin Hollis and Ted Benton in particular gave helpful critiques. In the final stages of clarifying my ideas and getting me to say what I mean to say, Stan Barrett, Frans Schryer, Peter Sinclair and Marion Stiasny have been particularly helpful.

Acknowledgments are due to the following for permission to quote from the works shown: to Professor Max Black for a diagram from 'The Social Theories of Talcott Parsons: a Critical Examination', 1961; to Prentice-Hall, Inc., Englewood Cliffs, N.J., USA, for a quotation from Talcott Parsons, Some problems of general theory in sociology, in 'Theoretical Sociology: Perspectives and Developments', ed. John C. McKinney and Edward A. Tiryakian (c) 1970; to Macmillan Publishing Co. Inc., for material from Talcott Parsons, 'The Structure of Social Action', copyright 1949 by The Free Press of Glencoe, Talcott Parsons, 'The Social System', copyright 1951 by Talcott Parsons, Talcott Parsons, 'Working Papers in the Theory of Action', copyright 1953 by The Free Press, a Corporation; to Macmillan Publishing Co. Inc., and Routledge & Kegan Paul Ltd for material from Talcott Parsons et al., 'Family, Socialization and Interaction Process', copyright 1955 by The Free Press, a Corporation, and Talcott Parsons and Neil Smelser, 'Economy and Society', copyright 1956.

Abbreviations

Amer U	The American University
ES	Economy and Society: A Study in the Integration of Economic and Social Theory
EST	Essays in Sociological Theory (revised edition)
FSI	Family, Socialization and Interaction Process
SECP	Societies: Evolutionary and Comparative Perspectives
SMS	The System of Modern Societies
SPMS	Structure and Process in Modern Societies
SS	The Social System
SSA	The Structure of Social Action: A Study in Social Theory with Special Reference to a Group of Recent European Writers
STMA	Sociological Theory and Modern Society
TGTA	Towards a General Theory of Action
TS	Theories of Society: Foundations of Modern Sociological Theory
WP	Working Papers in the Theory of Action

Introduction

This book is my attempt to give a reading to Parsons. The test of an adequate interpretation or reading is that when the reader has finished it, he can take any book or article of Parsons and fit it into the suggested structure of Parsonian thought. In order to do this, I must trace how his ideas developed and how problems that are unresolved at one stage reappear at another. It is also necessary to focus on the structure of his basic argument, not the substantive analyses he gives, for it is in terms of the former that an interpretation of the latter can be provided.

This is a book on theory, not substantive issues. Parsons' concerns are wide ranging: the kinship structure of the United States to international politics - ancient Greece to the future of the university system in the United States. As most of his discussions are based on widely accepted sources, what commands attention is the general conceptual framework in which he looks at the material. If Parsons were simply a prolific writer whose work contained some insights as well as some errors, then he would not have attracted the attention he has. His significance comes from his attempt to provide a general theory of social activity. It is on this level of general theory that I shall tackle him.

One of the problems in doing this is that Parsons has become a symbol. In particular for conflict sociologists and radical sociologists, he has become a symbol of the type of sociology they reject. By and large, they have arrived at the position they attribute to him by looking at his position on a number of substantive issues (e.g. social stratification and the existence of a consensus in society today). Their attack on him is based primarily on their rejection of the substantive positions he takes on these issues. They place their own gloss on these positions. That is to say, they attribute to him a set of views from which they would generate these positions on substantive issues. They have on the whole, assessed him from outside, rather than finding out why he takes the positions he does. They do not usually focus on those features of his theory he sees as central like the functional dimensions (FDs) and pattern variables (PVs). Moreover the consensus assumption is rejected without asking what role it plays in the theory. My approach to Parsons will be from a different vantage point. I am concerned with the internal coherence of his theoretical ideas. I will make arguments of the form: Given that Parsons wishes to maintain this position, can he also maintain this other position? If not, then what changes have to be made or can be made in his ideas?

One of the central concerns of this book is to present a 'cleared-up' version of Parsons' main theoretical ideas. His style is notoriously difficult to follow, and even he admits that there has been 'concern over the years with the difficulty of simply reading my work intelligibly' (Amer U, p.vii). My initial concern is to clarify Parsons' ideas to the best of my ability. I have said 'ideas' rather than 'theory' for one of the central contentions of this book is that Parsons has two different and incompatible theoretical frameworks running throughout his work-action theory and systems theory or structural functionalism. If this is the case, then a clear presentation of his ideas, sorting the two approaches out from each other, is a necessary first step to any assessment of his work. This book aims to clarify Parsons' ideas to the point where an assessment is possible, and make a start on giving such an assessment.

In order to help present Parsons' ideas clearly, this book will start with a first chapter on the philosophy of science. This will make explicit the way I am selecting and relating materials from Parsons. Many philosophies of science present a rigid picture of the scientific enterprise. Theories are seen as made up of very precise statements with fixed interrelations. Such a view tends to be a strait-jacket when one tries to come to grips with the somewhat amorphous nature of theory. What I want to do is develop a perspective that allows me to come to grips with the amorphous nature of theory without seeing theory as wishy-washy. In order that what I am doing is not seen as some sort of special pleading for sociology, I have used a fair number of natural science examples in this chapter.

Parsons claims that the foundation of all his work is the 'voluntaristic theory of action'. In his first book,

'The Structure of Social Action', he attempts to show that Marshall, Pareto, Durkheim and Weber all converged towards a synthesis of positivism and idealism, which he sees as voluntarism. In my second chapter, I shall argue that Parsons does not show how positivism and idealism can be reconciled. Instead of reading the book as Parsons suggests, as working towards a synthesis of positivism and idealism, I shall argue that the most comprehensible interpretation of it is as an attack on the utilitarian concept of the individual - rational, alone, and separate from society. SSA's central problematic is this account of man in general and the classical economists' account of the rise of capitalism in particular. Parsons' claim to have reconciled positivism and idealism is not, however, irrelevant. His failure to come to grips adequately with these types of positions leads to subsequent theorizing in both traditions. If this contention is correct then it would be possible to go through the rest of Parsons' work pointing to where a problem is tackled in an idealist way and where it is tackled in a positivistic way and showing that they are incompatible. Instead of doing this, which I feel would not lead to a great deal of insight, I have separated his two theories out and presented them separately.

Chapters 3 to 7 deal with Parsons' action theory. This defines its concepts in terms of the meaning of an action to an actor. Chapters 3 and 4 trace the development of this approach from a partially social to a fully social image of man. By a fully social image of man I mean an image of man that allows no room for the conception of an individual separate from social process. Chapter 5 discusses the major categories Parsons uses to discuss the patterning of meaning in society - the PVs and FDs. The relationships Parsons gives among the PVs and FDs and his analysis of function differentiation provide the basis of action theory laws, I shall argue. The next chapter looks at how man becomes social - the socialization process. The final chapter about Parsons' action theory argues that he has solved the problem of order too well - he has difficulty accounting for conflict, social change and deviance. The major theoretical problem for his action theory I shall argue, is creativity.

Chapter 8 examines Parsons' systems theory or structural functionalism. This approach involves defining concepts positivistically. His major contributions in this framework are the FDs interpreted as a classification of the types of consequences an activity can have on the system, and his claim that systems tend to differentiate into sub-systems focused on each of these FDs.

Chapter 9 looks at some of the ways he confuses action theory and structural functionalism and how this allows him to dodge various problems. Despite the confusion however, there are interesting ideas. The final chapter draws some of the material from earlier chapters together to give an assessment of Parsons' work.

It seems desirable to make several general comments on the nature and limits of my analysis. This book is concerned with a body of ideas. Parsons has written books and articles in conjunction with several other people (notably Bales, Platt, Shils and Smelser). Trying to separate Parsons' contributions from those of his co-writers seems a fruitless task. In any case, the style of what he has written with others, and what he has written himself, is sufficiently similar (and Parsons' style is distinctive) that it seems clear that Parsons has had a major influence on what he has written with others.

The problem of combining action theory and structural functionalism is one version of the perennial problem in social science of combining objective and subjective points of view or in currently fashionable anthropological terminology of combining emic and edic analyses. My claim is that Parsons does not succeed in combining these two approaches and what is of interest is demonstrating this and what the implications are for his ideas. Whether these two approaches can be combined I am not sure. The solution, if there is one, hinges I suspect on answers to certain philosophical questions, particularly the body-mind question.

The major limitation on this book is that I wish to look at Parsons as a sociologist. Parsons feels that human activity should be analysed in terms of four separate levels or systems - the biological, personality, social and cultural. Each of these involves looking at human activity from a different point of view. The social level or system focuses on the organization or pattern of relations among actors, while the personality system has as its focus the individual. The cultural system focuses on that which is shared and symbolic (e.g. beliefs, values) while the biological level, which Parsons adds in his later work, focuses on the individual's organism. The biological, personality, social and cultural provide four different perspectives from which human activity can be viewed. Each of these is independent - it cannot be reduced to one of the others - yet interdependent, what goes on at one level influences what goes on at other levels. Except for parts of chapter 6, dealing with Parsons' approach to the personality system, this book is about the social level. Basically I have restricted myself in this way because of limitations in my own knowledge.

In claiming to provide an interpretation of Parsons I am not saying that my analysis fits all the data - the data being the writings of Parsons. The sheer volume of his writings and the time span over which he has written, make it almost inevitable that he contradicts himself in minor ways and makes mistakes. What I have aimed for is a clear statement of the significant strands of his thought. There seem to be four major ways of attacking my interpretation - by criticizing the framework for analysis presented in the first chapter; by showing that I have not stuck to it; by pointing to a significant strand in Parsons' work that I have omitted; or finally by demonstrating that I am muddled.

1 The framework for analysing Parsons

The current image of science is one of men in laboratories conducting experiments, not one of men in offices wielding pens. Philosophers of science in particular paint a picture of science that leaves no real place for the thinker in his armchair. Sociologists often have accepted the philosopher's view of scientific activity as being that of men in white coats. In attempting to come to grips with Parsons, it is essential to have a view of science that gives a place to somebody who describes himself in the dedication of one of his books (SS) as 'an incurable theorist'.

Analysis of a sociologist's writings must involve implicitly or explicitly a view of the philosophy of science as one must select, order and criticize. Frequently this is done on the basis of an implicit view of how one should go about analysing a work. This seems dangerous, as the deficiencies of the analysis may lie not in the person's ability to analyse, but in the way he goes about doing it. Some examples may make this clearer. Should one focus on the person's values and state the political implications of his position as Foss (1963) does, or do a sociology of sociology as Gouldner (1971) (1) does? What would count as setting out and criticizing a theory? Should one, as Black (1964) and Dahrendorf (1966, ch.5) do, set out the premises from which (they claim) the whole position can be generated? Alternatively should one start from the key facts the person accepts or discovers? This range of possibilities indicates that a choice exists as to how to analyse Parsons and that the approach taken will affect what is treated as important in his work.

If I felt that any major school in the philosophy of science provided a satisfactory framework for analysing sociological ideas, then I would briefly elaborate this school's position and defend it against major criticisms. However the major philosophies of science have accepted a view of science that leaves no real place for the theorist. They have certain fundamental problems in them which come from the use of the analytic-synthetic distinction. An attempt will be made in this chapter to lay the groundwork of an approach to analysing man's ideas about the world that does not rest on this distinction. While I shall use this as the framework for discussing Parsons, this chapter is not intended as special pleading for a framework of analysis suited to Parsons in particular and sociology in general. Philosophers of science have accepted too positivistic a view of the scientific enterprise. To analyse Parsons or anybody else satisfactorily, it seems necessary to break out of the limits the philosophers' world view imposes and see how the investigation of the world is a more flexible undertaking.

THE ANALYTIC-SYNTHETIC DISTINCTION

The framework of much of present epistemology, (2) philosophy of science, and modern Anglo-American linguistic philosophy is the analytic-synthetic distinction. It can be traced back to Aristotle's conception of logic. As a prelude to breaking out of this approach, I shall look at how it leads men to see science and some of the problems this involves. For this purpose Kant provides a convenient starting point. He defines analytic and synthetic statements thus (1966, p.7):

> Either the predicate B belongs to the subject A as something contained (though covertly) in the concept A; or B lies outside the sphere of the concept A, though somehow connected with it. In the former case I call the judgment analytical, in the latter synthetical. Analytical judgments (affirmative) are therefore those in which the connection of the predicate with the subject is conceived through identity, while others in which that connection is conceived without identity, may be called synthetical. (3)

Kant's other important distinction is between 'a priori' and the 'a posteriori'. (4) For Kant all 'a priori' propositions were characterized by 'necessity' and 'strict universality' (p.3). If we are to have any secure knowledge, it must be 'a priori', Kant argues, and the basic question for Kant was, 'How are synthetic judgments "a priori" possible?' (p.13). For the world to be intelligible men must accept certain principles that order their experience. (5) These synthetic 'a priori' truths make the world comprehensible. What Kant appears to have overlooked (6) is that men do not always find the world intelligible. Often men find that their frameworks fail to order the world in a satisfactory (7) way. The implication of this is that either the principles that men have for ordering their experience may be true or false, or truth and falsity are not applicable to such principles. This will provide one of my starting points.

Since Kant's death in 1804, several of the assertions he claimed to be synthetic 'a priori' truths have been contradicted by scientific developments. (8) Believing that there can be no grounds for the truth of such assertions, many philosophers now reject their existence. Schlick (9) is typical of many in saying (1949, p.281):

> propositions are either synthetic 'a posteriori' or tautologous; synthetic 'a priori' propositions seem to it [Schlick's position] to be a logical impossibility.

Going back to the definition of 'synthetic' given by Kant it can be seen to be defined as a residual category. Most philosophers have, however, equated synthetic assertions defined residually (all nonanalytic ones) with a positively defined category of 'empirical'. (10) Having satisfied themselves that there are no grounds for the truth of synthetic 'a priori' truths, they have concluded that all synthetic assertions are 'a posteriori' and empirical. One assumption in this whole line of reasoning is that no assertion (except for analytic ones) that is not directly related to facts, is capable of playing any part in men's understanding of the world. Stated another way, this premise is that all assertions that form a legitimate part of men's knowledge are definitions or propositions that can be in some way assigned a truth value in terms of the facts. (11) If one accepts this (and I shall not), then the equation of synthetic with empirical seems more reasonable. By focusing on types of truths, Kant formulated the question in such a way as to preclude the consideration that there might be synthetic 'a priori' assertions which it does not make sense to call true or false (in the way these terms are understood by positivists) but which nevertheless have a part to play in our understanding of the world.

The type of position just discussed is positivistic. It is based on the acceptance of a world of facts outside of and independent of the observer in terms of which the legitimacy of all parts of science is to be determined. As this world of facts is the determinant of all scientific knowledge, this approach focuses on the experimenter determining these facts. Most philosophers of science have explicitly accepted this view that science is composed of definitions (analytic) (12) and synthetic propositions which are empirical. A typical instance of this position is Popper's statement that (1968, p.47)

> there can be no statements in science which cannot be tested, and therefore none which cannot in principle be refuted, by falsifying some of the conclusions which can be deduced from them. (13)

This view of science sees scientific laws as empirical generalizations of the type that, in principle, can be contradicted by a counter-instance (deductivism or falsificationism) or induced from observation statements. Popper explains the procedure he sees scientists as using thus (1960, pp.132-3):

> From a hypothesis to be tested - for example, a universal law - together with some other statements which for this purpose are not considered as problematic - for example, some initial conditions - we deduce some prognosis. We then confront this prognosis whenever possible with the results of experimental or other observations. Agreement with them is taken as corroboration of the hypothesis, though not as final proof; clear disagreement is considered as refutation or falsification.

Watkins, one of his followers, elaborates this view to get a hierarchy of empirical statements (1957, p.115):

> Observation-statements are the primary empirical statements. Instantial hypotheses, are empirical statements if they directly give rise to observational statements... A non-instantial hypothesis, or system of hypotheses like Newton's three laws which cannot be directly tested, is empirical if it in conjunction with empirical instantial hypotheses, gives rise to further instantial hypotheses.

Let us look at the process of trying to test Newton's law of motion by combining it with several empirical statements. Newton's first law of motion is: 'Every body continues in a state of uniform motion in a straight line or in a state of rest, unless acted upon by an outside force.' Add to this the following observation statement: 'This body is not in a state of rest.' The conclusion that follows from these premises is that the body is being acted on by an outside force. If the concept of force used in the formulation of Newton's first law is a closed (14) concept, then it will be possible to ascertain whether the situation we are examining is a confirmation or a refutation of Newton's first law. On the other hand if force is a more open concept, then whether we have a falsification of Newton's law is unclear. If 'force' is an open concept, then when one says 'Here is a body that is accelerating, and I am not aware of an outside force acting on it' a Newtonian can reply, 'Keep looking for something that might count as a force in the situation for this may be a clue to a new force that we are unaware of now.' What turns out to be crucial in the quotation just given from Popper is the term 'clear disagreement'. How does one tell 'clear disagreement' from 'disagreement'?

In order to work within the analytic-synthetic (= empirical) distinction, philosophies of science must see scientific laws as clearly specified generalizations about clearly specified facts. (15) Scientists must be seen as working with closed concepts. This yields a static picture of science where what is included under each category used is specified for the current state of science. Not to do so leads to a breakdown of the analytic-synthetic distinction and a more dynamic view of science.

Historically Newton did not state his laws with a list of what outside forces were and an operationalization for each. This led scientists to look for forces instead of rejecting the law on the basis of some 'falsification'. A supposedly exhaustive list of forces would have limited the vision of scientists, not expanded it. (16) Philosophers who accept the analytic-synthetic (= empirical) distinction, account for this by saying that when a new force is discovered either one has a new empirical generalization or a new definition of force. They contrast two static views - that before the force was discovered and that afterwards. Their problem is that they cannot account for the shift except in an 'ad hoc' way. In other words they can only state that there was such-and-such a definition of, or empirical generalization about force, and then later there was another definition or empirical generalization. They cannot explain why the new definition is a definition of force or why the new empirical generalization is one about force. No rationale for the shift can be given. A more dynamic view of science that will allow an understanding of these changes in a non 'ad hoc' way seems desirable.

One can see the dispute about operationalization in this context. (17) Philosophers who accept the analytic-synthetic (= empirical) distinction want to settle this dispute in such a way that the meaning of a term is (or is determined by) its operationalization. They want this in order to work with closed concepts that allow generalizations that are about clearly specified things. For instance, Carnap's method of establishing the empirical significance of terms shows only their empirical significance in one context (Schlesinger, 1968, p.50). He does not tell us how we know that we are talking about the same type of thing when we talk about the temperature in the middle of the sun, and temperature as measured by a mercury thermometer. Only if we distinguish between the operationalization of a term, and the meaning of the term itself, can we claim we are talking about the same thing in two different contexts. A clear understanding of how one term can have several operationalizations is required.

This would provide a non 'ad hoc' and dynamic account of how, for example, the concept of force was extended into areas like electro-magnetism. (18)

Having accepted Kant's definition of the situation, while rejecting his analysis of it, philosophers are in a strait-jacket of closed concepts imposed by the analytic-synthetic (= empirical) distinction. The way out will lie in an analysis that allows some assertions to be open and allows for numerous different operationalizations of scientific concepts.

PROGRAMMATIC ASSERTIONS AND PROGRAMMES

'The meaning of a word is its use in the language' (Wittgenstein, 1967, p.20). (19)

Wittgenstein's analysis of the word 'game' in his 'Philosophical Investigations' suggests that there is a family of cases covered by the term. While there are certain core applications (20) of the term which, to continue the analogy we might call the 'nuclear family', the range of potential application is not specified (which has its analogy in the uncertainty about how far to apply kinship terms). The existing set of uses of a word do not exhaust its possible uses. Wittgenstein, on the basis of this and similar examples, concludes that words do not have the sort of clear cut boundaries or consistent uses that would make a definition possible in the way that positivists want. All that is possible, Wittgenstein argues, is to describe the uses to which a word is put.

What then is the use of a definition in science? I suggest that its core use is to isolate what are the key features of the core use of the word being defined. Definitions give what we understand at present to be the essential features of the core usage. They are theories about use. With a new understanding of the use of a word, a new definition of the word will come about. This is a dynamic view of words which allows us to see the extension of the meaning of words in a way which is not 'ad hoc'. It does not involve simply contrasting the meaning of words at different times. Instead of the change in meaning being arbitrary, possible changes are built into the word. Reasons can be given for extending a word to cover new phenomena.

There are two aspects of the process of deciding whether a case comes under the word in question - isolating what are the key features of the core applications, and isolating what are the key features of the case in question. What counts is a similarity between the core usages and the case in question, but what exactly will count as a similarity is not given in advance but is a matter of thought, consideration, and analysis. As the criteria of what is to count as 'the same' are not given in advance, concepts are open and not closed.

A consideration of the term 'political party' may help to illustrate this approach. (21) In the late nineteenth century the core applications of the term 'political party' were to groups like the Liberals and Conservatives. Their key features were seen to be that they were one of two or more groups competing to hold power in a state. When Lenin came to power the concept was extended to include a group that had once been a group competing with other groups to hold power, despite the fact that competing groups no longer exist (or no longer exist within the state). With the rise of one party states in the third world the term came to be seen in terms of political mobilization systems. The key feature of the core case is no longer seen as being one of several competing groups for power, but as a political mobilization system. The core usage remains but is seen in a different light. To apply the term 'political party' to both the groups in late nineteenth century Europe and the third world now has involved a reinterpretation of both. The first is no longer seen as one of several groups competing for power but as a mobilizer of different interest groups, while the latter is not identified simply as a dictatorship and its hierarchy, but seen as a channel that feeds demands into and aggregates them for the political system.

Language is a flexible tool for coming to grips with the world. If political scientists had approached the concept of political party as the holders of the analytic-synthetic (= empirical) distinction would wish, they they would have refused to include the Communist and Fascist groups and the groups running various third world nations under the label 'party'. (22) They would have seen differences and not similarities. This too would have led to some understanding. However, the point is that by seeing similarities first by bringing a variety of cases under the term political party, political scientists had a way of exploring the world including the core application. Seeing similarities has not prevented the making of distinctions and the identification of different types of political parties. To identify somebody as a member of a particular kin group allows us to place him in relation to the rest of his kin group, and to understand him as part of this kin group. This does not prevent us from seeing him as a member of other kin groups, or from talking about him in terms other than as a member of a kin group.

The open-closed distinction can now be further clarified. To the extent that a concept is open, the range of extension of the core application is large. A completely open concept is one which could be extended indefinitely. For this to be the case, its core applications would have to be without any meaning. A completely open concept is an empty one - it lacks all meaning. To the extent that a concept is closed, the range of extension of the core application is limited. A completely closed concept is one where the potential range of application of the core usage and the present range are equal. It has a completely fixed meaning. A completely open concept is the opposite extreme - a concept with an infinite range of meaning and thus none. Most concepts lie somewhere between these two ideal-type cases. They possess a meaning for they have basic core applications but are not completely closed as their range of potential application exceeds their range of present applications. (23) I will use the word 'open' to refer to cases where the range of potential application is quite large. However it is important to remember with regard to most words that they are open in some way and are closed in others.

In a similar way to words, assertions can be open in some ways, and closed in others. This can be because the assertion contains one or more 'open' concepts or because the assertion as a whole is 'open'. For instance if one looks at the assertion, 'All events have a cause' then in addition to the concepts 'event' and 'cause' being open, the assertion as a whole can be interpreted in various ways such as 'constant conjunction' for Hume and 'productivity' for Bunge (1963). I shall call such assertions 'programmatic assertions'. They have a core use (24) but are stated as generalizations that go beyond their core application. Their scope of potential application is left unspecified to some extent and to this extent they are open.

A programmatic assertion goes beyond its core application but to just what or to what limits is not given.

Whether a particular case should be included under a programmatic assertion is a decision based upon looking at both the case in question and the core application. While we know what the core application is, in examining a new case we may come to realize new features of the core case. A programmatic assertion allows an exploration not only of new cases but also of the old case at the same time.

I have called these assertions 'programmatic' as they provide a programme of work or a project directed towards extending their coverage. That they provide men with such projects does not mean they are intentional statements of the form: 'I intend to look at the world this way to see what sense I can make of it.' Rather, as scientists accept programmatic assertions they go about exploring the world in a certain way. Such assertions are not programmatic in the sense that a programme given out before a concert which lists the music an orchestra intends to play, is. For instance the programmatic assertion, 'All events have a cause', might be seen as a statement about how a person intends to operate when investigating reality. He intends to see things in the light of mechanical causality. If this is a correct categorization of 'All events have a cause', then it would make sense to say that it is a true proposition about Joe's intentions (i.e., it is true to say that Joe intends to see things in the light of mechanical causality), while it is a false proposition about Harry. This procedure seems illegitimate, for we do distinguish between intentional statements and statements about the world. It seems unacceptable to say 'All events have a cause', which has the appearance at least of a statement about the world, is an intentional one. Men do not accept that they can ascertain the truth or falsity of 'All events have a cause' by seeing how people act. However if a person believes that the world is of a particular type - a causal one - then we can make certain inferences about how he will go about investigating it. The ability to make this type of inference however, is not equivalent to saying that the person who says 'All events have a cause' is uttering an intentional statement. Conventionalists, (25) who see scientific laws as mere tools or conventions that men use in investigating the world, tend to forget in arguing their position that what a man believes has a major influence on how he acts.

A set of programmatic assertions that covers some universe (e.g. the universe of physical events, or of deviance) will be called a 'programme'. A programme tells us what sort of universe we are dealing with and gives us a way to go about understanding it. It tells us about the types of things and relationships between them that can exist. In this broad sense, a programme is about the logical structure of the world. For Kant synthetic 'a prioris' provided the presuppositions required for understanding the world. Programmes provide not only this but also the substantive content of the world. For instance, the economist's programme, which involves economic rationality, structures the world in terms of means-ends chains.

Scientific theories are programmes, while most scientific laws are programmatic assertions. Programmatic assertions are neither completely open for then they would be vacuous, nor completely closed for then they would be sterile and rigid. However, how open a theory or law is varies from case to case, and with the time in its development to which we are referring.

Programmes and programmatic assertions are logically compatible with any possible universe. No empirical statement or series of observations can force one logically to give up or accept a programmatic assertion. Such assertions are incapable of being falsified or verified. One way of describing them is as assertions that one can make without fear of contradiction by the 'facts' in any possible universe, (26) including the most bizarre world dreamt of by a science fiction writer. Alternatively, to state the point in a more conventional manner, there is no such thing as a crucial experiment.

In the light of this discussion, the example given previously of Newton's first law of motion can be understood more adequately. It now can be seen why it made sense to say to a person who could not account for a situation to keep looking for a new force. If Newton's first law is understood as a programmatic assertion, then it cannot be refuted on the basis of facts. However, this is not to say that scientists are completely in the dark. There is a clear reference point to the idea of force in the notion of one object hitting another or pushing another. However it is not claimed that in every case such a force exists, only that a force exists. That is, scientists are saying that there is something similar enough to such a force that it will be legitimate to cover it under Newton's first law. This may involve a long search and a reinterpretation of the core usage. (27) However, this process may be worth while because if the case can be described in terms of Newton's first law, then an understanding similar to that which men have of one billiard ball hitting another one is possible. Programmatic assertions can be more or less useful in understanding the world. I say 'can' and 'more or less useful' because some programmes give us more understanding than others. (28) In fact, being aware that men cannot be forced by facts to cease accepting a programme, is an additional reason to be on guard against dogmatism.

Programmatic assertions are not empirical because there are no clearly specified criteria as to what is to count as an instance of the assertion. Nor are they empty analytic because they are about the world. They are synthetic 'a priori' ideas in the sense that they are about the world and thus synthetic and made logically prior to looking at the facts and thus 'a priori'. They are a type of idea that men use in understanding the world. If by synthetic 'a priori' is meant an 'a priori' factual assertion which is 'a priori' necessarily true or false, and this is what Kant and others mean by the term, then there are no synthetic 'a prioris'. Programmatic assertions are neither necessary nor necessarily true. (29) They are more-or-less arbitrary assertions which are evaluated in terms of their utility. They are more-or-less useful standpoints from which the world may be investigated. This type of idea when men think with it and act on it constitutes their basic cognitive faith. They are our basic understanding of the world. The relevant question is not whether scientists can have certainty (they cannot (30)) but whether there is a possibility of rational cognitive faith.

Assertions may be divided into several classes. Definitions, as was seen earlier, are attempts to isolate the key features of the core. They give what men understand to be at present the essential nature of the core usage. However, as men admit their understanding of the core usage to be somewhat open, they are tentative. Redefinition of the core is possible on the basis of new understanding. It seems useful to say that there is a new concept as opposed to saying that a redefinition has occurred when the programme within which the definition occurs changes. For instance 'force' at one time meant 'ehtical power' and occurred within a religious and ethical programme (Jammer, 1957, pp.16-23). When force comes to be seen in a mechanical programme, then the definition of force has changed. To say whether a redefinition has occurred or a new concept introduced, the term must be seen in its place in the programme not in isolation.

Another aspect of definition is that it may be in part demonstrative or ostensive. For instance a nineteenth century user of the term 'political party' knew that prime examples of them were the Liberals and Conservatives. The core uses, identified perhaps by proper names, or perhaps by their relationship to various other entities in the theory, are what a definition has to pick out. If a redefinition occurs, these cases, known demonstratively, must still be included. (31)

In addition to definitions there are programmatic assertions and fact claims. Fact claims include claims about non-observable entities (e.g. supernatural entities). Empirical statements are a sub-set of factual ones. They refer to observable entities and use concepts whose meaning is stabilized. In terms of open-closed and operationalized-unoperationalized, programmatic assertions are open and unoperationalized, non-empirical factual claims are closed and unoperationalized, while empirical statements are operationalized and closed. (32)

When analysing a theory it is not possible to tell from the structure of a sentence into which class of assertions it falls. One must look at it in relation to the whole theory. Its use must be examined. For instance when a Marxist says 'every social relationship is dependent on people's relationship to the means of production', he might (judging by the structure of the sentence) be making an empirical statement. However by seeing it in relation to the rest of his assertions it is clear that what counts as a 'means of production' and the nature of 'dependence' are open. Instead of making an empirical claim, he is saying something like this: 'If we analyse social relationships in this way, ultimately we can make sense of them.' He uses Marxism as a mode of analysis. Marxism is used this way not because its employers see it as a mere tool to help analyse the situation, but because Marxists believe that the universe of social relationships is of a certain type.

SOME PROBLEMS AND OBJECTIONS CONSIDERED

One approach taken by some holders of the analytic-synthetic (= empirical) distinction to a number of what I call programmatic assertions is to say that they are meaningless. For instance Warnock says (1961, p.107):

> For if S [every event has a cause] can be affirmed, whatever may be the course of events, it says nothing of what the course of events in fact is ... it is vacuous.

He argues that it is not analytic and that it cannot be refuted by facts. What I do not accept is the implication that as neither of these is the case, that it lacks any meaning. It does have a relatively clear reference point in the notion of mechanical causality. The generalization

'Every event has a cause' is not an assertion, however, that every event has such a cause, just that it has a cause. A scientist is affirming with this assertion that there is something similar enough to a mechanical cause in all cases for it to be legitimate to cover it under the assertion 'Every event has a cause.' This process may involve a ong search and a reinterpretation of mechanical causality. Yet it is worthwhile, because when he can describe the case being investigated causally, then he will be able to attain an understanding similar to that which he has of mechanical phenomena. The crime of the empiricists is that in trying to get rid of fuzzy ideas they have been forced to throw out many of the flexible tools with which we explore the world. However there is an element of truth in their position for as was noted earlier a completely open concept is an empty one lacking all meaning. Nevertheless one cannot assume that what has no completely stipulated meaning has no meaning. By insisting on closed concepts positivists are implicitly advocating using concepts which are necessarily sterile, rigid, narrow and inappropriate for investigating new phenomena.

Another related approach taken by a number of philosophers of science to assertions I would call programmatic is to call them metaphysical. They then assert that metaphysical assertions are not factual, essentially because their methods of determining their truth or falsity (verification or falsification) break down. Their role in science is seen as suggesting scientific theories (Popper, 1969, p.74), but within scientific theories metaphysics is 'committed to the flames for it can contain nothing but sophistry and illusion'. A typical example is early atomic theory, which has proved suggestive. What does not make sense is how it follows that early atomic theory, which is a very open programme, is about something beyond the physical. That the nature of the physical is seen in an open way does not make it metaphysical.

Gellner attacks arguments from paradigm cases by seeing them as a variant of the ontological argument. The ontological argument for God, put rather crudely, is that we can think of the concept of God, therefore God exists. The argument from the paradigm case is that if a word has a referential use, then what it is used to refer to exists. He gives an excellent illustration of this type of argument as it is sometimes used in linguistic philosophy (1968, p.34):

> What do expressions such as 'of one's own free will' mean? Why, let us look at their paradigmatic use. Should we not use it of a smiling bridegroom marrying

> the girl of his choice? Well then, 'that' is the kind of thing the expression means. What else could it mean? Ergo, free will is vindicated... The Argument from Smiling Bridegroom solves it all.

This seems a valid objection to some arguments produced by linguistic philosophers. The basic relevant difference between my position and that of linguistic philosophers of the type he is attacking, is that choice among different programmes and programmatic assertions is possible (see next section). Choosing between programmes involves considering a range of things in terms of them. One of the types of questions we can ask is whether one programmatic assertion is compatible with another we wish to maintain. I would suggest that the dispute about free will is best interpreted in this light. Is the programme which involves a conception of free will compatible with a programme that involved determinism? To 'answer' this question it will be necessary to look at both programmes - see how they are used to analyse things like nature, psychology and history. An argument about the compatibility of two programmes will force one to look at such things as Gellner claims we should (p.39), not avoid considering them as the linguistic philosophy argument allows.

Some of the arguments in this book, however, will be similar to those found in linguistic philosophy, for their ways of analysing ordinary language can be applied to the ordinary language of a discipline or of a particular theoretical approach. One can ask, for instance, which are the paradigm uses of the theoretical terms and when are the theoreticians using their words metaphorically. This provides the basis of an analysis of how theoreticians use their words and what their theories are. Establishing what a theory is, is not to accept it as correct. The techniques of linguistic philosophy can be applied to areas other than ordinary language. Doing this does not involve accepting the ends or doctrines of linguistic philosophy. I am certainly not out to show that through ordinary language we can solve all sociological problems.

I have been assuming for the sake of simplicity of exposition that words, programmatic assertions, and programmes have only one core. The objection can be raised that many words have two or more. How can one cope with this? The basic answer is to see the different cores as parts of different programmes. For instance, Parsons gives two different definitions of deviance (SS, p.250):

deviance is a motivated tendency for an actor to behave in contravention of one or more institutionalized normative patterns

and (ibid.)

deviance is the tendency on the part of one or more of the component actors to behave in such a way as to disturb the equilibrium of the interactive process (whether a static or moving equilibrium).

What violates institutionalized expectations need not upset the system's equilibrium (33) and vice versa. Deviance has two different core uses for Parsons. This is analysed by seeing the first definition of deviance in relation to action theory (34) and the second in relation to structured-functionalism. (35) The problems of multiple cores may be dealt with, not by focusing on the particular word or assertion, but by seeing it in its overall context.

PROGRAMME DEVELOPMENT

Having discussed the nature of programmatic assertions and programmes and considered some objections, the question becomes how to use them to investigate the world. Related to this is the question of which programme to accept. I am trying to answer the traditional philosophy of science question of how one decides to accept a theory.

I will not be able to provide any ultimate tests for the truth or falsity of any programme. No certainty that we have knowledge seems available. This does not mean however that it is impossible to choose between theories. I shall aim to provide grounds for rational faith in our understanding, not chase the 'will-o'-the wisp' of certainty. I will discuss how we can test our theories, and on the basis of how well theories pass our tests, we can choose between them.

Programmes order the world we are trying to understand. One question asked is: 'Will conceiving of the universe in this way lead us to interesting questions, problems, and better answers?'

It makes sense to talk of more and less developed programmes. A developed programme is one that has been successfully elaborated to deal with many of the problems in its area. In developing a programme we show how the core applications can be extended to cover other cases. We demonstrate that it is possible to understand the new case and the core case in a similar way. If there are several competing programmes, the one that appears capable of the most extensive consistent development should be chosen. This may not be the theory which at present is furthest developed. For instance if a previously accepted theory has run into trouble (i.e. has failed to deal with some area in the same way it has dealt with others) and a new one has solved this problem, then the new theory may be legitimately considered the one capable of more extensive consistent development. In the 1920s Einstein's theory was less developed than Newton's yet many people felt that eventually Einstein's theory could be alaborated to deal with the phenomena that Newton's had, and more.

I have talked about consistent development of a programme. The way we test for this is by taking our programmatic assertions as closed empirical ones. The basic advantage of doing this is that by treating them as closed empirical statements, we can use the normal methods of the holders of the analytic-synthetic (= empirical) distinction for testing theories. For instance, to see whether we have consistently developed Newton's first law, we specify what we will count as a force and test this operationalization in as many different situations as possible. Should we be unable to develop the law in its operationalized form (i.e. we have what Popper (1969) would call a falsification and Kuhn (1966) an anomaly), then we have been unable to develop the programme consistently by this particular way of closing it.

At this point it is important that we were only treating the programme as closed, for this means we now have two choices. One can reject the programme or some part of it. Alternatively, one can try to develop the programme or the part of it that failed to be developed in the manner attempted, in some other way, and see if some other consistent development of the programme is possible. Which of these a scientist will do should depend upon which is likely to lead to a programme that can be consistently developed. This is a matter of judgment dependent on factors such as whether there is another plausible way of effecting closure on the programme; how successfully have other parts of the programme dealt with other areas; whether there is, or the scientist can think of, an alternative programme that appears able to solve the problem. While a scientist can give some justification to whether he continues to accept a particular programme, he cannot prove he is right. In the final analysis there is an element of faith in whatever choice men make. Science is in part an art.

In the light of this it is possible to understand a basic difference in approach between experimentalists and theoreticians. The experimentalist is concerned with testing for consistent development of a programme and so must treat it as closed empirical generalizations. An engineer applying science must also treat scientific laws as closed. The theoretician on the other hand, sees in his practice scientific laws as open. In practice no absolutely rigid line can be drawn between experimentalists and theoreticians. For the experimentalist, concepts are less open - he is willing to do a little bit of extending the core application but not much. (36) Perhaps the situation can be summarized as: an academic believes writing articles organizes facts; an experimentalist believes ideas order facts, while a theoretician believes ideas represent problems.

It can now be seen why the analytic-synthetic (= empirical) approach to science appears so plausible. Holders of this distinction focus on experimentalists. Positivists see people testing theories, not developing theories. (37) They present a series of static pictures of science with arbitrary transitions between them. Science is seen as men in white coats in laboratories, or interviewers ringing doorbells, not people in studies wielding pencil and paper.

The element of faith involved in which programme to accept opens up other possibilities of criticism. One's faith is open to various ethical and political objections. A programme that sees some men as inferior to others on account of the colour of their skin, can be objected to on humanitarian grounds. This faith is not a good faith. Sociological theories can be objected to on the basis of their political implications. This is not to say that theories should be accepted on ethical or political grounds alone, just that these have a legitimate role to play in whether theory should be accepted. Another legitimate type of criticism of theories is on the basis of the philosophical implications. For instance if certain forms of behaviourism involve a particular answer to the body-mind problem, then objections to that solution of the body-mind problem are objections to the form of behaviourism, though not necessarily a definitive one. As a rule, to the extent that it is practical, one should be aware of several conflicting theories, as one can aim only at a reasonable faith and not at certainty. One should be aware of alternatives as what is reasonable depends on what other possibilities there are. Being aware of several programmes and ideally working with more than one, also helps avoid dogmatism. (38)

REDUCTION (39) AS A PROGRAMME

The problem of reduction is most familiar to sociologists in connection with psychology - can social acts be reduced to psychological facts? To philosophers the problem is associated with the 'naturalistic fallacy' in ethics (40) and the body-mind problem. (41) It seems possible to extend the relevance of this problem to certain relationships between theories. I would like to suggest that a number of theoretical disputes can best be understood as an attempt to reduce one theory to another. If one programme covers a certain universe and there is another programme which covers some or all of that universe, then the relationship between them may perhaps be usefully seen in terms of a reduction. For instance, to deal with a problem to be discussed in chapter 9, there are three possible relationships that can exist between sociological theory and economic theory. First, economic theory can be deduced (42) from sociological theory or some part of it. (43) In this case given that sociological theory is wider in scope and that economics can be deduced from it, men should accept sociological theory as it will have greater explanatory power (as it explains economic theory and more). In Popper's terms, it has more potential falsifiers. Second, economic theory can be reduced to sociological theory or some part thereof. This involves showing that what was of worth in economics can be reformulated in terms of sociological theory. At the extreme this might involve showing that there was nothing of worth in economic theory. This would involve showing how the programme of sociological theory was able to account for everything covered by economic theory more adequately and in a basically different way. (44) The third possibility is that it is impossible by means of a reduction or a deduction, or some mixture of both to subsume economics under sociology. In this case economics is independent of sociological theory (45) and sociologists must give up their claim to have a better theory than economics. Not only must they give up the claim to have a better theory, but they must find good reasons for separating the field of economic activity out of social activity if sociological theory cannot account for economic activity as well as economics. If holders cannot separate out economic activity, and economic theory gives a better account of economic life, this is a good reason for giving up sociology. Reductions and attempted reductions are a way of seeing conflicts between theories in so far as there is no conflict over what the facts are. When a theory is reduced, it is 'undermined'; its props are taken away, rather than that it is attacked on the basis of factual evidence from outside. A reduction is based on an examination of the fundamental concepts of a theory (46) rather than the detailed evidence pro and contra it. (47) I agree with Einstein when he says (Jammer, 1960, pp.xii-xiii):

> In the attempt to achieve a conceptual formulation of the confusingly immense body of observational data, the scientist makes use of a whole arsenal of concepts which he imbibed practically with his mother's milk; and seldom if ever is he aware of the eternally problematic character of his concepts... And yet in the interests of science it is necessary over and over again to engage in the critique of these fundamental concepts, in order that we may not unconsciously be ruled by them.

The term 'reduction' involves a point of view - that of the theory being subsumed. From the point of view of the other programme, it is an 'expansion'. For instance, if in chapter 9 it can be shown that economic theory can be subsumed under sociological theory, then the explanatory power of sociological theory will have been expanded. One important way that a reduction or expansion can be made convincing is to show not only why a better explanation of the phenomena is possible, but also why the old theory was held to be plausible. For instance, a reduction of witches to hallucinations and germs explains in terms of the hallucinations why people previously believed in witches.

The most frequent type of objection made against reductions is that they involve a category mistake. (48) Rorty gives an answer that is, I feel, satisfactory for the reductions involved in most theories. (49) He shows how a theory of germs and hallucinations has replaced a theory of witches. (50) He points out that a person attempting to replace demon language is not claiming that witches, hallucinations and germs are all of one category. What people call demons need not be in the same category as what we now use to explain demons (i.e. hallucinations and germs). He notes that there is no need to make an identity claim between demons and hallucinations and germs (1966, p.38):

> there is no simple way of filling in the blank in 'What people called demons are nothing but ------.' For neither 'hallucinatory contents' nor 'germs' will do. The observational and explanatory roles of demon must be distinguished.

Similarly if we expand one programmatic assertion to include what was previously covered under another programmatic assertion, then we do not need to claim that the two programmatic assertions involve similar types of categories.

CONCLUSION

This chapter has been addressed to problems in how any theory should be analysed. What I want to do now is point to a few implications of this framework for analysing Parsons.

One of the important implications of this approach to analysing ideas is that Parsons' positions will be seen as theories not as conceptual frameworks. (51) Conceptual frameworks by this approach are seen as setting out the types of entities and the relations between them that can exist. Definitions contain implicit theories. How men divide up the world is not seen as an arbitrary matter. The idea of a reductive or expansive programme will be important in this regard.

This approach to analysing theories also indicates where one should begin one's analysis. One of the core cases is clear, can one sensibly examine how the theory might be developed or extended. If the core case has problems, then it is these problems that must be sorted out first. In my view, it is precisely here that problems do crop up, the biggest of which is that voluntarism does not reconcile positivism and idealism. This leads Parsons to have two as opposed to one programme running through his work. It is to problems about the centre of his programmes that this book is addressed. Basically there is no point examining the periphery before the centre.

Stated another way, Parsons is a theorist working on developing a programme. Thus it is not surprising that it is 'far from easy to specify precisely what are the empirical referents of his categorical scheme' (Mulkay, 1971, p.78). What I would say is that Parsons uses open concepts. I do not deny that the problem of effecting closure on his concepts is a major one. However there is an analysis of a theory that should be done before one ask how to apply closure to its concepts. (52) Only after the core cases are clearly specified, does it make sense to ask what the limits of their extensions are. In light of this discussion the central questions of the book can be stated thus: 'What are Parsons' programmes?' and 'Are they worth trying to implement?'

The analysis of the nature of theory in this chapter, allows me to push Bershady's (1973) analysis of Parsons further than he feels safe in doing. Bershady (pp.68-73) sees Parsons trying to do a similar thing for the analysis of social activity as Kant tried to do for physics. Kant endeavoured to provide a basic minimum framework (space-time) in terms of which all physical laws had to be expressed. Parsons, Bershady argues, is trying to do a similar thing for social science. His conclusion is that Parsons does not succeed in achieving this objective and doubts whether it can be (p.151). If the views on epistemology presented in this chapter are accepted, one can go further and say that Parsons cannot produce such a framework. Thus while I find Bershady's book a most sophisticated one on Parsons, I do not find it helpful in understanding Parsons to analyse him as doing that which in principle cannot be done.

2 Parsons' voluntaristic theory

Parsons' main conclusion in SSA is that Marshall, Pareto, Durkheim and Weber converged on a single theoretical schema. In order to take into account key facts required to understand human society, they were forced to move away from positivism and idealism. However, both positivism and idealism have a 'permanently valid precipitate' (pp.718-19), which Parsons claims to have made the basis of a 'voluntaristic theory'. The rest of his work, Parsons (SSA, pp.E-F; 1964b, p.316) claims, is an elaboration of such a theory.

SSA, however, should be read as the book of somebody who thinks he is coming to grips with positivism and idealism, but whose actual focus is different. His convergence claim is too strong as he does not show that the position arrived at is not eclectic or 'ad hoc'. However his analysis does provide an indication of what he sees as central to a good theory. Even if the convergence claim is accepted, voluntarism is not an adequate reconciliation of positivism and idealism. The central concern of SSA is to attack the rationalistic, individualistic account of society given by utilitarianism considered as a theory of action (not a philosophy), and the account of the rise of capitalism given by classical economists. Despite the attack on utilitarianism, Parsons takes the unit act, understood in a means-end way, as his core case, and argues for an understanding of society in general subjective categories and indicates what he sees as key features of society that a theory should take into account.

The focus of this chapter is on Parsons' own programme, not on the particular writers he is analysing. Whether they shifted position and whether they incorporated the elements Parsons describes them as doing is outside the scope of this book. To say whether his interpretation of each is adequate would involve an analysis of each and that would take several chapters at least. (1)

WHAT PARSONS SAYS HE IS DOING

Parsons claims that Marshall, Pareto, Durkheim and Weber converged on a single theoretical schema. This schema, which he calls voluntarism, contains the permanently valid precipitates of idealism and positivism. This has to be interpreted as meaning that these writers had a non 'ad hoc' solution to the problem of how to combine these approaches and that this solution can be set out as he sets out voluntarism. What I wish to argue now is that voluntarism may be too eclectic - it cannot be shown to be a non 'ad hoc' solution.

A non 'ad hoc' solution could be provided either by a clear theoretical statement or the acceptance of a core application with fairly clear ways of being extended to other areas. In the case of a theoretical statement, one would have to be able to specify why and how each element from a tradition is to be used in the analysis as opposed to an element from another tradition. Merely to list the elements necessary to a theory without expounding a systematic set of relationships among them is not to demonstrate arrival at a non 'ad hoc' position. In the case of accepting a core case, the relationships among the elements must also be specified. Otherwise there is no clear indication of how to extend the core application to other applications. In such a case, one cannot claim to have a theory, for a theory always has an infinite range of applicability (i.e. there can be an infinite number of cases the theory applies to). Parsons, I shall argue, describes voluntarism in such a way that it may be 'ad hoc'. Voluntarism is too eclectic to count as a point of convergence of Marshall, Pareto, Durkheim and Weber. It may be open to the same type of attack as Parsons makes on utilitarianism. Utilitarianism, he argues, involves an assumption of a natural identity of interests which is not integrated with the rest of the utilitarian analysis. That voluntarism must be shown to be non 'ad hoc' is a standard that Parsons accepts (SSA, p.486; cf. also p.354):

> It will not, however, do merely to say that both the positivistic and the idealistic positions have certain justifications and there is a sphere in which each should be recognized. It is necessary, rather, to go beyond such eclecticism, to attempt, at least in outline, an account of the specific modes of inter-

relation between the two. It is in this connection that the voluntaristic theory of action assumes a place of central importance.

I have said voluntarism 'may be "ad hoc"', for there is another way of looking at what Parsons is doing. He can be seen as analysing each of these writers to see what specific points they have that should be included in a satisfactory programme. Looked at this way, the points where voluntarism may be 'ad hoc' become problems which his subsequent theorising should tackle. His subsequent action programme does take account of many of these problems, I shall argue in later chapters. Seen like this, voluntarism as expounded in SSA is a set of programmatic commitments which Parsons is making. To the extent that these problems can be solved in a way compatible with voluntarism, the position arrived at is not 'ad hoc', though Parsons in SSA does not establish this to be the case.

The question now is whether Parsons' voluntaristic theory, or as he also calls it, his theory of action, can be shown to be non 'ad hoc'. In his schematic outline of the categories a voluntaristic theory should use, he gives a generalized formula for a system of action (SSA, p.78):

A system of action =
numerous unit acts
+ elementary relations of unit acts in a system
+ relations emergent from unit acts being grouped into units called actors
+ relations emergent from the relations of individuals

These elements are held together with plus signs. The problem is that we are not told how to interpret the plus signs and this means that the interrelations between them are unspecified. Thus it is not clear whether voluntarism is an 'ad hoc' solution or not.

That Parsons describes his system of action with plus signs follows from his concept of emergence. Emergent properties, he says, (SSA, p.739), 'cannot be derived by a process of direct generalization of the properties of the unit act': they can vary independently of the properties of unit acts (SSA, p.32). For Parsons, this follows from the existence of another level of organization which comes from systems of action being organic. The emergent properties of systems of action have a different ontological status from the units of action systems. Parsons in elucidating the concept of emergence gives the following example (SSA, pp.739-40):

It is impossible, from the data describing a single rational act with a single clearly defined immediate

> end and a specific situation with given conditions and means, to say whether or in what degree it is economically rational. The question is meaningless, for the economic category involves by definition the relation of scarce means to a plurality of different ends. Economic rationality is thus an emergent property of action which can be observed only when a plurality of unit acts is treated together as constituting an integrated system of action.

That the question of economic rationality is meaningless depends on an objective conception of economic rationality. Parsons accepts Pareto's conception of economic rationality which is based on his conception of logical action - an action which by the standards of modern science actually produces the results intended (SSA, pp.264-8). Thus to say an action is economically rational is to say that it is the least expensive way of attaining a result, given the valuation of different things, by the standards of modern science. In other words, economic rationality is defined positivistically by a standard external to the system of action. If, on the other hand, one conceives of an action as economically rational when the individual doing it is attempting to minimize costs, an isolated action may be economically rational. (2) An economic action becomes one that has a certain type of meaning to an actor. I shall argue later that Parsons does develop this conception. What is important for the present argument is that whether a property is emergent or not depends on one's theoretical approach, not on the nature of the property. (3)

By calling economic rationality and common values emergent properties of a system of action (SSA, ch.19), Parsons is saying that the only way he has coped with these features is by adding them on in an 'ad hoc' way to his unit act framework. (4) Unit acts are the building blocks of the theory of action he claims (SSA, p.77) and are composed of a situation, an end, a means and a standard governing the choice of means (SSA, pp.43-51). Yet despite calling the unit act his basic frame of reference, he says (SSA, p.734):

> it is primarily recognition of the empirical importance of these emergent aspects of total systems which characterizes the voluntaristic theory of action.

A great deal of SSA does focus on common values in particular and argues that Marshall, Pareto, Durkheim and Weber incorporated these in their theoretical approaches. What Parsons has not shown, however, is that they have done so in a non 'ad hoc' way. Voluntarism with its acceptance of common values as emergent - held on to the system with plus signs - may be 'ad hoc'. This analysis shows how it is possible for Pinney to make the objection that (1940, p.177)

> It is not clear from the discussion whether the value element is Marshall's own value attitude or an objective element in his analysis. The latter is certainly not demonstrated.

From the point of view of Parsons' subsequent theorizing he can be seen as making a commitment to incorporate common values and means-ends analysis (the unit act) into the same programme.

There is another way in which voluntarism may be 'ad hoc' - its acceptance of the expression of values. Parsons says (SSA, p.693):

> here in the phenomena of Gemeinschaft is to be found another case where acts may best be interpreted as modes of expression of attitudes rather than as means to specific ends.

He describes this as an extension (SSA, p.694) of the unit framework but does not show how his core case (the unit act seen in a means-end way) is to be extended to the new area. Parsons argues that some of Weber's and Pareto's (SSA, pp.269-77) work involves seeing the actor as directly expressing his own values. The problem again is that this may be 'ad hoc'. As will be seen, this problem recurs in his later work in the form of how to relate instrumental (means-ends) and expressive (action seen as an end-in-itself) action. In chapter 4 it will be shown how he incorporates both in his action programme. Parsons recognizes the problem here for he says that the expression of value attitudes has (SSA, p.682; cf. also 1935, p.306) 'an unavoidable residual character of which the reader by this time will have learned to be suspicious' and it says a great deal for Parsons' analysis that he is able himself to point to one of its major problem areas. Later, in SS, he recognizes even more clearly that his unit act in SSA (SS, p.8) 'is applicable only to cases where the action is positively goal-oriented' and that a wider conception of the unit of action is required.

Having argued that voluntarism may be 'ad hoc', I wish now to argue the stronger position: in so far as it is seen as a reconciliation of positivism and idealism, it is 'ad hoc'. The basic problem with Parsons' argument, that these writers converged on a programme reconciling positivism and idealism, is that it tends to be of the form: 'The writer came to recognize the importance of "x" particular factor.' However, positivists did not suddenly discover that men have subjective awareness or idealists that there is a material environment. Theorists did not discover that people exist in situations, that people follow norms and have ends. All this in a general way has been known since time immemorial. The question has always been how to account for and describe these 'facts' and the nature of their interrelations. Positivism and idealism are both answers as to how to describe and interrelate these 'facts'. In addition to his characterization of the theory of action in terms of unit acts, Parsons also sees it as an understanding of human activity in terms of four independent variables - heredity and environment, the intermediate means-end sector, and ultimate value system and effort (SSA, pp.718-19; p.251). This is inadequate, for one must specify how these are to be understood to show a reduction of positivism and idealism to a programme containing their 'permanently valid precipitates'.

Parsons gives as a conclusion to his analysis of Marshall, Pareto and Durkheim (SSA, p.469; cf. p.699):

> It seems legitimate to conclude from it [this analysis] that neither the radical positivistic position nor the related utilitarian view is a stable methodological basis for the theoretical sciences of action. (5)

Yet earlier he says (SSA, p.76):

> It is not denied that it may be possible to state the same facts in terms of other conceptual schemes, in particular such as will not involve normative elements. Schemes of that character which have been advanced, such as the behavioristic scheme, are, in the author's opinion, much less adequate as tools for statement and analysis of the facts of human behaviour than the action scheme. But this remains for present purposes an opinion. No attempt is made in this study to discuss such an alternative scheme critically or compare it systematically with that of action in empirical application.

This latter statement is, I think, an accurate one about SSA; SSA does not attempt to show that behaviourism is inadequate despite the fact that Parsons sees it as a major positivistic position. What is significant in a book attacking sociological positivism is its omissions. Not only behaviourism but things such as technological determinism are conspicuous by their absence.

Parsons defines positivism as 'the doctrine that positive science is man's sole significant cognitive relation to external reality' (SSA, p.421; cf. p.61). Aside from being a weak definition, for it basically shifts the problem to that of defining positive science, thus raising philosophical problems he wants to avoid, it does not cover a lot of sociological positivism. The positions he calls radical anti-intellectualistic positivism (e.g. social Darwinism, behaviourism) are not positively defined by such a definition. His failure to come to grips with positivism is significant for his later work, as a large proportion of this is positivistic.

Parsons says that the basic method of the idealist tradition is 'Verstehen', which he describes thus (SSA, p.485):

> An entity is verstanden when it is given a place in a system of meaningful relationships, by which it acquires 'Sinn'. If it is itself an ideal entity, for instance, a proposition, this takes place directly. If not, if it is rather a spatiotemporal object or event, the method of 'Verstehen' involves a further step - this entity must be symbolic interpretation be assigned a meaning which meakes it congruent to such an ideal system.

In other words an idealist does not understand an activity in isolation, it is understood only in a context - it cannot be observed by a neutral detached scientist looking at it in isolation. Idealists, in contradistinction to positivists, have categories of meaning as their fundamental categories. This tends to lead them to seeing events as unique, and to rely on intuition. Parsons' discussion of intuition (SSA, pp.586-91) omits a discussion of the good reasons why the method is used. Its use involves the abandonment of the positivist conception of a detached scientific observer. Parsons does give intuitionist theories empirical status (SSA, p.590):

> The intuitionist theories ... are strictly 'empiricist' theories. And that there is perception of meaningful wholes can hardly be denied. (See the immense amount of work on perception by Gestaltists.)

Perception of meaningful wholes is what positivists do deny. If Parsons is to come to grips with reconciling positivism and idealism he must analyse why positivists deny the perception of meaningful wholes. Positivists want to see cold hard isolated facts in the world; each feature of the world has its own independent causal efficacy. Idealists see man's culture and/or ideas as central and refuse to treat an item in isolation.

Because Parsons glosses over these types of issues, he does not adequately show in SSA that Marshall, Pareto, Durkheim and Weber converged on a position that reconciled idealism and positivism. His basic problem is that he is too glib. He says that he is concerned only with positivism and idealism in their sociological variants and will treat philosophical questions only where necessary (SSA, pp.20-7). The problem here is that positivism and idealism have various variants (e.g. an ontology, an epistemology, a philosophy of history, a methodology of science) that all feed into each other in various complex ways. They comprise what Wittgenstein would call a family of uses. The sociological uses of these terms are too intertwined with the other use for philosophical questions to be seen as residual.

This assessment of what Parsons claims to do cannot be seen as surprising. It is a bit much to expect him to analyse four major thinkers, assess their contributions to understanding society and provide a satisfactory solution, even if only on the sociological level, to what is perhaps the longest running dispute in Western philosophy. He is simply too glib and this is not the place for glib answers.

WHAT PARSONS IS DOING

The best way of getting at what Parsons is actually doing in SSA is through considering what Althusser would call his problematic. (6) While it is indicated at numerous points in SSA, it comes out most clearly in the essays he wrote before this book. His problematic is the utilitarian, individualistic, rationalistic economic account of society and especially its account of the rise of capitalism. If one sees SSA in this light it is possible to see why he discusses what he does.

After finishing his PhD thesis on various conceptions of capitalism, he wrote a series of articles on people such as Marshall, Sombart and Weber, dealing at length with their account of the rise of capitalism and relating them at numerous points to the laissez-faire account of capitalism's rise. (7) He also directly tackled the status of classical economic theory and its tendency to claim to provide a complete account of all human activity (Parsons, 1932). He characterized the laissez-faire account of the rise of capitalism or free enterprise thus (1931, p.130):

> The things which really need explanation are not the specific forms of behaviour and organization but the removal of barriers and the development of certain arrangements facilitating exchange, communications etc., such as money and credit, which are generally themselves in the developing rationality. This is on the whole the orthodox Anglo-Saxon view of economic history: the barriers must be removed, but once they are removed, modern capitalism - or free enterprise - becomes established of itself. It needs no specific

> propelling force - and if it consists merely in rational conduct, why should it?

If SSA is considered as an attempt to show the inadequacies in this type of account of society and the rise of capitalism and to designate some of the ways it can be superseded, (8) it makes sense. Parsons starts off with the Hobbesian problem of order: if each man rationally pursues his own individual ends, a war of all against all will ensue. To avoid this implication, utilitarians have used three main strategies. The first is to ignore the problem and implicitly hope the reader will assume that men's interests fit together naturally. Dodging an issue or being unaware of it does not solve it. In addition, the fair implication to draw from a writer omitting mention of the relationships among men's ends is to assume they are random. If they are random, then one cannot account for social order as Hobbes showed. The next strategy for a utilitarian is to add some sort of metaphysical prop to explain an identity of interests. This inconsistency characterizes social contract theories.

The third strategy used is to attempt to account for the ends, but in doing so utilitarianism has tended to 'break down' into behaviourism (9) or some other radical positivistic position. (10) This Parsons calls the utilitarian dilemma (SSA, chs 2 and 3) (11) and sees utilitarianism as unstable. Parsons sees SSA as examining another way out of the utilitarian dilemma (SSA, p.102; cf. p.124):

> the central problem may be stated thus: How is it possible, still making use of the general action schema, to solve the Hobbesian problem of order and yet not make use of such an objectionable metaphysical prop as the doctrine of natural identity of interests? ... To repeat its [SSA's] principal concern will be with one way of escape from the inherent instability of the utilitarian system.

Parsons looks at the writers in relation to the utilitarian view of man rationally pursuing his own individual ends, which, from the point of view of society, are random. He wants to do this in a way that is compatible with the 'general action schema', which uses subjective categories. What he sees as crucial to Marshall is the introduction of 'activities' involving non random ends related to the activities of men in society. What he finds unacceptable is (SSA, p.175) 'a profound laissez-faire bias which is in need of very serious correctives'. Pareto he sees as introducing non-logical (i.e. not rational or irrational) action and in particular ritual action; distinguishing economic and social utility and thus showing the inadequacy of purely utilitarian preference curve analysis for determining welfare; seeing society as pursuing an end and thereby accepting the structural element of (SSA, p.249) 'a single common system of ultimate ends', recognizing that common values vary from society to society; and using clearly subjective categories. Parsons likes Pareto's cyclical view of change with one societal type following another and his stress on force and fraud because it provides a needed corrective to the view of the rise of capitalism by the spread of rationality.

Parsons sees Durkheim as starting from a critique of the core economic laissez-faire case - two individuals exchanging goods to their own advantage. For this exchange to be possible there must be an element that the utilitarians do not include in their analysis - a set of rules that govern the exchange. Durkheim also rejects the explanation of social change in terms of an increase in human happiness because what constitutes happiness changes as society changes. Thus social changes cannot be explained in terms of men acting rationally to maximize their happiness and removing obstacles to this. This removes one of the key underpinnings of the nineteenth-century utilitarian idea of human progress. While in 'The Division of Labour' Durkheim accepts a positivistic explanation of the increase in the division or labour (population increase), in 'Suicide' he attacks and rejects numerous positivistic explanations (e.g. climate), as he also does when considering religion. In 'Suicide', Parsons sees Durkheim pursuing his analysis further and recognizing a social component in individual ends (what are individual wants is seen as formed by society). With his anomie analysis, Durkheim has transcended the utilitarian dilemma, for this analysis (SSA, p.337)

> amounts to carrying the Hobbesian problem down to a deeper level. The level of social instability which Hobbes analyzed presupposes a plurality of individuals who are capable of rational action, who know what they want. But this is itself an unreal assumption.

Durkheim's discussion of egoistic suicide shows that individualism need not be seen as a theory about human activity but can be interpreted as a social ethic. Parsons then sees Durkheim as analysing how social order is maintained by people's acceptance of common values. Durkheim's analysis of ritual and religion is seen in relation to the maintenance of social order and as an analysis of non-rational action.

This, I think, summarizes the key points of Parsons' analysis of Marshall, Pareto and Durkheim. What is striking is that most of what he chooses to discuss bears upon the utilitarian view of a rational individual pursuing his own ends and the account of the rise of capitalism based on this. Now we have all read enough of these writers and the secondary literature on them to know that he could have chosen numerous other points. Thus it seems reasonable to conclude that his problematic is the utilitarian economic view of man as read in relation to this. The first half of SSA forms a fairly coherent whole which does not read as an attack on positivism. Parsons has built up the key elements to his core case for society. Instead of a society held together by the advantages people get from exchanging with each other, he sees society as held together by common values. (12) Men accept these values in some way and have the ends they hold formed by society. (13) At times men act directly on their values (expression of value attitudes).

In formulating his image of society in opposition to utilitarianism and classical economics, Parsons is in many ways taking the same starting point for his analysis as Marx. He reacts to it by stressing the importance of values and religion in explaining men's activity. Given this, his failure to discuss Marx's account of how values, religion and ideas are shaped by the economic base is unacceptable. As Parsons' starting point is an attack on what Marx would call bourgeois economics, he is unlikely to be a liberal in a classical sense. As will be discussed later, Parsons is a liberal humanist but he underpins this position in a rather unconventional way (see chapter 7).

In the second half of SSA, Parsons' concern in discussing Weber is slightly different. He first outlines Weber's account of the rise of capitalism in the West and his comparative studies on the role of religion in society to show that an alternative to the laissez-faire economists' account of the rise of capitalism is possible. He sees Weber as accepting the key features of the core case of society just outlined, as Weber sees society in subjective categories, stresses the importance of common values and beliefs, particularly in shaping men's interests, and accepts the expression of value attitudes. Since he sees Weber as accepting the basic core of his image of society, he is concerned with showing that this type of analysis can be done scientifically. Writing for the largely positivistic Anglo-Saxon academic audience, Parsons' main preoccupation is to show that one can use subjective categories without engaging in metaphysics. He sees Weber's main polemical attacks as being directed against objectivism and intuitionism of the idealist variety, as they both deny the possibility of general laws using subjective categories. He agrees with these polemics of Weber but then argues that Weber did not carry them far enough. Weber's own work he criticizes for its 'type atomism' - his construction of ideal types which do not allow the elements to vary independently (cf. also Parsons, 1966, pp.8-29). As will be discussed in chapter 5, this is an indication of what sort of programme he wants to develop.

What I hope is now clear is that SSA can be read as an attack on utilitarianism in general and its account of the rise of capitalism in particular. Read this way, the book has many parallels with Lukacs' 'History and Class Consciousness' (1972). Like Parsons, though from a different point of view and written earlier, this collection of essays is concerned with attacking the positivistic atomism of bourgeois thought and asserting for Marxism the importance of culture in an adequate analysis of society. (14) Parsons' focus in SSA seems strange to us because we have seen the debate about the rise of capitalism in Marxist - non Marxist terms. Thus it is easy to overlook what his problematic was.

CONCLUSION: PARSONS' BASE LINE FOR HIS SUBSEQUENT WORK

There would appear to be two polar types of relationship between his analysis in SSA and the rest of his theorizing: either there is a sharp break between SSA and his later work, or a significant measure of continuity can be found. The first, if it were the case, would be interesting and would require a focus on the reasons for the break. Atkinson (1971, esp. pp.9-33) (15) does see such a break and makes it central to his discussion. (16) My interpretation on the other hand sees a significant measure of continuity between SSA and Parsons' later work. However this does not mean that Parsons developed a unified conceptual scheme as he claims; rather his later works can be seen as a process of working out some of the muddles of SSA and never resolving others.

What I want to do now is to indicate briefly how this analysis of SSA relates to the rest of Parsons' work - at least as I see it. His claim to have dealt with positivism and idealism, while his actual focus was on utilitarianism, leaves him believing he has solved the problem of reconciling them without actually having done so. The result of this is that running throughout the rest of his work are two approaches to theorizing. The first, action theory, involves the subjective point of view and is in the idealist tradition. The key features of this will be discussed in chapters 3 to 7. Chapter 8 discusses the key contributions and his approach to systems theory, which is in the positivist tradition. Chapter 9 will illustrate how he oscillates between these. Both types of programme run throughout his work and he oscillates continually between them. He does not start from a definite position and later introduce 'crucial equivocations' that tend to shift his position into another, as J.F. Scott (1963) maintains. Now if this oscillation is the case, it will be possible to go through the rest of his work and say, 'Here, because Parsons is muddled about idealism and positivism, he is giving incompatible definitions of key terms.' To focus merely on this oscillation seems unproductive, for the aim of this work is to clarify his theory. In order to accomplish this task, it seems best initially to go behind his oscillation and separate out the two approaches to theorizing in his work.

Parsons has been called both an action theorist and a structural-functionalist. Bershady describes his position (1973, p.163) as an 'unstable amalgam of positivist and "historical" premises'. To use anthropological terminology, he has emic and edic points of view running throughout his work. As Parsons is unaware of this, it is necessary in order to give him a reading, to separate these two perspectives from each other. Only then can the implications of running these two perspectives together be clearly seen.

As Parsons did not make his attack on utilitarianism a clear focus in SSA, utilitarian elements continue to be found in his later work. However, he commits himself to transcending utilitarianism and moving in the direction of a social as opposed to individual view of man. He says (SSA, p.387):

> The most fundamental criticism of utilitarianism is that it has had a wrong conception of the concrete human personality. So not only desirability, but even happiness, comes back - as a concrete state of the individual who is integrated with a set of social norms.

Sociology he sees as the study of human activity in so far as it can be understood 'in terms of the property of common-value integration' (SSA, p.768). Chapter 3 will be concerned with analysing his partially social, partially individualistic, image of man. The following chapter will argue that when he develops his analysis of how values are integrated in action he moves to a fully social image of man. His basic argument as to why a war of all against all does not occur is that men accept common values. In chapter 3, I will look at his analysis of different societies in relation to a core case of a society where values are fully accepted. In chapter 4, when I discuss his analysis of institutionalisation and how values and meanings are accepted, the core case shifts to an ego-alter interaction. Another feature of this analysis of SSA will also be discussed in chapter 3 - his failure to integrate expressive action satisfactorily. Finally, in chapter 5, I will examine how he fulfils his commitment to seeing society in general subjective terms when I analyse his 'functional dimensions' as a classification of types of meaning. If I succeed in doing all this, then this analysis of SSA will have given a valuable guide to his later work.

3 Tying man to society: the partially social image of man

In SSA, Parsons attacked utilitarianism, yet accepted the unit act understood in a means-end way as his core case. From this tension results a strand in his work that can perhaps best be described as social utilitarianism. It is social in that the ends are seen as social (e.g. a love relationship, honour, happiness for someone else) as opposed to being based on individual advantage. The classical economists' and Hobbes' view of man as motivated by egoistic greed is rejected. The ends are social also in that they are formed by society. Society is not threatened by a war of all against all or held together only by the advantages men gain from exchanging goods and services with each other. Instead society ties the individual to it by forming ends that fit into that society's system of common values.

By seeing ends as formed in society, Parons focuses on what for a utilitarian would be an unproblematic backdrop to a person's ends. This leads to seeing a social component in ends that seem, at first sight, highly individual. Accepting Durkheim's analysis in 'Suicide' of how human happiness depends on society, Parsons sees an end like one's own pleasure as having a social component. However Parsons lacks an analysis of how men accept ends; and implicitly at points underpins his analysis with a somewhat utilitarian view of man detached from social process in this position. As he deepens his analysis of how men accept social ends, he moves to a fully social image of man, and transcends the problem discussed here, as will be seen in the next chapter.

Social utilitarianism is useful as a framework for ordering some of the work done between writing SSA (1937) and TGTA (1951), but is of decreasing relevance to Parsons' later work. However, he does not like to admit that his framework ever shifts - it only develops. Thus, for instance in 1961 (TS, p.32) he says: 'Action treats behavior as "goal-directed."' This chapter is concerned with tracing a movement in Parsons' thought that leads him to a position where he can reformulate his programme. It is not meant as an exhaustive treatment of his work between 1937 and 1951, but is meant only to pick out a major strand running through his writings. Much of his work from this period (e.g. on vested interests) is best seen in the light of his analysis of institutionalization which will be discussed in the next chapter.

SOCIAL ENDS

Utilitarian social theories attempt to explain and describe all of men's actions in a means-ends framework. (1) The core case for the classical utilitarians is a man pursuing his own clearly defined personal end by the most efficient means he knows of. After describing a man's activities in this way, utilitarian theorists attempt to build up an analysis of society or some section of it in terms of actions so described. The introduction of social ends solves some, but not all, of the problems of this programme. While Parsons does not formulate much of his analysis in terms of social ends, in the next section I will argue that it helps to clarify several of his analyses (e.g. of the professions).

Parsons in SSA sees the idea of ends being social as opposed to individual as one of the major results of Durkheim's analysis of anomie (p.382):

> The element of ends as it appears in the means-end schema is no longer by definition 'individual' but contains a 'social' element.

The classical utilitarian framework sees men as having ends for themselves - individual ends - which are seen as existing prior to or outside of social interaction. Parsons, on the other hand, sees man as having ends that grow out of his social interaction. (2) Man is seen not as wanting things purely for himself; rather much of what he seeks is certain types of social relationships. For instance, an end somebody might have is a love relationship which, to exist, involves the actions of two persons. The person is seen not as only wanting to receive but also to give love. Other actions like eating a steak are not seen purely as a way of satisfying one's hunger, as the classical utilitarians would hold, but rather have also a social component; steak is not just fuel, but is good food for a person like me to eat.

One basic problem of any means-ends analysis that

claims to be a total analysis of society is that of accounting for the ends. While some ends can be explained as a means to other ends, (3) there will be one or more ends which are ultimate ends (i.e. ones that are not means to other ends). The introduction of social ends does not solve this problem. Parsons in SSA dealt with a special case of this problem on the whole. Utilitarian theorists, by not giving an account of ends, are implicitly assuming that they are random. If they are random, social order (which depends on some integration of the ends of individuals with each other) is impossible (SSA, chs 2 and 3). In this analysis lies the implicit assumption that common ends, a system of ends or common values, are sufficient to solve the problem of social order. Recent writers like Olson (1971) and Barry (1970) have shown that there is a major problem here. Olson states his central thesis thus (p.2):

> Indeed, unless the number of individuals in a group is quite small, or unless there is coercion or some other special device to make individuals act in their common interest, 'rational, self-interested individuals will not act to achieve their common or group interests.'

The rationale behind this is that a self-interested individual will weigh the cost of his contribution against the difference his effort will make to the outcome. For instance, to use an example Barry develops, the person deciding whether to vote or not will weigh the effort involved in his voting against the probable difference his vote will make to the outcome of the election. In most cases this difference is negligible, so the rational self-interested individual will not bother to vote. Using some basic economic concepts, it is possible to state the problem quite precisely. Any individual will judge whether to act or not, on the basis of whether the cost to him of acting is larger or smaller than the difference his action will make to the outcome. In other words, he will act only if the cost to him is less than what is from the point of view of the group the marginal return (4) resulting from his effort. In many cases his cost will be more than his return, so he will not act. The problem is that everybody acts this way according to the theory. Thus nobody to whom a joint return will come, if they all act, will find it worth while to do 'their share'. Consequently actions in which, if each person performs (e.g. voting), the average return exceeds the average cost, will not be done according to this theory. Now the simple facts of the matter are that many actions of this type do get done (e.g. most people vote). Ergo, the means-ends framework cannot even explain a group of people acting in their own interest. (5) The problem is not one that could have been formulated by classical utilitarian theorists such as Hobbes, Locke and Mill, for the marginal concepts were formulated only in the late nineteenth century. While Parsons never recognizes this problem, it will be argued that his theory provides an answer. (6)

The introduction of social ends solves some of the problems Barry and Olson bring up. Whether it solves any particular problem is a matter of whether, empirically, people happen to have a social end that would provide an explanation for the problem in question. For instance, Barry assumes that an individual has the end of obtaining a government beneficial to his interests. From this assumption, he shows that in most cases it is not rational for a person to vote, as his vote is unlikely to affect the outcome of the election. However, there are other ends, to which voting could be a means, that remove the problem. The obvious end to solve this problem is the social relational one of participating in electing a government. This social end, it should be noted, is compatible with the end of electing a government favourable to one's interests. The 'bandwagon effect' that political scientists talk about can be seen as a particular instance of this social end. It involves voting as a means of giving one's support to the winner. Parsons' own analysis of voting sees it as a means of asserting one's solidarity with groups with which one is involved (STMS, p.235). The essential point for the present argument is that the introduction of social ends into the action programme extends it in such a way as to make possible the solution of the type of case Olson (7) and Barry see as problematic.

Another problem with the means-end programme is how to describe adequately all actions in relation to the core case. Freud's discussion of the unconscious can be seen as making a major contribution to this problem. For instance, his analyses in 'The Psychopathology of Everyday Life' (n.d.) can be interpreted in terms of analysing acts as means to unconscious ends. In terms of conscious ends (i.e. the agent's declared intention when he is not lying), these actions are inexplicable in a means-end way. By taking Freud as extending the notion of ends to include unconscious ends, Freud can be seen as showing how a means-ends analysis can be extended to encompass actions that had previously not been explicable in this way. (8) One point worth noting about introducing unconscious ends, as there is a parallel with social ends, is that to introduce them changes the view of conscious ends. For instance, a person who is arranging items on his desk to get a tidy desk (conscious end) is likely to be seen also as having an unconscious end that permeates his conscious end. Other writers have shown that the means-ends framework can be applied to new areas not by developing new concepts but by the perceptiveness of their analysis. For instance, Laing and Esterson (1970) show that schizophrenia can be seen as a 'rational' response to an unusual environment.

The introduction of social ends extends the core case of the classical utilitarians to give a more adequate description of most actions. Eating is not just a way of satisfying hunger but has a significant social component. Even where a person accepted the fuel approach to food, one can see a social component in his end of fuelling himself (probably a Puritan self-image). The point is parallel to the earlier one about the introduction of unconscious ends. Once accepted, they change one's perception of conscious ends.

Parsons, however, realizes the descriptive inadequacy of the means-ends framework, for he draws a distinction between instrumental and expressive or consummatory action. This distinction seems reasonable. Instrumental action is action whose meaning to the actor is that it is a means to some end. It is possible to see consummatory or expressive actions in this way. For instance, one can see making love as a means to the end of expressing love. However, as an accurate subjective description, this seems inaccurate for many cases. Making love is in itself expressing love, and this is how many people feel it. One might 'make love' as a means of expressing love, but this would be a different type of action and one which appears worth distinguishing from 'making love' as an expression of love. Thus Parsons makes a subjectively accurate distinction with the instrumental-consummatory distinction. However, this creates a basic problem. His assertion of the existence of consummatory action (action which is an end in itself) is incompatible with his previously quoted statement: 'Action treats behavior as goal-directed.'

However, the existence of this problem helps one to understand why Parsons gives the analysis of expressive action he does in TGTA and SS. He tries to assimilate expressive action as fully as possible to the instrumental. In the left-hand column in Table 1 are the four problems he sees ego having when engaging in instrumental action in relation to alter. To facilitate comparing the expressive case, I have placed the parallel problems for the expressive case in the right-hand column. (9)

TABLE 1

Instrumental problems in relation to alter	Expressive problems in relation to alter
disposal (alter as consumer)	receptiveness of alter
remuneration	responsiveness of alter
access to facilities	occasion and relations to third parties
co-operation with alters (terms of)	problem of expressive loyalty - alter as source of a pattern of gratification

He talks (SS, p.147) about the '"economy" of expressive orientations', and (TGTA, p.214) 'the distribution of rights to response, love, approval and esteem' which are "relational possessions"' (TGTA, p.214). There is a parallel in the expressive system to the 'terms of exchange' in the system of instrumental actions (TGTA, p.214). By drawing this range of parallels between instrumental and expressive actions, Parsons can be seen as attempting to pick out key features of the core case that can be extended to cover expressive action. He is not willing to take the final step and cover expressive action under the core case. In his refusal, which I think is correct, he retains the problem that was noted in the previous chapter, that the expression of value attitudes might be an 'ad hoc' addition from the point of view of the unit act. However, those like Jarvie (1964) (10) who wish to see all action as rational and thus instrumental could do worse than to read Parsons. (11) Unlike Jarvie, he has at least the beginning of an analysis of how to extend the means-end framework to cover what are normally seen as expressive actions.

The final problem of the utilitarian programme I wish to discuss applies only to those versions that want to see the means in a moral way (e.g. Parsons and Merton). Where one sees the means as all being morally equivalent (e.g. as in economics), the problem does not arise. The problem is clearest in Merton's famous deviance classification (1968), so I shall discuss it in relation to that. He sees deviance as the violation of institutionalized expecttations and defines deviance in terms of the relations between 'institutionalized means' and 'cultural goals' (i.e. in terms of the relations of means to ends). The problem, put simply, is that to the extent the means are institutionalized, they are not means, but partake of the character of ends, so that their violation is deviant. If they were strictly means, this would not be so. There are ways that Merton can try to solve the problem - for instance, by talking about more or less institutionalized components of human activity - but they tend to destroy the simplicity of the schema. (12) Parons sees four of his deviance categories filling those of Merton (SS. p.258: FSI, p.145), or it seems reasonable to suppose that he has this problem in his own theory. His claim that his categories fit Merton's (13) shows that he does not recognize that Merton's schema has this problem. The claim itself, however, seems wrong for some cases. He says (SS, p.258): 'Merton's "innovation" and "ritualism" are our two compulsively conformative types'. Merton classifies most crime for financial gain (illegitimate means to the cultural goal of success) as innovation. I balk at calling a bank robber a compulsive conformist.

The same problems that Merton has with institutionalized means exist for Parsons' unit act framework. He sees a unit act as composed of a situation, an end, a means to the end, and a selective standard governing the choice of means which is normative (SSA, pp.43-51). When he discusses the concept 'normative', he says (SSA, p.75):

> The term normative will be used as applicable to an aspect, part or element of a system of action if, and only in so far as, it may be held to manifest or otherwise involve a sentiment attributable to one or more actors that something is an end in itself, regardless of its status as a means to any other end...

The problem here is that this assimilates the category of means governed by a normative standard into the category of ends, and the means-ends framework disappears. I will discuss in the next chapter how Parsons gets out of this problem, but for present purposes will remark only that the introduction of social ends does nothing to solve the problem.

SOME ANALYSES TYING MAN TO SOCIETY

In this section I want to look at some specific analyses of Parsons to see how he binds man more closely to society. They represent a movement on the more empirical level between SSA's position of attacking individualistic utilitarianism and the social image of man to be discussed in the next chapter. I shall elucidate these analyses in terms of the concept of social ends just discussed.

By examining the motivation of professional and business behaviour Parsons challenged the radical difference between them that the utilitarians saw. The normal approach to professionals at this time was to see them as altruists who apply technical knowledge to problems in a disinterested way, in contrast to businessmen who egoistically pursue their own interests. Questioning both sides of this, Parsons sees business and the professions as essentially similar. A clear example of the type of approach to the professions that he is attacking is M. Logan (1953, p.49):

> A profession is a vocation whose practice is founded upon an understanding of the theoretical structure of some department of learning or science and upon the abilities accompanying such understanding. This understanding and these abilities are applied to the vital practical affairs of man. The practices of the profession are modified by knowledge of a generalized nature and by the accumulated wisdom and experience of mankind, which serves to correct the errors of specialism. The profession, serving the vital needs of man, considers its first ethical imperative to be altruistic service to the client.

Parsons finds this type of approach, which sees a vast difference between the professions and business, as problematic, for both are in the same society. He says that both businessmen and professionals aim at objective achievement and recognition. These two are normally combined together in the goal of success. Where this is not the case there is a tendency towards commercialism in medicine or dishonest business practices in industry. However, if the 'institutional structure is working at all well' (EST, p.63), it is not to a doctor's advantage to violate his professional code. The goal of recognition is a social end. What Parsons does with it is to tie the individual into society. He sees a wider range of activities being in the individual's interest than do the classical utilitarians. Introducing social ends like recognition allows an extension of the core case of what is a self-interested action.

It is necessary to discuss one more aspect of Parsons' conception of a professional before returning to comparing professionals and businessmen. Parsons starts analysing the professions by asking what are the complex of social conditions needed to apply science in society. The question is analogous to one of Durkheim's in 'The Division of Labour': 'What are the noncontractual elements of contract?' Utilitarian analyses, Parsons noted, tend to see the application of science as nonproblematic. He sees himself as replicating the logic of Durkheim's analysis as he presented it in SSA, but for science, not contracts. His basic answer is that for science to be applied there must be an occupational role stressing rationality, specificity of function, universalistic as opposed to particularistic criteria of judgment (EST, pp.34-49) and affective neutrality as opposed to affectivity (EST, p.160). (14) Later, Parsons extends this analysis to argue that architects are unlikely to achieve fully professionalization as part of their concerns are aesthetic (Amer U, p.100). In other words they are not directly implementing science and are not thus completely governed by a role stressing rationality, specificity of function, universalism and affective neutrality.

Parsons sees precisely the same elements characterizing the role of a business executive, particularly one in a bureaucracy, as he sees characterizing professionals. The result of this is to tend to assimilate business to professional activity. What a businessman does is to apply universalistic criteria of judgment of a situation rationally to a specific function or task in an affectively neutral way. This leads to a technical view of the economy. Economic action becomes competent action based on a body of knowledge. Given this, how can one object to it on ideological grounds? This image of economic activity remains central to Parsons' later work, though it gets refined in various ways. For instance, in Amer U (p.7) he says, 'managerial competence plays a paramount role in the conduct of productive organizations.' (15)

Parsons' seeing recognition as an important social end for economic actions can be seen as a particular case of a more general view that all of alter's responses to ego 'may be called sanctions'. As men's ends are social, the actions of others are always relevant from the point of view of social control. Giving recognition becomes a form of social control. Man is locked into society.

RESIDUAL UTILITARIANISM

In TGTA, Parsons says that an actor's orientation to a situation can (p.58):

> be divided into two analytically independent categories: a category of elements of 'motivational orientation' (appearances, wants, plans) and a category of elements of 'value'-orientation (cognitive standards, aesthetic standards, moral standards).

The way Parsons interprets this involves a residual utilitarian element in his theory and implicitly contains an interesting theory of morality. In the next section I will look at the version of the PVs he relates to these orientation categories.

This division of man is like the old tripartite division of man into intellect, emotions and the will (Swanson, 1953, p.130). However two of the modes of motivational orientation, the cognitive and the cathectic, are seen as basic. Man thinks and wants. The evaluative mode is on a different level (TGTA, p.59):

> The evaluative mode involves the various processes by which an actor allocates his energy among the various actions with respect to various cathected objects in an attempt to optimize gratification.

There are usually a range of options open to an actor, and evaluation involves trying to pick the one that maximizes the actor's overall gratification. Parsons is making 'reason the slave of the passions'. The evaluative mode is the equivalent of Freud's reality principle.

In addition to the modes of motivational orientation, Parsons also has modes of value orientation. These, he says, serve to narrow the range of alternatives open to the actor and help him/her to foresee long run consequences (TGTA, p.71). What Parsons has in effect done is to see an actor with types of energy, desires - call it what you will - separate from social process. These types of energy (the motivational modes of orientation) are then guided by various standards. In that the actor accepts the restrictions they impose, he is tied into society since Parsons sees values as shared. The actor is using the values standards as a way of maximizing his long run gratification. Thus he is the utilitarian individual separate from social process. The following quotation illustrates the type of position (TGTA, p.71):

> The evaluative mode involves the cognitive act of balancing out the gratification-deprivation significances of various alternative courses of action with a view to maximizing gratification in the long run. The value standards are various recipes or rules (usually passed from person to person and from generation to generation) which may be observed by the actor in the course of this balancing-out procedure.

Parsons here is committed to a theory of morality. Moral action by this approach is the pursuit of gratification within a general definition of the situation. As the actor aims at a pattern of gratification, he must follow various rules of thumb to enable him to achieve it. While I could elaborate this theory of morality further, what is important now is that it would be unacceptable to Parsons and this is why he never sets it out clearly. He wants values not to be explicable in terms of other variables (1935), yet here sees values in terms of a relation between cognition and cathesis.

The following is the definition of a social system that incorporates the key features of this analysis (SS, pp.5-6):

> a social system consists in a plurality of individual actors interacting with each other in a situation which has at least a physical or environmental aspect, actors who are motivated in terms of a tendency to the 'optimization of gratification' and whose relation to their situations, including each other is defined and mediated in terms of a system of culturally structured and shared symbols.

This can be seen as the culmination of one strand of Parsons' thought. In SSA he attacks utilitarianism for its implicit assumption that men's ends are random. Central to an adequate view of society, he argues, must be a recognition of a set of common values of a system of intermeshing ends. In the last sections I discussed how understanding ends as social tied man more tightly to society. Then Parsons, by separating motivation from the standards that guide it, retains something - I'm not sure I'd call it an actor or an individual - separate from social process. Man is related to value standards that are still in some way outside him. Thus his position contains a residual utilitarian element. His definition of a social system sees actors aiming at gratification in the classical utilitarian manner but, unlike the utilitarian case, he focuses on the culture that shapes the values and ends as central.

PATTERN VARIABLES AND MOTIVATIONAL CATEGORIES

Parsons introduces various of the distinctions he came to see later as PVs during essays he wrote in the late 1930s and 1940s. However it is not until writing TGTA that he attempts to deal with the distinctions as PVs. When he introduces them in TGTA he calls them a 'derived, classificatory system' (p.76). In this section I shall consider his derivations (16) of them and the conception of them that would result if this derivation were possible. While his derivation contains faults, what is more important is that the conception of the PVs involved is unsatisfactory. Parsons has another, and more satisfactory, conception of the PVs than the one discussed here which involves residual utilitarian elements. The alternative satisfactory version of the PVs will be discussed in chapter 5 and I shall do my major elucidation of the concept then and discuss the nature of PVs only as it bears upon the derivation here.

He defines a PV as (TGTA, p.77)

a dichotomy, one side of which must be chosen by an actor before the meaning of a situation is determinate for him, and thus before he can act with respect to that situation.

There are four pairs of PVs: affectivity-neutrality; specificity-diffuseness; quality-performance (which is also called ascription-achievement); and universalism-particularism. (17) These are dichotomies, not continua. Every action is characterized by one PV from each PV pair (TGTA, p.76). In terms of the PVs Parsons classifies roles, norms, values, and a whole host of other things.

Parsons describes his method of derivation thus (ibid., p.91): (18)

our method of derivation through the establishment of primacies among types of interest and the resolution of ambiguities intrinsic to the world of social objects.

He claims to derive affectivity-neutrality and universalism-particularism from 'the absence of any biologically given hierarchy of primacies among the various modes of orientation' (ibid., p.76). As there is no biologically given hierarchy of modes of orientation, the first question that Parsons sees for the actor is whether to evaluate or not. If he does not evaluate and accepts immediate gratification, he chooses affectivity; if he chooses to evaluate, he choose neutrality (ibid., p.77). If evaluation is seen as weighing immediate gratification possibilities in terms of overall gratification possibilities, it appears possible to consider this as not occurring in certain situations. However, this is unsatisfactory, for Parsons says that every action is characterized by one PV from each PV pair and says in his derivation of universalism-particularism that this is based on the person evaluating (ibid., p.89). He cannot hold both that affectivity is the choice made when the person chooses not to evaluate and that all choices must be made. Consequently his derivation of affectivity-neutrality and universalism-particularism are incompatible.

It is possible to find more logical problems in his derivations of these two PV pairs. However, what is more important is the conception of the PVs that is involved in linking them to the motivational categories. For instance, affectivity, if linked directly to gratification, will have to mean something like a feeling (either warm or cold), and at points Parsons accepts this conception (WP, p.51): 'affective activity is not as such specifically oriented to the maintenance of, or conformity with pattern.'

He also has a conception of neutrality in line with this (WP, pp.51-2; cf. SS, p.267):

In the case of affective neutrality on the other hand,

> there is by definition a potential conflict between the particular gratification interest and the stability of the cathectic system. Orientation in this situation can take the form of the feeling of 'obligation' to maintain conformity with the pattern, so there is a sense in which we may say that affective neutrality constitutes 'cathexis of the pattern'. (19)

The problem with this conception of affectivity-neutrality is that we do have norms and values about affectivity. We have norms such as 'you should love your wife or husband.' If affectivity-neutrality and universalism-particularism are derivable from the motivational categories, then they must be personality level concepts. If they are personality level concepts, then Parsons cannot classify roles, norms and values in terms of them (much of one of his books, SS, consists of doing this) without reducing the social system to a personality level. The problem in these 'derivations' of the PVs comes from Parsons' residual utilitarianism. He is working in terms of an individual separate from social process who is deciding how to relate to that process.

Parsons' two other PV 'derivations' - of quality-performance and specificity-diffuseness - can be dealt with much more easily. They are not derivations but elucidations. I shall return to PVs in chapter 5 and consider their nature there.

4 The social image of man

With the formulation of a clear conception of institutionalization, Parsons provides the underpinning to a fully social image of man. This action programme has as its core case a view of an ego-alter interaction that sees what both individuals do strictly as social process. The traditional liberal and utilitarian concept of an individual separate from social process is eliminated. Parsons' objections to utilitarianism in SSA become more thoroughly rooted as he develops an alternative foundation for his action theory which eliminates any conception of an individual separate from social process.

This programme, which I shall call his social action programme does not come out of a vacuum. Even before writing SSA, Parsons is praising Pareto for seeing residues as characteristics of men in society not 'of an abstract human nature' (1932, p.341). In SSA he says (p.387; cf. also p.248 and p.464):

> The most fundamental criticism of utilitarianism is that it has had a wrong conception of the concrete human personality. So not only desirability, but even happiness, comes back - as a concrete state of the individual who is integrated with a set of social norms.

Parsons describes one of the steps forward he sees himself making in TGTA thus (EST, p.359):

> the insight that the major axis around which the expectation-system of any personality becomes organized in the process of socialization is its 'interlocking' with the expectation-systems of others, so that the mutuality of socially structured relationship patterns can no longer be thought of as a 'resultant' of the motivation-systems of a plurality of actors, but becomes directly and fundamentally 'constitutive' of these motivation-systems.

In TGTA he makes a number of remarks that are at variance

with the social utilitarianism discussed in the preceding chapter and are in line with a social action programme. For instance, he says (TGTA, p.66):

> Only in a figurative sense does an actor 'have' patterns of value-orientation. In a strict sense he 'is', among other things, a system of such patterns.

As a general statement with regard to those parts of TGTA and SS that fit into an action programme, I would say that TGTA is the book of somebody actively trying to move out of social utilitarianism, containing most of the key elements for doing so, but unable to put these together systematically. SS, on the other hand, is the book of somebody who has found the social action framework, but has not followed it through fully enough to eliminate all elements of his former programme.

In this chapter, I will be primarily concerned with clarifying the central features of Parsons' social image of man. I will discuss institutionalization and his view of the key features of any ego-alter interaction. Then in commenting on this I will discuss how it allows Parsons to transcend some of the problems discussed in the previous chapter, provides a view of man where culture is liberating not repressive, and clarifies the relationship between instrumental and expressive action. Next I will discuss how Parsons defines the world to fit with his core case.

The programme discussed in this chapter is within the idealist tradition for two related reasons. The first is that it takes the subjective point of view. What is going on is described from the points of view of ego and alter. Related to this, the meaning of what is going on is seen as dependent on ego and alter, not on some given external reality that a neutral scientist can observe. Man is seen as creating his own meanings, not as having them dictated by an 'external reality'.

THE CORE CASE OF SOCIAL ACTION THEORY - THE INSTITUTIONALIZED EGO-ALTER INTERACTION

At the centre of Parsons' action theory is an analysis of the central features of the interaction of any two actors. On the basis of this core case, which is an interaction between ego and alter, Parsons builds his social action theory. The core case identifies the essential features of action independently of time, place and culture. This analysis can be seen either as providing an ideal type of action and/or as a thought experiment where all features of the interaction due to it occurring in a particular culture, time and place, are stripped away. In other words, this analysis characterizes any interaction regardless of when, where, or in what culture it occurs. This enterprise is similar in type to Schutz's analysis of the conditions and characteristics of 'normal' social interaction (Schutz, vol.1, 1962). The methodology, though implicit, is the same as Schutz's - a phenomenological reduction. I shall present action theory by first setting out this 'core case' and then examining how this has been extended. Schutz presents his own work in this way. After setting out the characteristics of our 'taken for granted' world he analyses the homecomer (Schutz, vol.2, 1962, pp.106-19) and the stranger (ibid., pp.91-105) in relation to his 'core case'.

The feature that Parsons sees as key to ego and alter's interaction is that their actions are institutionalized. This he defines thus (SS, p.38):

> In so far as, relative to the actions of a plurality of actors, conformity with a value-orientation standard meets 'both' these criteria, that is from the point of view of any given actor in the system, it is both a mode of the fulfilment of his own need-dispositions and a condition of 'optimizing' the reactions of other significant actors, that standard will be said to be 'institutionalized.'

That the interaction between ego and alter is institutionalized is a result of them having developed a pattern of gratification related to a pattern of norms. Parsons calls this the 'theorem of institutional integration' (SS, p.43) and says it is the 'fundamental dynamic theorem of sociology' (SS, p.42). He states the theorem thus (SS, p.42; cf. pp.545-55):

> This integration of a set of common value patterns with the internalized need-disposition structure of the constituent personalities is the core phenomenon of the dynamics of social systems.

Parsons does not at any one point set out how he builds up to this view of institutionalized ego-alter interaction as the core phenomenon of his social action theory. My basic concern in this section will be to set out how he builds up this core case as clearly as possible.

Both individuals (ego and alter) are interested in maximizing their gratification (SS, p.69). However, what will be gratifying for each actor is not given in advance, as Parsons starts from the assumption that motivation for the actor is undifferentiated (WP, p.208; cf. FSI, p.109; EST, p.59):

> We may start from what may perhaps seem to be a radical assumption about motivation, namely that, 'for purposes

of the theory of action' motivation is best treated as 'originally' undifferentiated with regard to the system in which it is used. According to this conception, for the personality as a system, motivation consists in a single unitary 'urge to gratification'; it is simply an urge to 'get something', to level the existing state of motivational tension. The specification of goals, the 'content' of what the actor wants, is thereby assumed to derive, not from any inherent structure of the motivational system, as such, but from the 'orientations' which have developed in processes of action themselves. (1)

In other words the individual has a potential for gratification,but what he will find gratifying he discovers through interaction. Becker's description of learning how to enjoy smoking marihuana is a good description of learning to find certain sensations pleasurable (1966). The assumption of undifferentiated motivation allows Parsons to see men as fulfilling need-dispositions acquired during the course of social interaction. Social process cannot be seen as the fulfilment of the needs or drives an individual has prior to involvement in it. The basis for a social contract view of society - that it makes sense to talk of a man prior to involvement in society - is eliminated.

Parsons qualifies his assumption of undifferentiated motivational energy by saying that there may be some organically given drives. However, he argues that even when activities provide outlets for drives, the manner of gratification is learned socially (TGTA, pp.110-14; SS, p.9; WP, pp.39-40). For instance the sex drive alone cannot explain the myriads of different sexual practices. This qualification is important to his learning theory when he applies it to babies. As will be discussed in chapter 6, drives provide the initial gratification in terms of which a baby acts.

In addition to seeing motivation as undifferentiated, Parsons sees gratification as social in nature (WP, p.35): 'The mutual interdependence of actors for essential gratification is not in need of comment.' Comment seems necessary. If, by this, Parsons means only that men must enter into exchanges with others to satisfy needs like hunger, then he is in the utilitarian position he attacked in SSA. An alternative is to say that gratification is social in nature. This is not to say that an individual cannot find gratification in what he does alone. In a parallel way to which an end pursued in isolation can be social, so too can gratification pursued alone be social. (2) Gratification obtained through interaction is, however, basic. The assumption of an undifferentiated motivation to social gratification or, to modify Freud, a social pleasure principle, is important for it leads to ego and alter interacting.

With ego and alter interacting it is important that in addition to having the ability to cathect, (3) each has a cognitive potential (SS, p.7). (4) Since gratification is social in nature (e.g. being in a love relationship), the gratification of each is contingent on the actions of the other. As what the other will do is uncertain, (5) each seeks to interpret and establish using his cognitive ability what he wishes the other to do and what he himself is doing. This leads to cognitive signs and symbolism. Cognitive symbolism is based on each trying to make clearer than it would be simply through signs (nature of the behaviour itself) what he is doing and what he wants the other to do. A set of symbols takes time to develop, for criteria of sameness are involved (WP, p.33; then SS, p.10):

> Sign behaviour of any sort (involving either 'signals' or symbols in Morris' sense) implies a certain differentiation of the most elementary form of action system, and also the extension of action process in time, in such a way that the concept of expectation (and memory) becomes relevant.
>
> ...the concept of expectation which involves some sort of 'generalization' from the particularities of an immediately current stimulus-situation ... On the human level certainly the step is taken from sign-orientation to true symbolization.

At the same time that cognitive symbolism is developing, ego and alter are developing and organizing their gratificational structures relative to each other. Each is concerned with organizing his activities in such a way that an activity brings several types of gratification to him (e.g. being with alter gives him gratification from being loved and from playing cards). The development of cognitive and cathectic relationships proceed together and (WP, p.32) 'a symbol "always" has "both" "cognitive" and "expressive" meanings.' Each is oriented to a pattern of gratification and thus is willing to engage in acts which seen by themselves are deprivational but seen in terms of an overall pattern are gratificational. Parsons says about the actor (TGTA, p.14):

> He will often perform actions which, taken alone, are self-deprivational but which, when seen in the wider constellation of his need-disposition system, represent the most gratifying total balance of action possibilities which could be performed under the circumstances.

In contrast to this perspective, behavioural psychologists tend to see man's and rats' behaviour in relation to isolated gratifications. Ego and alter are not oriented to immediate gratification but consider, in choosing what to do, future gratification as well. Through having ego and alter orient to a pattern of gratification, Parsons builds in to his analysis of any particular situation a time perspective. In Freudian terms one might say he derives the reality principle from the pleasure principle.

As ego is dependent upon alter for his gratification and vice versa, each learns to interpret the cognitive and cathectic content of each other's activity and to communicate his own wishes as this makes a gratificational difference. After a time when a set of symbols has been established and learnt by each, if one of them arbitrarily changes the significance (either cognitive or cathectic) of what he does, the other will be unable to obtain as much gratification (SS, p.11): 'Even the most elementary communication is not possible without some degree of conformity to the "conventions" of the symbolic system.' Parsons does not see these 'conventions' in his social action programme as a means to attaining gratification (6) but rather gives them moral significance (WP, p.41):

> such a symbol system must have a normative aspect. Not only must the 'meaning' of the symbols be learned but both communication and contingent gratifications are dependent on their 'proper' use, that is, on maintaining conformity with the 'standards of the system'.

And (WP, p.38; cf. also SS, pp.11-12; WP, p.42):

> A set of expressive signs or symbols in this sense comes to be organized as a system. As such, a principal condition of its serving the communicative function in either its cognitive or its expressive aspect is necessarily that the actors are oriented to conformity with the normative standards.

By making the standards normative, Parsons is saying that when people have established a way of acting, they have a morality. When an action is institutionalized, ego has come to find the action satisfying in itself and to expect alter to respond in a way that he finds satisfying. A pattern of such actions is what Wittgenstein would call a 'form of life'. Having accepted this form, ego and alter see it as having moral significance. The standards are not just means to attaining favourable responses, each actor has come to accept them as being worth while in themselves.

It is important for this, that ego and alter have established the meanings of the actions, and are not just interpreting them. What is, say, a friendly action is not just a matter of interpretation; ego and alter between them establish what they are doing as friendly. The distinction between the mode of motivational orientation and the standards of value-orientation disappears. A certain type of action is not something an actor 'has' or 'plays'; rather, it is something he is (EST, p.107). An actor does not have friendly actions as something separate from him, he is friendly. The value is internalized, it is part of him. There is not a part of the actor separate from social process in Parsons' social action programme. The distinction between the mode and standard of orientation drops out of Parsons' work after SS, as, on the whole, he has moved out of social utilitarianism.

This programme closely intertwines how one sees a situation and how one should respond to it. Both are part of the same process (Parsons, 1965, p.94; cf. also Amer U, p.62):

> This, essentially, is what I mean by the internalization of a value-pattern - that it comes to define meanings for the personality system as such.

He criticizes Freud's distinction between ego and superego for its failure to see this. The distinction, he argues, assumes that an external reality is given independently of the actor who adjusts to it and applies superego standards to it. Freud, he argues, fails to see that both definitions and evaluations of an object are part of the same cultural pattern (WP, ch.1). If one sees somebody as a friend, then the form of action called for is friendly. (7)

To sum up all of this, in the core case of interaction, ego is doing something that expresses a pattern he has internalized and which he expects will lead to a favourable response on the part of another. If the action is institutionalized, this will occur unless the other person makes a mistake. (8) The pattern of interaction in a two-person or larger group is the meaning in action theory of the term 'system'. While this is a stable system, it is not a system in equilibrium. If an equilibrium exists, then if something causes the system to move away from the equilibrium, forces will come into play that will tend to restore the equilibrium. However, as will be discussed in chapter 7, if ego is seen to do something that does not fit with the institutionalized patterns, a vicious circle of deviance tends to be established. The notion of an equilibrated system exists in structural-functionalism or systems theory and will be discussed in chapter 8.

SOME COMMENTS ON THE CORE CASE

Built into Parsons' core case is a consensus. What is involved in a consensus for social action theory is more than just everybody agreeing. They must also know that they are in agreement. When an action is institutionalized, ego not only fulfils his own need dispositions by acting in a certain way, but also expects, and reasonably so, that his action will meet with a favourable response by alter. This requires agreement and known agreement on the meaning of actions. As there must be realization of agreement by the actors, a consensus in social action theory is not a pure additive relation of one view plus one view plus one view. For instance, consider two people who each want to go to bed with each other, yet neither feels able to bring the subject up.

The term 'consensus' that occurs in social action theory should be distinguished from the term 'equilibrium' that occurs in systems theory. A consensus exists when people are in agreement and know they are about the meaning of things. To say a consensus exists is not to say that everything is functional. It is possible for everybody in total agreement to go to their doom. Nor is it possible to say that where an equilibrium exists, a consensus does, for it is known that some disagreements may produce stable situations.

Parsons' emphasis on a consensus fits with the phenomenological approach of Schutz who is concerned with analysing the 'world as taken for granted' (vol.1, 1962, pp.74-6). In addition to a similarity of focus, the ego-alter interaction serves to underpin several of Schutz's analyses. For instance both his 'general thesis of reciprocal perspectives' (ibid., p.14) and his 'world of contemporaries as a structure of typifications' (vol.2, 1962, pp.37-56) follow from the institutionalized ego-alter interaction that Parsons takes as his core case. Like Schutz, Parsons is best seen as providing an analysis of the 'humdrum' of social existence. His core case can most easily be seen to make sense in terms of what we take for granted. For sociological theory it is perhaps best to have a core that focuses on things like language or money. When sociologists focus on man's disputes, they often overlook the 'backdrop' of the interaction. Although our disputes may be of greatest concern to us, if our taken for granted world looms largest in our activity, then this may be the place to start (not finish) our analysis. A core case that deals with what Schutz sees as the central feature of social life cannot be rejected out of hand as implausible.

The primary importance of the consensus assumption is that it allows Parsons to talk sensibly about the social meanings of action. By using the consensus assumption, he is able to talk not only of the meaning of an action to a particular person, but also of its social meaning. Sociologists often wish to discuss the social significance of an action, not meaning by this the consequences of the action but its meaning for society. They frequently use the word 'significance' instead of 'meaning', as 'significance' is ambiguous between meaning and consequences. This allows the writer to duck the problem of what is involved in saying that an action has a social meaning. Parsons' consensus assumption can be seen as a theoretical ploy, and a brilliant one, to move from the level of meaning at the individual level to meaning at the social level. It provides a way of interpreting statements such as 'Kennedy's death was a national tragedy', and 'Inflation is occurring.' (9) Parsons asks the question (WP, p.36):

> In other words are the meanings of signs, in their expressive significance, each 'private' to each actor, or is there such a thing as a 'common' meaning; if so what are the conditions on which it depends?

Clearly there are both expressive and cognitive common meanings - we can understand other people. Parsons' presentation of institutionalized action is his analysis of the conditions upon which the fact that we can understand others depends. This is a primary fact about social life. While one can and frequently does misunderstand others, the very fact that one is aware that one may be doing this, is dependent on the fact that at some previous point one has been aware of understanding others. While at times man's misunderstandings loom largest in our awareness, we should not forget the vast set of understandings of others that is basic to our being aware of these misunderstandings. To repeat the type of point made when comparing Parsons and Schutz in a stronger way - given understanding of others is primary, perhaps here is where we should start our analysis. At a minimum, our theoretical viewpoint must allow understanding of others as a primary fact. If meaning was private, society would not be possible.

There is an overlap at this level between Parsons and ethnomethodology. Garfinkel (1967, p.ix) gives Parsons, along with Schutz, Gurwitsch and Husserl, as the major influences on him. Both Parsons and ethnomethodologists accept a view of man creating social reality. Nature, the environment and man are seen as defined by man, rather than as in the positivist tradition, the environment being a set of givens to which man adjusts. Cicourel (1968) sees a fundamental feature of social interaction, the 'negotiation of reality'. While not in as strong a sense as Cicourel, the outcome of the ego-alter interaction is a negotiation of reality, for neither ego's nor alter's reality is predefined but results from the interaction. However, from the point of accepting man as the creator of his reality, ethnomethodologists and Parsons go in different directions. Ethnomethodologists focus on how men create social facts as objectively real by their on-going accomplishments. Parsons on the other hand focuses on the types of patterns these social facts form as will be discussed in the next chapter. There is also a complete difference in the 'feel' of what each does. Ethnomethodologists see the world as precarious and have the romantic-existentialist's demand that the ordinary be extraordinary and capable of being written as a thriller. Parsons, on the other hand, while making social order a central concern, appears to feel comfortable in the world.

Gouldner reacts to this tone in Parsons by saying that he (1971, p.139, my emphasis in quotation marks):

> rejected the pessimism that had long tinged German Romanticism and whose gloom had deepened in the post-Bismarckian and post-Schopenhauerian period; he crystallized a more 'optimistic' and more activist formulation of sociological Romanticism. In short, Parsons Americanized German sociological Romanticism.

The shift that Parsons has made is not just a matter of tone, style, or focusing on the more 'attractive' features of life. The optimism is built into the structure of the programme. A crucial difference between Parsons and Freud (1963) is that culture (civilization) is not seen as basically repressive. Man for Parsons discovers gratification through building culture - in fact, the theory might be called 'Civilization and its Contents'. In Marcuse's terminology, Parsons has eliminated surplus repression. (10) Parsons' starting point is similar to the position Marcuse achieves at the end of his analysis of Freud (1969, p.169):

> Libido can take the road of self-sublimation only as a 'social' phenomenon: as an unrepressed force, it can promote the formation of culture only under conditions which relate associated individuals to each other in the cultivation of the environment for their developing needs and faculties.

The basic interactive relationship is seen as non-repressive. Ego and alter establish a way of interrelating where what each does is intrinsically rewarding and brings forth favourable responses from the other. As a result,

Parsons can provide the base for a radical criticism of any social situation in which repression exists. A baseline that does not include repression means that any repression that exists calls for explanation.

The view of any action incorporated in this core case provides a solution to the instrumental-expressive action problem that was discussed in the last two chapters. The expressive component of an action is the part that corresponds to the intrinsic satisfaction that ego gets from doing the action. The instrumental component refers to the expectation of a favourable response from alter. Any institutionalized action contains both an expressive component - the action as an end in itself - and an instrumental component - a means to an end. In the language of the definition of institutionalization, the expressive component is for the actor 'a mode of gratification of his own need-dispositions' (SS, p.387) while the instrumental component is 'a condition of optimizing the reactions of other significant actors'. In the last chapter, I argued that Merton's concept of 'institutionalized means' was a contradiction in terms and that a parallel problem existed for Parsons' unit act. Now it can be seen that Parsons has transcended the problem, and why the instrumental-expressive categories largely drop out of his work after SS. (11)

It is now also possible to make sense of a major dispute in moral philosophy. Utilitarian moral philosophers based their moral prescriptions upon the assumption that actions could be described in strict means-ends terms. This is not possible for one major class of actions - institutionalized actions. One of the major reactions to utilitarian moral philosophy came from people such as Pritchard and Ross. What they did was to stress the importance of expressive action. Pritchard in particular is clear that morality deals with actions that are ends in themselves. He says (1968, pp.10-11):

> the view involves that when, or rather so far as, we act from a sense of obligation, we have no purpose or end ... The attempt to base the sense of obligation on the recognition of the goodness of something is really an attempt to find a purpose in a moral action in the shape of something good which, as good, we want. And the expectation that the goodness of something underlies an obligation disappears as soon as we cease to look for a purpose.

What the intuitionists and some others who have reacted to the utilitarians have done is to stress the expressive component of action. However, given that both the instrumental and expressive components are present together in any institutionalized action, both are only partial answers to the problem. By focusing on one feature of action, they each gain plausibility. However, given a more adequate description of action, it can be seen that any satisfactory set of moral prescriptions must take account of both components of actions.

THE WORLD SEEN IN SUBJECTIVE CATEGORIES

In order to extend a core case where ego and alter are seen as defining their reality, the world must be described in subjective categories. Parsons does provide subjective definitions of key sociological terms such as institutions (SS, p.39), allocation (SS, p.114), facilities (SS, p.119), stratification (SS, p.132) and class (EST, p.328). His definition of a possession is a good illustration of how something that is often seen objectively is defined subjectively. The key feature of possessions and property is not physical or a relationship between an individual and an object, but a social relationship among people (SS, p.119):

> the possession as such, is 'always' a right or a bundle of rights. In other words, it is a set of expectations relative to social behaviour and attitudes. It is never as such a physical object, but always consists in 'rights in' or relative to physical, social, or cultural objects, rights of use or of control of disposal.

Parsons' social action programme as has been discussed allows him to transcend some problems in his unit act framework. He drops this framework and uses roles as his least complex social unit. He defines these subjectively (SS, pp.38-9):

> A role then is a sector of the total orientation system of an individual actor which is organized about expectations in relation to a particular interaction context, that is integrated with a particular set of value-standards which govern interaction with one or more alters in the appropriate complementary roles.

Faris quotes this definition and then says that a role for Parsons is 'the response of the other' (1953, p.103). The definition he cites does not back up this contention. Somebody is not acting as a policeman whatever he does in uniform, to use Faris' example; he is only a policeman when he acts in appropriate ways. This is not to say Parsons is not confused about roles. He is, though Faris does not see how. Parsons also has a positivistic systems theory definition of role (SS, p.25):

> what the actor does in his relations with others seen in the context of its functional significance for the social system.

The point to note here is that Parsons does oscillate between the objective definition just cited and the subjective social action theory one. (12) However, the aim of this chapter is to clarify Parsons' social action theory and objective definition of role will be discussed in chapter 8.

A core case which sees ego and alter as defining reality and a set of subjective definitions of the features of society makes sense only if these features are central to explaining what goes on in society. As argued in chapter 1, definitions are implicit theories about the key features of a case. Parsons' concept of structure as 'those elements of the patterning of the system which may be regarded as independent of the lower-amplitude and shorter time-range fluctuations' (TS, p.36) can be (13) seen as a claim that this is indeed so. He claims that the most permanent features of social interaction are values, norms, collectivities and roles. This is what constitutes the structure of any social system. Parsons here is claiming for instance that a person who sells goods door to door groups together the range of actions involved in this, on the basis that they are all part of the salesman role. Other possible bases of grouping activity together (e.g. geographical) are, he must say, less permanent. In the next chapter, I shall look at the PVs and FDs, Parsons' two main categories for analysing the structure or patterning of social systems.

One objection to this whole approach to analysing society might be that it reifies people. The answer to this is that yes it does reify people in the sense that it claims that people do reify themselves and others. This seems to me a tenable claim about how people normally interact. Even Sartre says that men must live in bad faith. However, as I shall argue later, Parsons' problem is that he does not allow for a creative breakdown of this reification. It should be noted that in this context many of the pejorative implications of reification break down. If it is accepted that men normally reify each other (in fact so doing is a necessary condition for social interaction), then the accusation that one is reifying another loses much of its force. Acceptance of this will lead to another approach to what is involved in reification.

CONCLUSION

Parsons has locked man firmly into society. Man is fully social. In the preceding chapter it was seen that social ends made all responses of other people a form of social control on the individual. The control of society over the individual is now made complete - not only do others react to him in such a way as to control him - he also has internalized values and controls himself. That man is controlled by social process is not to say he is repressed. The culture he builds while it controls him also allows man to fulfil himself. The problem with this perspective, I shall argue later, particularly in chapter 7, is that it excludes human creativity.

The next three chapters examine various extensions of the core case of the social action programme. Chapter 5 discusses how Parsons sees the meanings men create patterned in terms of the FDs and PVs, while chapter 6 discusses learning. Chapter 7 will bring together material from chapters 4 to 6 in order to look at how Parsons deals with conflict, change and deviance.

5 The patterning of meaning: pattern variables and functional dimensions

The centre of Parsons' work (1) for many people is summed up in Figure 1.

	universalism neutrality	affectivity particularism
specificity performance	A adaptation	G goal-attainment
quality diffuseness	latency (tension- management and pattern- maintenance) L	integration I

FIGURE 1

The object of this chapter is to elucidate the meaning of this diagram in Parsons' social action programme. In terms of the PVs and FDs, he discusses the patterning or structure of a social system. These variables are ways of describing certain features of the consensus which is inherent in his core case. They are, as fits with this core case, categories of meaning. In terms of the relationships among the PVs and FDs, Parsons establishes certain limitations on the possible patterning of the meanings involved in action.

Parsons' classification of PVs and FDs and their interrelations is the basis of his answer to a long running concern in his work. Even before SSA, he argues for the necessity of a system of ultimate ends (1935, p.295), while the existence of a set of common ends is central to his argument in SSA. The PV and FD classifications are a way in his social action programme of extending his analysis of the consensus. A consensus by itself is insufficient to provide a viable pattern of interaction. In addition (SS, p.52):

> the 'content' of the common patterns of value-orientation must be such that the reciprocal orientations of the interacting actors will mesh with each other. There is a variety of different patterns according to which such meshing is conceivable, but in 'any given' system of interactive relationships the patterns must have been selected from among these possibilities in such a way as to be compatible with the stability of the interaction process.

In this chapter I will start with a discussion of the PVs which are a classification of orientations, then discuss the FDs which are a classification of the types of meanings of actions, then functional differentiation. Next I will discuss the way the PV and FD classifications are linked by Parsons to delimit the possible stable patterns of interaction. Finally I will discuss examples of how the FDs can be applied to suicide and homicide.

It should be stressed that this chapter focuses on the FDs in social action theory. One of the major sources of confusion in Parsons is that he also has a completely different interpretation of the FDs in systems theory. Within systems theory or structural functionalism they are a classification not of the meanings of actions but of the types of consequences an action can have for a system. For instance an adaptive action is one that has adaptive or maladaptive consequences for the structure of the system. This type of interpretation of the FDs is an extension of what in a loose way is called functionalism. I am reserving discussion of it in detail until Chapter 8.

PATTERN VARIABLES

PVs are used to characterize orientations. Orientations, I shall argue, are the subjective counterparts of behaviour where behaviour is seen as the physical processes the actor goes through. This position can be elucidated in opposition to that of Whyte, who says (1964, p.255) that Parsons is not concerned with the actions of people. (2)

> Parsons is instead concerned with 'the orientation of the actor to the situation.' In the world of Talcott Parsons, actors are constantly orienting themselves to

> situations and very rarely, if ever, acting. The show is constantly in rehearsal, but the curtain never goes up. Parsons focuses on the process whereby the individual sizes up his social environment and makes up his mind about what he might do. At this point he stops. It is precisely at this point that some of us wish to focus our attention.

Whyte then, to support his claims, quotes Parsons' saying (1964, p.256):

> the 'Theory of Action' is clearly not a theory of behavior in the more immediate sense, particularly concerned with the physical movements of organisms ... It is rather a theory that is concerned with the analysis of certain mechanisms which control behavior in this latter sense, which therefore in the old-fashioned, behavioristic sense, are not visible not immediately observable, which I think in the organism operate overwhelmingly in the brain.

Parsons also states, concerning the relationship between orientations and actions (TGTA, p.4):

> Action has an orientation when it is guided by the meaning which the actor attaches to it ...

and (TGTA, p.161): (3)

> action itself is the first order derivative from the orientation; that is, it is caused by the orientation.

This last remark in particular is open to the interpretation that the relationship between orientations and actions is a causal temporal one as Whyte suggests. However, I suggest that it is best read in conjunction with the previous quotation. In this case, orientations are what make behaviour, action. If one focuses purely on the relations between the organism and its environment, then this is a focus on pure behaviour. What makes behaviour, action is that the actor is orienting. It is because the actor attaches subjective significance to what he does that it is action, not behaviour (SECP, p.5). Orientations for Parsons are a fundamental component of action. If an actor orients in a certain way, it means that he acts in that way. For instance to say that an actor orients affectively is to say that an actor acts affectively.

It is not possible to deduce from a person's observed behaviour what PVs should be used to describe it. For instance, consider a white employer who hires only white people. From this fact, one cannot tell whether he is acting universalistically - hiring all whites as he can understand their way of speaking - or particularistically - hiring a person of his colour of skin. The point of view of a detached neutral scientific observer is inadequate - 'verstehen' is required. As orientations are the subjective counterparts of behaviour, a simple description of the behaviour will be inadequate for ascertaining what the subjective counterpart is.

As was discussed in chapter 4, roles for Parsons are defined in terms of orientations. Thus, a classification of orientations provides a classification of roles, and he uses the PVs to classify roles. This enterprise seems an extremely worth-while one. Normally sociologists classify roles as they are classified in ordinary life, which tends to be in terms of function loosely defined. The result is a list of roles that ranges from funeral director to mother. Some are found only in one society, others in most. The basic problem is the list is endless. By classifying roles in terms of the PVs, Parsons arrives at a limited number of possible types of roles. This raises the possibility of stating some regularities about roles. Any laws one states about roles when classified in terms of PVs will be applicable in numerous contexts. A law about a funeral director's role, on the other hand, will tend to be so specific that it rules out contrary cases. This criticism does not apply where a writer has attempted to classify roles by some scheme, though most classifications do not claim to be as exhaustive as the PVs (in terms of which any role can be classified). Similar remarks apply to Parsons' classifications of norms, values (4) and need-dispositions (5) in terms of PVs.

Permit me to reassert the importance of classifying roles and other things in terms of a schema like the PVs, for I am fed up with reading studies which use variables such as male-female. I know that they are easy to operationalize and a lot of things correlate well with them. However, the age-old questions need to be asked: 'What is the nature of man?' and 'What is the nature of woman?' Any answer is clearly relative to a given time and place. Consequently the use of variables such as male-female in sociology constitutes reification of the worst sort. Is it not about time sociology grew up? (6)

Parsons' acceptance of the PVs as a classification of all orientations implies a reductive programme. All other ways of orientating must be shown to be particular instances of some set of PVs. This programme commits one to showing that the meaning of any orientation can be subsumed under the PVs by a reduction or to deriving it by introducing appropriate restrictions to some set of PVs. Parsons discusses this problem only briefly and argues for instance that traditionalism refers to PV choices over time (TGTA, p.90). In order to illustrate how this reduction might be carried out, I shall look briefly at reification as the term is normally understood.

If a person reifies himself or another person, then he sees himself or the other person as a thing. I shall consider the case of a person reifying another person. This person will be seen objectively; he will be considered as a fixed bundle of attributes that can do certain things and will react in distinct ways to certain situations. The person who reifies him might say: 'He is frightened by bank managers and will stutter when he walks into the bank manager's office.' He would see no potential for change. Within Parsonian action theory the problem is to describe the person's orientations when he reifies another. (7) As he judges the other objectively, one of his orientations will be universalistic. He sees the other not as somebody special (particularistically), but in terms of a set of characteristics that any number of people could have. In addition, he is concerned with the other's capabilities, not the sort of person he is. Thus, he orients to the other in a way characterized by achievement, not quality. Treating the other person as a thing, the reifier sees the other's reactions to situations in a detached way. He does not emphathize with the other. He orients to him neutrally, not affectively. The fourth orientation he has to the other is specificity. He sees the other in particular situations with a well-defined range of interests and does not have a general diffuse orientation. Thus the orientations of a person who reifies another are characterized by universalism, achievement, neutrality and specificity. In contrast to this way of orienting to others, the most 'human' way would appear to be the exact opposite - in terms of particularism, quality, affectivity and diffuseness. Later in this chapter it will be seen that the 'reification' set of PVs characterizes adaption while the 'humanistic' set characterizes integration. This reification example shows how one might (8) go about reducing some orientation to one characterized in terms of the PVs. To arrive at a more definitive judgment on the PVs, this type of reductive project must be attempted on a large number of ways in which people characterize orientations. What can be said is that they appear to be a useful addition to social action theory.

THE FUNCTION DIMENSIONS

The label 'functionalist' is frequently applied to Parsons, yet few people attempt seriously to assess what difference his use of the FDs makes to his 'functionalism'. In so far as he differs from the anthropological functionalism of Malinowski or Radcliffe-Brown, a part of the difference rests with the use of the FDs. Parsons has written an article in which he says that these categories are 'the master-classification of functional imperatives of any social system, or indeed any system of action' (1964a, p.65) and criticizes Malinowski for his failure to grasp their importance (1964a, p.66):

> I should maintain, then, that Malinowski's late classification of the functional imperatives of culture, or as I should prefer to say of a social system, could well have constituted a basic starting point for a general theoretical analysis of social systems in their own right, not just as derivatives of basic biological needs. Unfortunately, however, this notable contribution stands as a virtually isolated fragment.

Given that Parsons himself believes that his position is importantly different from Malinowski's, the statement that he is a functionalist in the normally understood meaning of the term should be the conclusion of an analysis, not (as for Gouldner, 1971) (9) a premise.

In Parsons' social action programme, the FDs are a classification of action in terms of the meaning of the action. At one point Parsons (1964b, p.330) talks about 'the four basic functional meanings' and if he had used this term more often he might have avoided a great deal of confusion both in his own thinking and in how others read him. However, as his basic term is 'functional dimension', I shall stick to it. In this approach an action can have adaptive (A), goal-attainment (G), integrative (I), or latency (L) meaning. An action with goal-attainment meaning is one which is seen to be a direct enactment of the values of the social system in question; adaptive acts are ones that are seen as producing facilities for the attainment of goals. Integrative acts are ones that assert the solidarity of the social system's members. Latency acts are ones that help manage tension and maintain the pattern. Parsons' view that acts can be functional or dysfunctional within this approach can be interpreted as meaning that acts can have either positive or negative meaning. For instance, a dysfunctional adaptive action is one that is believed to take away from or diminish the facilities the social system has for achieving its goals. This approach is not concerned with whether an action is adaptive, but with whether it is believed to be.

This conception of the functional dimensions comes from (10) a set of categories which Bales developed for the analysis of task-oriented small groups. He analyses the interaction of a group of people who have been given a clearly specific problem to solve. He takes as a given (and reasonably, in his experimental situation) that the groups do aim to find an acceptable solution to a problem that has been set for them. Bales claims to classify actions according to how they appear to the actor to whom they are addressed (1950, p.39). The meaning of an act to an alter is presumably a result of two things, the act itself and how alter perceives the act. To a paranoid, almost all acts appear hostile and would have to be classed as type twelve (shows antagonism). Bales never gets into this problem and in fact implicitly makes a consensus assumption that allows him to classify the acts from a group point of view. In Parsons, this consensus assumption is explicit and, as was discussed in chapter 4, provides a way of talking about the meaning of actions on a social level. The FDs are Parsons' major classification for discussing such meanings.

	instrumental	consummatory
external	adaptation	goal-attainment
internal	latency	integration

FIGURE 2

Parsons claims that the four FDs are an exhaustive set and can be generated by crossing the two 'axes of differentiation' (1964b, p.330): instrumental-consummatory and external-internal (11) (1964b, pp.330-1). This can be seen in Figure 2 (1964b, p.331). The external-internal distinction subsumes, he claims (1964b, p.330), the self-orientation-collectivity-orientation distinction which he originally proposed as a PV pair. This attempt to cross axes of differentiation to obtain the FDs does not work. External-internal is a systems theory concept which will be discussed in chapter 8. The problem with elucidating these concepts in action theory is that it does not make sense to talk of external and internal meanings - or at least the ways in which one might elaborate external and internal meaning bear no relationship to the functional dimensions. Yet is possible to give a distinction in action theory that gets at what Parsons is trying to get at by the distinction external-internal. This distinction is specific-general or concrete-symbolic. Using this distinction, Figure 3 can be drawn.

	instrumental	consummatory
specific (concrete)	adaptation	goal-attainment
general (symbolic)	latency	integration

FIGURE 3

By this diagram, goal attainment actions are ones where the actor is achieving specific or concrete goals or ends. Adaptive actions are ones the actor sees as providing the means to such goals. Integrative actions are ones where the actor is attaining general or symbolic ends. The consummatory activity he is engaging in is generalized. For instance a friendly action is one that symbolizes the friendship. On the other hand, going to a circus with a friend would be a specific concrete end and thus a goal-attainment action. Latency actions are ones which having the meaning of providing general or symbolic means. These actions are not ends in themselves but are seen as providing general ways of getting to one's goals. For instance, learning might be seen as a general way of attaining goals. All these actions can be negative as well as positive. An action for instance could be seen as a failure to attain a specific goal.

This spelling out of each of the FDs in terms of instrumental-consummatory and specific-general gives a close fit with how Parsons describes each of the cells except for latency. What I want to argue now is that this characterization of latency solves a number of problems that are in Parsons' characterization of this FD. He identifies latency with values and the basic pattern of meaning. The problem here is that he also characterizes latency acts as instrumental, and one's basic pattern of meaning and values cannot be a matter of expediency. He also describes latency actions as being both pattern-maintenance and tension-management actions. The problem here is that a person could feel he is 'letting off steam' (i.e. tension management) and at the same time feel that he is tending to break the pattern down (negative pattern-maintenance). The action is both functional and dys-functional at the same time as two different things are involved in this characterization of L. The problem arises as tension-management's referent would appear to be the personality. Given Parsons' assertion of the indepen-dence of the personality level and social system level, this is unacceptable. Blain (1970) makes a similar point to the above, but on a more general level. Parsons says that integrative acts focus on the inter-unit level while latency acts focus on the intra-unit level. Thus Blain argues that the referent for latency is always at a different level than that for integrative acts. There is an interesting bit of 'empirical proof' of this conceptual confusion. Sydiaha, in a study using Bales' categories, has the lowest correlations between two repeated scorings of recorded interviews in Bales' categories 2(.70) and 10(.71) (1961, p.394). These are two categories which Parsons includes in latency (WP, p.74).

If one sees latency actions as general or symbolic means, then one fits them under the instrumental category as Parsons claims, avoids the previous discussed problems, and can subsume under the category most of what Parsons wishes to fit into it. For instance, in small problem-solving groups, passive agreement and disagreement are seen as latency actions. Passive agreement or disagreement is seen by the group's members as increasing or decreasing on a general level the ability of the group to attain its specific and general goals. On a societal level, Parsons sees educational institutions and the family as engaging primarily in latency activities. From a social point of view, raising children and educating them has the meaning of providing the children with the general means of attaining what they want. Parsons in his later work calls latency the fiduciary sub-system and says that this sub-system (Amer U, p.8) 'acts as a trustee of some interests in the society, e.g. conservation groups belong to the fiduciary sub-system insofar as they protect the societal interest in the natural environment.' While this definition fits into systems theory or structural functionalism as an activity is defined in terms of its consequences, not its meaning, the idea behind this conception of latency fits the interpretation of latency as generalized means. Where people see themselves as preserving the environment, they see their actions as providing general resources (means) for society.

Given that the four functional dimensions are interpreted this way, and that Parsons claims they are an exhaustive classification of all actions, a reductive enterprise is called for. Just as one is committed to showing how the meaning of all orientations can be reduced to the PVs, so too one is committed to showing that the meaning of all actions can be reduced to the four FDs. This is for Parsons a totally untouched reductive programme. What is involved is similar to what is involved in the previously discussed PV case. The relationships between the PVs and the FDs, which will be discussed later in this chapter, are helpful in carrying out this reductive programme.

If one removes the assumption of consensus which allows us to talk about the social meaning of action, it is still possible to use the four functional dimensions as a typology of types of meaning. It can be the meaning to the actor who performs the act. Second, they can be used to classify the meaning of the act to the person to whom it is addressed. The meaning of the action, as was noted earlier when discussing Bales, will depend on both the action and alter. Third, one can ask the meaning of the act to a group of people. The act may be addressed to more than one person, or even if it is directed to one, may be reacted to by several. If there is a consensus, then the meaning of the act will be the same for everybody and we are back to the social meaning position. Alternatively, if cognitive dissensus exists in a social system, then a complete description of the act will include its meanings to different people. A description of the act might be something like this: to 30% of the social system's members, including ego, the action had an adaptive meaning; to 60%, including the person addressed, it had latency meaning; to 10%, goal-attainment; to none did it have an integrative meaning. This approach becomes interesting when one starts to talk about the different roles of the people to whom the act appeared as of one sort rather than another. For instance an action might appear as adaptive to the political elite and disintegrative to union members.

At this point a critic might say, 'I see how A, G, I and L can be seen as categories of meaning, but why call them functional dimensions?' This objection can be approached in two ways.

The first answer is to say that the term 'functional' does describe dimensions of meaning. People's basic categories of meaning concern things seen in terms of their functions defined in some loose way. People see their own actions and other things in terms of what they are, meaning by this some intrinsic quality of the act. To see the world in terms of 'doing' categories, as opposed to categories describing states of being, seems to be in some way a rather Puritan view of the world - which fits with Parsons' background as the son of a Congregational minister (Mitchel, 1967, p.2). At one point, he says that a person is defined by his deeds (FSI, p.57): (12)

> in the process of socialization, 'ego' comes to be 'he who' in relation to alter does so and so under given conditions. 'There is no other meaningful

answer to the question what ego is, if ego as personality is conceived to be a system of action.'

The second line of approach to the previously raised objection is that Parsons consistently mixes, without realizing it, his social action theory interpretation of A, G, I and L with his systems theory one. This can be seen by comparing the references given in this chapter's footnotes for the action theory interpretation with those in chapter 8 for the systems theory interpretation. These references are to the same books. It can be argued that the names he gives the functional dimensions betray the confusion. Goal-attainment suggests people pursuing goals and this fits action theory, while adaptation suggests an adjustive mechanism suitable for a systems theory. The A, G, I and L categories are central to both the action and systems programmes and mean different things in each, so it would be better to use two separate terms to refer to them. Thus, basically this critic would be right.

Parsons' confusion about the term 'functional' is, however, typical of a general confusion in the functionalist approach to sociology. While Parsons' use of 'function' involved in the term 'functional dimension' has little to do with the nature of functional analysis, as this analysis is seen formally, it has a great deal to do with how functional analysis is actually used.

Isajiw points to the central problem of functionalism by asking whether 'x has the function of A for system y' means 'x is a cause of Ay' or 'Ay is a cause of x' (1968, pp.28-9). There have been several good philosophical analyses of functionalism, for example Hempel (1959), Nagel (1967), and Rudner (1966, pp.84-111). These seem to be acceptable models of explanation, yet they disagree on this question which Isajiw sees as central. Hempel focuses on explaining that which has the function, while Rudner focuses on explaining a 'G' state (a state of the system which tends to be maintained). When one meets this sort of variation on such a central question, it seems reasonable to assume, especially if nothing seems wrong with the forms of explanation presented, that these analyses are prescriptive, not descriptive. That is to say, they tell us of ways that functional terminology could be used rather than the way it is used. Consequently, in order to understand what underlies functional terminology, I wish to look at its 'use'.

The problem Isajiw started with is the essential characteristic of its use - one is not sure what is being explained. In order to illustrate this and to clarify the usage, I shall look at a classic example of functionalism - Davis' account of religion. In 'Human Society', he sets out 'to offer a scientific explanation of religion' (n.d., p.509). What is to be explained is religion. Yet we find that his central claims are about religion's effects on society (n.d., p.524; then p.529):

> The relation of these (sacred objects) to society is not a symbolic relation but only a functional one: the effect of the beliefs and rites with respect to sacred symbols is to create a more cohesive society.
>
> Religion, then, does four things that help to maintain the dominance of sentiment over organic desire, of group ends over private interest. First, it offers, through its system of supernatural belief, an explanation of the group ends and a justification of their primacy ... In these ways religion makes a unique and indispensable contribution to social integration.

These claims may help to explain why a society is cohesive, (13) but they do not give a causal explanation of why religion exists. At this point, the normal philosophical analysis tends to add a step (e.g. a Darwinian survival argument). There are, I assume, a number of such steps that could be added, some plausible, some implausible. The point is that such steps are not added and the defence that they are obvious is untenable.

What then is the structure of Davis' analysis of religion? The usual step at this point is to discount his original statement that he is interested in explaining religion and say that he is interested in explaining the effects of religion. The plausibility of this step rests on there being no suggested way in which the claim that religion is integrative can be seen as an analysis of religion itself. I would like to suggest that Davis can be interpreted (14) as engaging in a reduction of the meaning of religion to an integrative meaning. His argument can be seen as attempting to establish that for a society, religion has an integrative meaning. (15) In this way his discussion of religion can be seen in an action theory as an explanation of religion.

If this analysis of how functionalism is used is accepted, then one can understand why functionalism is frequently accused of teleology. For instance, if Davis' argument about religion is seen as one which argues that religion has an integrative meaning to a society's members, then this position can be recast teleologically. This would be done by saying that the 'integrative needs' of society caused the religion. This claim is seldom actually made by functionalists. However, from the analysis of how functionalism is used, it can be easily inserted as a way of clearing up the muddle. Sociologists could have spared themselves the sterile dispute over teleology, whose only use seems to be to provide an introductory theory class topic, if they had analysed how functionalism is used.

Another way to tackle the question of usage is to ask why Marx and Marxists do not use functionalist terminology. Kingsley Davis says that Marx's claim that religion is the opium of the masses can be reformulated in functionalist terms (1967). It could be, but the point is, it is not. And the interesting question is why.

Perhaps the best place to start is Marx's discussion of profit in 'Capital'. He argues that though in some cases profit is just a by-product of, or means to, another activity, given the nature of the capitalist system, all activity of a certain type can usefully be treated together. The occasional idiosyncratic (i.e. non-profit) motive does not affect the type of consequences that profit-making activity has on the system in which it occurs. If one wishes to run a left-wing newspaper, one still has to make a profit because of the nature of the capitalist system. Identifying profit-making activity is not a problem, what its consequences are is.

Returning now to the question of the opium of the masses, it can be seen that the focus is on the effects of religion. Religion has the consequence of making the worker more willing to accept his class position. Marx does not wish to claim that the subjective significance of religion for people is that it means contentment with one's lot. To do so would create problems about true and false consciousness. Second, the Marxist is morally opposed to religion having such a meaning. (16) The Marxist has no desire to bring in indirectly any claims about the meaning of religion when he says that it is the opium of the masses. (17) Consequently he avoids using functionalist terminology.

Thus Parsons, in calling A, G, I and L functional dimensions, is using the term 'functional' as it is frequently used in the literature, though not as it purports to be used in the literature according to the philosophy of social science. His confusion is typical of a muddle that exists in the functionalist approach.

The other term Parsons frequently uses for A, G, I or L is 'functional problems'. This term also strikes me as unfortunate. It would be better to name them 'functional opportunities' or 'functional possibilities'. The advantages of these terms are that they eliminate cognitive bias in the concept and also eliminate the suggestion that there is necessarily something external to the actor or social system that must be coped with. In addition and related to the last point, as values are internalized for

Parsons, the genesis of the action can easily be primarily internal.

FUNCTIONAL DIFFERENTIATION

No action is exclusively in one FD - we may have many reasons for doing one action. The classification is an analytic one. No action could be exclusively a specific consummatory act. To some extent it would also be general and symbolic and a means, if only peripherally, to other ends. However, to the extent that the meanings of action do get separated from each other, they separate into A, G, I and L actions. Parsons calls the process of separation a meaning-'functional differentiation'. A fully differentiated social system would be one in which its members distinguished clearly and distinctly four different categories of meaningful action or subjectively grouped classes of meaningful activity. I shall call such a class of meaningful activity a sector.

A sector should be distinguished from a sub-system of the type Parsons uses in his systems theory. A sub-system in systems theory (e.g. the adaptive sub-system) is a system of a larger system. This sub-system is capable of being broken down into A, G, I and L components. In a sector, on the other hand, all actions have the same type of meaning. For instance, all adaptive actions in the adaptive sector will have an adaptive meaning and be characterized by the appropriate PVs (see next section of this chapter). This approach does not exclude the possibility of there being a system of adaptive actions. However, such a system will be composed entirely of adaptive acts and is not equivalent to a sub-system of the type Parsons discusses in system theory.

This approach sees functional differentiation as proceeding only as far as the four sectors. Further functional differentiation does not make sense because one cannot make sense of the idea of say an adaptive sub-sector of the adaptive sector. An additional reason why further functional differentiation does not make sense will be clear after the relationship between the FDs and PVs is discussed. Thus the image of society, when fully differentiated into sectors, is one in which all adaptive activity is in one area of society, all political in another, and so on. One might think of a society with four institutions.

Suppose we call the latency institution the family. This 'family' would be very unlike the family we know in our society. It would engage in latency activity only.

Thus a decision as to whether to have children or not, if seen to have an effect on the relationship between a society and its environment, would be taken not by the family but by the polity (G). Alternatively, this approach can be seen in terms of the meaning of actions becoming more differentiated without presupposing a differentiation of institutions. Thus a decision to have a child is seen as being in one way a political decision and in another an economic (as potential labour), etc. The different aspects of the act become clearer as functional differentiation proceeds and are related to as distinct separate meanings.

There appear to be two different ways in which this programme can be developed. The first is to claim that 'people group all acts in a sector together'. For instance, one might claim that people see as one sector of activity all latency institutions - the family, the education system and their religious devotions. To say they see them as one type of activity is to claim that people link these subjectively more to each other than they do to any other activities. A critic might object at this point and say that people see religious activities both in a latency dimension (devotion, basic underlying faith that supports all their activities) and in the integrative dimension (attending church is an action with meaning in terms of their status in society). Consequently the meaning of an activity does not differentiate along the lines of the functional dimensions. A possible response to this criticism is to say that ordinary language may mask some meanings people actually separate. People could use the word 'religious activity' to cover private devotions and attending church, yet still have these as significantly distinguished activities. 'Significantly distinguished' here means that the person associates his private devotions (L) subjectively more with raising his children (L), than his private devotions (L) with church attendance (I). The type of evidence that might support this is when in places other than his home town, the person no longer attends church as it is no longer a social occasion for him, yet still continues his religious devotions.

The second possible way of developing their programme is to say that any subjectively grouped set of activities will tend to be in one functional dimension but that these various sets may not be that closely tied to each other. While this is a weaker claim than the first, it nevertheless is a social action theory law about how meaningful activities are patterned.

One way in which it would be possible to develop either of these two approaches to functional differentiation would be to get the participants in one of Bales' small task-oriented groups to tell in their own words how the discussion had gone. One could then compare their description of the interaction and see if it corresponded with the phase-movement account of it that could be compiled from the scoring of the interaction by an observer. (18) A phase is an interval of time in which acts in one particular functional dimension predominate. A phase-movement account of an interaction gives the order and duration of each phase in the interaction. (19) While there are some complexities (20) involved in developing the functional differentiation hypotheses in this way, the advantage is that a closing of the functional dimension concepts for small task-oriented groups is available in Bales' categories. (21)

PATTERN-VARIABLES AND FUNCTIONAL DIMENSIONS

The FDs are related by Parsons to the PVs in a way that can be read off the box diagram at the start of this chapter. Parsons is claiming that a definite relationship exists between these two classifications. For instance, if a person's orientations are characterized by quality, diffuseness, affectivity and particularism, then the action will have an integrative meaning. This is one reason why an interpretation of the FDs in action theory is required and possible.

Parsons, however, is muddled on the nature of the relationship that exists between the PVs and FDs. For instance, he mentions (WP, pp.163-4, my emphasis in quotation marks):

> the conception of four dimensions, which correspond to the four system-problems of Bales and which are 'defined' in terms of the pattern variable concepts ...

On the next page he mentions (p.165, my emphasis in quotation marks):

> the four dimensions which in chapter three we 'derived' by bringing together the four system-problems of Bales and four of the five pattern-variables of Parsons and Shils.

The two statements are incompatible. If the FDs are defined in terms of the PVs, then they cannot be derived from the four PVs and the four system problems of Bales as this implies that the four PVs are insufficient by themselves to allow one to derive the FDs. Similarly, the four systems problems of Bales cannot both be equivalent to the four FDs and the four PVs be necessary to the derivation of the functional dimensions. This type of confusion can be shown to exist in several places, but I will let the one example suffice.

In addition to Parsons' confusion about the nature of the linkage between the FDs and PVs, when he tries to justify the particular linkage between a given FD and set of PVs, he uses a systems theory conception of the FDs (WP, pp.179-90). Thus, when he puts forward one of his main social action theory laws - the relationship between four FDs and four sets of PVs - Parsons has his feet firmly planted in mid-air. The easiest way of putting some foundation under the PV-FD link is to base it on some 'thought experiments'. The argument would run that if a person is orienting in a universalistic, neutral, specific and performance manner, then he must see the situation in adaptive terms. As a consensus assumption is made, how he sees the situation is how others see it too and so it can be said that from a social point of view the action is adaptive. A similar type of argument and in more detail is required for all the PV-FD relationships. Certainly something is needed to fill this gaping hole in the middle of Parsons' social action programme.

This linkage between the PVs and FDs can be seen as a means of arriving at the 'real' meaning of an action to an actor or society. For instance, an actor may claim that he is engaging in an activity for adaptive reasons. If however, one notes that his orientation is characterized by affectivity, particularism, performance and specificity, it is fair to conclude that in fact the activity has goal-attainment (G) meaning for him. One would then start to examine why the actor wishes to say that what he is doing is 'just' instrumental. One possible explanation might involve the Puritan work ethic. To be able to develop this section of the action theory programme it is necessary in cases like this (i.e. where the person says the action is in a particular FD but has the 'wrong' orientation), to produce some explanation of why the actor is distorting the significance of the action.

Cicourel criticizes non-ethnomethodological approaches for their failure to develop rules for how the researcher assigns meaning to the behaviour of actors (1968, ch.1). While he takes pains to place the interactions he discusses in a context by describing their backdrop as seen by the participants, he does not escape this criticism he makes of others. He basically broadens the problem to developing procedural rules for assigning meaning to the actor's activity and its backdrop. The PV-FD link can be seen as providing part of an answer, for, if it is correct, one can check whether assigning the meaning of latency to the act is correct by checking if the PVs are appropriate.

Durkheim's analysis of religion can be interpreted in terms of this law relating an actor's orientations to the social meaning of an action. Religion cannot be seen as bad science, for the attitude that people have when engaged in religious activity is unlike those that characterize technical manipulative activity. Religious activity on the other hand is characterized by orientations that express solidarity. Consequently, religion should be seen as integrative and not as adaptive activity (as bad science). Malinowski's point that the Trobrianders clearly separate magical techniques and practical techniques in their gardening (1948, pp.1-67) can be seen as an argument that subjectively the differentiation of meaning does exist. From an action theory point of view, that would appear to be how Durkheim should be seen. (22) However, whether religion has an integrative or latency meaning is, to my mind, an open question.

One major problem (that Parsons never faces), created by the PV-FD link is what to do about actions characterized by other than the four PV combinations that relate to the FDs. As he claims that the FDs are exhaustive, one might expect him to claim that only these four PV combinations are possible. However, he gives a table of types of value components of role-expectation that lists all sixteen logically possible combinations of PVs (TGTA, Fig.4). TGTA and SS, in particular, give numerous examples of actions characterized by PV combinations that are other than the four sets that fit the FDs. As Parsons claims that the FDs are an exhaustive classification, he has a major problem here. He never tackles this question. What he would appear to have to say is that actions characterized by PV combinations other than those that fit the FDs have mixed meanings. For instance, such an act would have not an unambiguously integrative meaning, but rather (say) a partial integrative meaning and a partial meaning of some other sort (perhaps adaptive).

This solution creates another problem (or opportunity) for developing the programme. His functional differentiation hypothesis, that social systems tend to differentiate into four sectors, means that such acts should tend to disappear. Here Parsons seems to be consistent, for many of his analyses of actions not characterized by the appropriate PVs (i.e. those that correspond to the FDs) see such actions as unstable or difficult to maintain in meaning. (23) Those which were written prior to his development of the FDs can be seen as confirmation of the adequacy of the FD-PV tie-up. For instance, he says that a universalistic, affective, diffuse orientation is difficult to maintain (SS, p.85). He gives as a possible example of this, 'religious universalism' (SS, p.85), which he says 'easily shifts into a denominational particularism' (SS, p.85) which makes it possible for it to fit a PV set that characterizes a FD. I'm not sure what he has in mind, but he could possibly be interpreted as saying that men tend not to love God defined in some universalistic way, but the God of 'my' people. Many of history's innumerable religious wars could be offered as evidence.

FUNCTIONAL DIMENSION CLASSIFICATIONS

In this section I shall discuss classifications that I have worked out myself of suicide and homicide in terms of the FDs. The purpose is to illustrate briefly how such classifications work and their usefulness. Both suicide and homicide are actions people do for many different reasons. The FDs provide a classification of these reasons. An act done for an adaptive reason is very likely to require a different explanation than one done for an integrative reason. By breaking up the categories of suicide and homicide, it is possible to understand how such a proliferation of theories has developed in these areas (Figure 4).

A		G
	e.g. Samsonic	e.g. 'neurotic' - acting out
	e.g. some political protests	e.g. cry for help
L		I

FIGURE 4 Types of suicide

An adaptive suicide is one where it is seen as a means to some end. Jeffreys' notion of Samsonic suicide (1952) would appear to fit into this category. In certain African tribes a person believes that, if he kills himself, he will become a ghost capable of taking revenge on other people. Alternatively, the person may know that, by killing himself, he will force society to make the person he names as responsible for his death suffer (by a fine, or even death). Another example of adaptive suicide would be a 'suicide squad' in wartime. Their deaths are seen as a means to attaining some vital military objective.

Many of the suicides studied by psychologists and psychiatrists appear to be goal-attainment suicides - ones where the meaning of the suicide is a direct fulfilment of goals. Many psychological theories of suicide stress the loss of a loved object (usually a person). Freud postulates a death-wish. Suicide comes to be explained in terms of this death-wish or an attack against a loved person with whom the individual has identified himself. The stress in many studies is on the fairly recent rejection by a loved one. If the descriptions in such studies are accurate, the suicides would appear to be goal-attainment ones.

Sociologists appear to have focused more on integrative suicides - ones which are focused on the person's desire to be integrated with others. This type of suicide is often a 'cry for help' (Farberon and Heidman, 1961). The 'successful' suicide is often the culmination of a series of attempted suicides and frequently its 'success' appears to be 'accidental'. Sociologists tend to focus on this type of suicide as they usually rely on official suicide statistics. The fewer persons close to an individual there are, the less pressure on the authorities not to classify the death as suicide. Another example of integrative suicide is provided by Firth (1961). He suggests that Tikopian suicide attempts involved a gamble with death, with the stakes loaded in favour of death, yet with a win being reacceptance into the society. An individual after committing an offence may start swimming out to sea or may set out alone in a small canoe. He is taking a big gamble, for if the weather is bad and/or the rescue fleet does not organize quickly, he is doomed. However, as he has thrown himself onto the care of his society, he acknowledges its authority and makes his reintegration into society possible.

A latency suicide is one that is concerned with the assertion of basic patterns of meaning. An example would be the monks in South Vietnam who poured kerosene on themselves and lit it. One point to note here is that the FDs focus on the meaning of an action, not the value placed on it. Thus these monks were seen not as acting out some neurotic fantasy but as making a political protest, though reactions to this were both pro and con.

The basic attraction of this classification of suicide is that it causes one to give up the search for a theory of suicide. Suicide is done for too many different reasons for one theory to fit them all. However, the classification suggests some useful starting points for explanation. It also helps one understand why sociologists and psychologists have tended to differ on this subject. Sociologists have tended to focus on integrative suicides, psychologists on goal-attainment suicides. If the action means different things, then one should not expect agreement on the theory of why it was done (see Figure 5).

Homicide

A		G
	e.g. detective story murders	e.g. bar-room brawls
	e.g. feuding revenges	e.g. kin murders
L		I

FIGURE 5

The normal crime novel is a whodunit - there is a long chain of reasoning connecting the murderer to his victim and his ultimate objective. This type of literature thus sees murder as adaptive. Theorists who have seen murder as the result of a subculture of violence (e.g. Wolfgang, 1966) focus particularly on bar-room brawls. Most of these would be goal-attainment suicides. The category of integrated homicide appears filled. An example would be many murders of close kin (usually husband or wife or vice versa). These are usually the result of a breakdown of a marriage that has built up over a long period of time. (24) Murders resulting from feuds between two clans would often be examples of latency homicides. Here killing somebody from the other clan is asserting that one's own clan will not permit its members to be killed without revenge being extracted. Another example would be the death penalty. The purpose of this classification is again to suggest that no one theory of homicide is possible and, in addition, these categories may provide the basis of sufficiently homogenous groups of actions that theories of each type of homicide may prove practical.

CONCLUSION

Parsons' major social action theory categories of structure (meaning relative permanencies in the patterning of meaningful action to the actors) are roles, collectivities, norms and values. These he classifies in terms of the PVs. Then he makes a major extension of his analysis of patterning by classifying these also in terms of the FDs. By linking the PVs to the FDs, he has gone a long way towards saying what patterns or structures of meaningful actions are possible and/or stable. By discussing the viable ways action can be meaningfully structured by actors, Parsons has opened up new possibilities in a little-explored section of action theory. This analysis of patterning is similar in many ways to that of Gestalt psychologists. Like Gestalt psychology, the range of patterns that can be formed is seen as limited in certain ways. However, instead of being an analysis of the patterns an individual can form, it is an analysis of those patterns a society can form.

In his analysis of functional differentiation and the linkage among PVs and FDs, Parsons is providing social action programme laws. That is to say he is making claims to which closure may be applied about how meaning is patterned and how that pattern tends to change. In addition he is claiming to do so in categories applicable to any culture. These claims are significant in the context of two major disputes in the philosophy of social science. First, it is in direct opposition to Winch's (1958) position that the form of life of a society can be described only in terms participants use themselves. Second, his social action theory laws are in direct contradiction to the claim, of some, that seeing action as meaningful precludes scientific laws. Parsons' claims to provide universally meaningful categories, and laws about actions described in terms of them, eliminates one major source of embarrassment for people who want to argue against Winch. They have examples to illustrate their positions. If these examples are accepted, the debate is over.

6 Socialization

Parsons' analysis of learning and socialization is of central importance to his account of society, for it is through socialization that a society's patterns of meaning are passed on to new members. His analysis of the mother-child interaction is built in terms of the ego-alter core case discussed in chapter 4 and the FDs and PVs as presented in chapter 5.

After discussing what type of theory he has, I shall describe the process of socialization from the point of view of the child. Parsons describes the process both from this point of view and that of the different interactive systems the child is in. By presenting the process from one point of view, the structure of the explanation can be made clearer. Clarification seems required here, for Parsons is muddled on several points. In addition, I find the exposition of his learning theory by Baldwin (1964) to be substantially different from my understanding of it. I dislike saying that Baldwin is wrong in his exposition, for I am aware that if one looks hard enough one can find textual support in Parsons' writing for most positions. However, as Baldwin's exposition is internally inconsistent on some central points, it seems fair to reject it. For instance, he says both that the cycle of socialization from the point of view of the child is A - G - I - L (p.176) and L - I - G - A, (p.189). (1) In addition, clarifying the analysis from the point of view of the child will facilitate the comparison of Parsons and Piaget which forms the last section of this chapter.

TYPE OF THEORY

'Socialization' is meant in a fairly literal way - the process of becoming social, which includes for Parsons becoming moral. As action theory takes the subjective point of view, what is moral is seen from the actor's point of view. What is moral will vary from one actor to another. This account of how a person becomes moral is not an attempt to explain particular moral beliefs (e.g. that men should be kind), but moral beliefs in general. In this aim, it is similar to Freud's theory, which attempts to account for morality in terms of the superego arising from the Oedipal situation. To use a somewhat vague distinction, the theory focuses on the form and not the content of morality.

Gouldner argues that academic sociology in general and Parsons in particular lack a sociology of morals or values, because sociologists think that to produce one would undermine the autonomy of these values (1971, pp.140-1). This they wish to avoid because they see morals as one of the important supports of the status quo which they are upholding. Gouldner's claim is in some ways rash, (2) for without knowing what such a theory would look like, it is difficult to say what its effect would be. For instance, Marxists offer an explanation of the economic base of a society in terms of the previous economic base of the society and economic factors forcing the individual to play his part in the present economic structure of a society. This explanation does not undermine the autonomy of the base. In the rest of this chapter, I shall present morality as the outcome of a social process. I will leave it to the reader to judge whether the account in this chapter knocks a nail into academic sociology's coffin, or breathes new life into a not so dead corpse. At the least, I am showing that Parsons does have an account of morality and that the omission of a sociology of morals from him is in part an omission in Gouldner's understanding of the theory, not in the theory itself.

There is a major type of objection that moral philosophers are likely to make against the type of theory being set out in this chapter. This is that moral action is by its nature free action. To say that a person performed a good act implies that the person could have done otherwise. Moral acts can take place only where man can choose. (3) This is usually expressed by saying 'Ought implies can', but it can be put the other way, 'Ought implies cannot.' Any sociological theory of morality, an ethical philosopher may argue, will be deterministic. As it eliminates choice, it eliminates morality and thus cannot be a theory of morality. (4)

The theory of morality to be put forward is deterministic. If morality involves free will, and 'morality' as we understand the word appears to involve a free will framework, then this is not a theory of morality. However, it is a theory of what men, including moral philosophers, have called moral activity. If moral philosophers wish to maintain that man can act morally only when he acts freely, then the answer, from the perspective taken here, is that morality as so defined has no applicability to human affairs. In other words, if the type of approach taken here is accepted, then moral philosophers have two choices: either to decide morality is irrelevant, or to change their conception of it. Part of my purpose in setting out the particular sociological theory of morality I do in this chapter is to illustrate a general type of approach. Even if this particular theory is unsatisfactory, it points to the possibility of a type of theory. Gouldner is right in pointing to a general absence of theorizing about morality in sociology, and this at least shows one way of tackling the problem.

A large part of this absence can be explained by the usual focus of theories of learning in both sociology and psychology. Learning is seen as the acquisition of ideas or knowledge. People are normally seen as learning that rather than learning how. If one thinks of a child learning information and what things mean, then one gets a cognitive focus to one's theory. If, however, one thinks of a child learning how to act in certain ways (e.g. as a male), then one gets a moral focus to one's theory. For Parsons, learning involves both learning information and how to act (TGTA, p.12):

> Learning is not merely the acquisition of 'information' (that is, specific items of cognitive orientation) about the properties of the object world; it is also the acquisition of new 'patterns of orientation'. That is, it involves acquiring new ways of seeing, wanting, and evaluating.

Parsons accepts the implication of this perspective that a theory of learning is a theory of becoming moral. For instance, while he discusses a child learning to please his mother, he says (1965, p.88):

> This is a mode of 'organization' of the ego with reference to its 'relation' to a social object. One can clearly say that, at the same time, it is learning to act in conformity with a set of norms.

Parsons' definition of structure as 'symbolically generalized meaningful orientations' must be interpreted very broadly. Meaningful must mean both cognitively and cathectically meaningful, for, as was seen when the ego-alter interaction was discussed, he sees gratification as socially learnt. In addition, he has attacked Freud for seeing only the superego as primarily socially formed and has said that man's cognitions and cathexes are also learnt (WP, ch.1).

The second major feature of Parsons' socialization theory is that it focuses on the acquisition of programmes. The idea of a programme was introduced in chapter 1 in connection with the problem of analysing a sociological theory. I would like to suggest, however, that its range of application is not limited to the philosophy of science, but covers all of human cognitive understanding. The difference between scientific understanding and the rest of understanding does not lie in the one being within a programme and the other not. Rather the difference lies in the way the programmes are used and extended in science. Rather than enter into a philosophical justification of the application of programmes to all of human understanding, I hope to show in the rest of this chapter that the concept is useful.

It is my contention that Parsons in FSI chapters 2 to 4 is concerned with the processes that lead to a child's acquisition of programmes. He is concerned with how a child acquires ways of relating to the world, not with how new items of information that fit into a previously existing framework are learned. His basic interest is in things like a child learning to see himself and act as a member of a family, not in a child who, knowing his eight times multiplication table, learns the nine times table, or how a child learns a particular dinner manner. These latter two he calls 'performance processes', as they basically involve applying a previously learned method to new material; the former is called a learning process (TGTA, p.123). This conception of learning is narrower than the one normally used in learning theory, which counts the acquisition of any new item of information as learning.

The opposition of this type of approach to behaviourism can be clarified by comparing Parsons' conception of human activity to Chomsky's of language. Chomsky attacks Skinner's account of language learning by claiming that behaviourism is in principle incapable of accounting for people's ability to speak a language. Speaking, Chomsky argues, must be understood as the development of a capacity. For a person to be able to speak he must be able to form sentences that he has never heard before and may, in some cases, never have been uttered before. As such, language use cannot be seen as resulting from any form of stimulus-response conditioning. Any form of behaviourism involves the person acquiring responses by doing a random variety of things, one or more of which is reinforced in some way or another. However when people come to utter a sentence they have never uttered before, they can do so reliably (1959). In other words, people when talking are engaged in rule-following behaviour. Following a rule or exercising a capacity allows one to see language use as both predicable and yet involving new (from the behaviourist point of view) actions. Similarly Parsons, by focusing on things like how a child learns to please his mother rather than how a child learns specific acts that please mother, is concerned with the development of a capacity (to be a loving child). Alternatively stated, the child is learning to engage in rule-governed activity. The rules of central concern to Parsons are moral norms. Thus Parsons' and Chomsky's account of human activity are both fundamentally opposed in their basic conception of that activity to behaviourism. Both see human activity in a similar way, though their explanations of it are different.

One more comment on Parsons' type of theory should be made. It is a theory of socialization. By treating the child-parent interaction as socialization, Parsons is presupposing the outcome of the interaction. To wrench a term out of its normal context, socialization is a concept that commits us to theorizing in the 'future anterior' (Althusser, 1969, ch.2). To see the process as socialization involves seeing the parent as the determiner of the outcome and the child as passive. Recent theories in this field have tended to move away from this assumption. (5) When Parsons' approach is compared with Piaget's, this limitation of his theory will be seen in a more detailed way to indicate a major weakness in his programme.

PARSONS' ACCOUNT OF SOCIALIZATION

Parsons describes the various phases a child goes through in becoming socialized in terms of a FD diagram. This FD diagram is in terms of the types of meaning that the child attributes to the situation (FSI, p.203):

> This question of the empirical source of the disturbance should, however, be distinguished from that of its 'meaning' with reference to each of the action systems with which we are concerned. For it is the meaning which events acquire for a specific action system that defines the inputs into that system ...

In this section, I shall first describe each phase of the process and then the logic underlying it (see Figure 6).

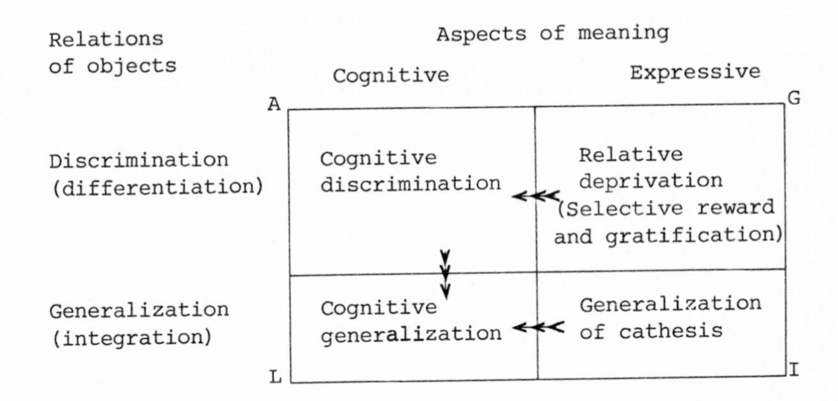

FIGURE 6 The socialization process (6)

Initial situation - a stable state in which the child is obtaining goals

The child is assumed to be, at the beginning, in a stable interaction pattern in which there are one or more goals he is obtaining. Parsons says (FSI, p.204):

> Empirically there may also be pressure from him (to grow up), but we will ignore this since we have assumed a stable state of the mother-child system.

That one has assumed something else is not a reason for ignoring the facts. It is a reason for changing one's assumption. I assume that Parsons means to say that this pressure is of little significance to the outcome. However, when we come to look at the work of Piaget, it will be seen that he at least, and I believe correctly so, attributes considerable significance to this pressure. That 'empirically there may also be pressure from him' is the basic reason that Parsons' theory must be supplemented by Piaget's. Theories must account for the facts, not assume them away.

What this assumption does is make the child passive and the mother the determiner of the outcome of the interaction. Thus Parsons ensures he is analysing a mother-child interaction that is socialization.

G Relative deprivation

In relation to his previous level of goal attainment, the child finds he is not achieving as much. Actions of his that had previously led to responses on the part of other(s) that he valued he no longer perceives as leading to these responses. The child relative to his previous level of satisfaction is deprived. He feels frustrated. Looked at from the outside, what is happening is that the agents of socialization are demanding new 'more mature' behaviour from him by refusing to relate to him in terms of the previous 'less mature' level.

A Cognitive discrimination

Next the child discovers that there are various new particular actions, which, if he performs, enable him to obtain a higher level of satisfaction of his old goals than he could in the previous phase. Parsons calls these mechanisms of primary adaptation (FSI, p.218). In this phase the child learns particular means to his old goals. As he starts to attain his goals by the new particular means, his satisfaction increases and frustration declines.

For a child cognitively to discriminate a range of new particular actions that will enable him to obtain his old ends, it must be assumed that there are present in the situation cues which can be discriminated by a child at the particular stage of development. In addition, acting in accord with these cues must produce some satisfaction in terms of results (FSI, p.197). That this will occur seems plausible, for the agents of socialization will usually try to make quite clear what they want the child to do and reward him for doing it.

Given that there are available cues in terms of which the child can perceive new means to his old goal and that the child aims at the gratification involved in his old goal, he will engage in a range of adaptive acts. The relationship of adaptive FD acts to goal attainment FD acts is the means-end relationship. The child acts instrumentally to attain his old goals. This phase movement (an increase in adaptive acts) is induced by a change in the situation. Parsons here has assumed that what is normally called learning - the acquisition of discrete bits of a repertoire of some type - will occur. His assumptions here boil down to the fact that the child wants to learn because he is not getting the same amount of gratification as before, that there is something to be learnt, and that the child can learn it. From this it follows that the child learns the new particular means.

L Cognitive generalization

The child in his A phase activities has acquired a range of particular means to sections of his old goal. In the L phase, he comes to see his activities not as a series of discrete separate actions but as a general class of behaviour that is demanded of him. These actions take on a general meaning. He comes to act in terms of a new relationship to his situation.

When a child has formed such a general class of actions, he can engage in new acts within this general class of action. This is parallel to a person who understands a grammar rule being able to utter new sentences. As the child continues to act in terms of the new pattern of meaning, and these actions are successful, he gains faith that the world is structured this way.

In the discussion of the ego-alter interaction in chapter 4 it was mentioned that symbolism takes time to develop, for criteria of sameness are involved. The use of symbols involves the ability to abstract some features of a particular case and see other cases as similar in terms of these features. Parsons moves the child from the A to L phase by assuming people have an ability to generalize, which the child exercises. The psychological programme that focuses on this type of process is that of the Gestalt psychologists. It should be possible to describe, in more detail than Parsons does, some of the ways a child generalizes in terms of various Gestalt theories.

I Generalization of cathexis

The child now comes to cathect, acting in accord with the new pattern of meaning. The agents of socialization have continued to reward the child in relation to part of his old goal. By rewarding him in relation to only part of it, forcing him to find some new means to this part, which are then generalized, the agents of socialization force a division of the old goal into two sections each with a general type of means to it. The child comes to cathect both these patterns of means as ends in themselves. The pair of ends in themselves thus developed are qualitatively different from the old goal and serve to replace it. For instance, instead of care, a child desires security and autonomy. If the child achieves both, he is cared for, but care has ceased to be his goal. Rather he now has two new and qualitatively different goals from care - security and autonomy.

Parsons' explanation of this depends upon seeing motivation as undifferentiated, with the exception of a limited number of biological givens (e.g. hunger) that are important only at the first stage of learning (the first year approximately). A person learns what is gratifying through social interaction. Whether an activity is found gratifying or not is not basically dependent upon its internal or intrinsic nature, but whether one has learned to find it so. The problem here is how one learns to find activities gratifying. Parsons' answer is that it is a 'cathexis on the means'. A cathexis on the means would appear to be the result of an association of means with some goal. The activities leading to an end gradually come to be linked to the end. The child starts with some biologically given pleasures and pains (e.g. feeling pleasure at eating; hunger). The processes leading to satisfying ends come to be desired in themselves and, as such, ends. As a result of a cathexis on the general class of means learned, the child moves to an integrative phase. The set of activities that were previously but a means to an old goal have become desired in themselves. On the basis of these new ends that the child has acquired, he asserts his membership in the 'collectivity of socialization'.

And again

After another stable period, the process will begin again. Parsons here sees socialization as a process of forcing the child to pull himself up by his own bootstraps. The child has an end (initially the satisfaction of his biological needs) and develops a means to it. This means comes to be cathected in itself, that is to say that there is a transfer of cathexis from the end to the means. This means, now in the status of an end, is then used to force the child to learn a new set of means which in their turn become ends.

Some comments on the theory

This approach sees the child-adult interaction as socialization and thus depicts the child as passive. Given that adults control the child's environment and that the child seeks goals, the adults can change the child's behaviour by forcing him to seek new means to his goals. The child is socialized by being forced to seek gratification in a series of social systems which are presented to him as a set of changes. The changes result not from any internal dynamic of the action system in question (the child's personality), but from the external changes to which he reacts.

It is not just the means-ends aspect of this theory that makes it passive. The principle of the cathexis on the means works through the child coming to like that which he does. Gratification is not seen as a dynamic force leading to a child upsetting the applecart, but something that binds that which the child does into his pattern of action. This, and the seeing of change as externally induced, are part of the conservative strain in Parsons' thought. In addition, he sees the tendency to generalize in a conservative way - that the child will come up with the 'accepted' generalization is implicitly assumed.

What Parsons means by a voluntaristic theory of action can now be clarified. Man creates his meanings in the sense that they are not given by external reality. However, man does not create reality in a creative way (meaning a novel way). What gets institutionalized is what already exists in the cultural system. Parsons' voluntaristic theory of action does not see man as free, for then one cannot account for social order. (7) It does see the meanings man attaches to action as dependent on his volition.

The socialization process can be seen as a swindle performed by society on the child through its agents of socialization. Just enough gratification is presented to the child in a new pattern to get him to accept it. Once he has reorganized the world cognitively and cathectically in terms of these new possibilities, the possibilities can be taken away from him. The question at this stage is what stops a new cycle of learning being started by his frustration. The answer would have to be that it is a lack of conditions for one of the subsequent phases. For instance, there may be no particular acts that the individual can learn, or the particular acts discovered may be only 'ad hoc' amendments and the person cannot generalize them.

The difficulty in learning new structures helps to explain why people's moral codes are fairly stable. It is not so much that man is virtuous by nature that leads men generally to act morally, but that it is not that easy to learn to sin. Man retains his virtue because of a lack of suitable temptations. Like the lady who maintains her 'virtue' as a result of never being asked, man retains a moral code as the conditions required to learn another are more complex than is generally assumed. While Parsons does not stress this point, it is of considerable importance to his general programme. Given the centrality of people's values in his theory, it is important that they be relatively stable. His analysis of socialization provides a rationale for this claim.

One of the situations in which we can expect most of the conditions for learning a new 'moral' code to be present is where people are likely to 'sell out'. An individual may join a political party or a bureaucracy with the intention of using it purely instrumentally. He will, however, have to learn a set of new particular actions, a rationale will be available to group these into a general class and conditions are favourable for him to develop a cathexis on this class of action. Thus one of the cases where people do change their values seems to be where the learning process presented can occur easily.

The theory is developed in such a way that the focus is on the meaning (as the child sees them) of inputs to the child's personality. From an interaction point of view the child is passing through a series of social systems. The agents of socialization change their behaviour pattern towards the child and he is forced to cope with the change. From the nature of the analysis it is clear that Parsons is right when he says (FSI, p.63):

> For simplicity we will refer to mother and child, but recognizing that 'agent of care' is the essential concept and that it need not be confined to one specific person; it is the function which is essential.

However, at the end of his analysis, he concludes (FSI, p.108):

> neither boy nor girl can, if our analysis is correct, be adequately socialized without a parent - or some substitute - of the 'opposite' sex ...

Leaving aside the problem that 'adequately' here probably is defined normatively, not empirically, the conclusion does not follow. Given that it is the 'function' and not the 'specific person', and as a person can act as somebody of the opposite sex, the reverse is correct. Should Parsons wish to deny this, an argument would be required and one is not given. While Parsons may have started to use the term 'mother' for simplicity, it leads to him being simplistic instead of developing the theoretical import of his position, which does not focus on a biologically given individual. This alternative conclusion is a much more interesting conclusion, for it means that a wider range of child-rearing arrangements are possible that is normally assumed. For instance, two homosexuals, one playing the male, the other the female role, should be able to raise a child.

What the child learns

Through socialization the child develops a personality structure that leads him to play roles that complement those which the agents of socialization play towards him. Parsons sees the basic building blocks of the personality system as need-dispositions and it is helpful to clarify their nature before discussing the order in which they are learnt. His definition is (TGTA, pp.114-15):

> Need-dispositions, we have said, are tendencies to orient and act with respect to objects in certain manners and to expect certain consequences from these actions. The expectations of consequences is nothing more than the cognition of a certain object as leading to a certain set of consequences and the cathexis of an object in the light of its antecedent relationship to a more cathected set of consequences. In other words, the expectation is nothing more than the cognition and cathexis of a means object qua means to an end.

This concept attempts to straddle his action programme and his systems programme. The word 'need' and the use of 'expect' in the definition fit with an action theory focus on meaning. Needs, when they are seen as social, and expectations involve the use of 'verstehen' to ascertain what they are. On the other hand the word 'dispositions' and the use of 'tendencies' fits with systems theory. While I will leave a full explication of dispositional concepts to chapter 8, the crucial point for the present argument is that they are defined in a positivistic manner from the point of view of an external neutral observer. It can now be seen why Baldwin (1964, pp.158-62) sees need-dispositions as a category requiring clarification. The analysis of Parsons in terms of action theory and systems theory allows one to go beyond pointing to a muddle to saying why it exists. While recognizing that the name 'need-disposition' and how it is defined is an attempt to straddle two approaches, I shall retain the term to avoid the confusion of adding new terminology. However, need-dispositions in this chapter are to be understood only in their action programme meaning.

At various points in FSI, Parsons uses 'internalized social objects' as the fundamental building block of the personality. He says that (FSI, p.56):

> It is that structure in the personality which regulates the orientation of the individual to an object (or class of objects) in the situation, by defining for ego the 'meanings' in the relevant respects of that object, and which has stability over time and a range of adaptability to changing conditions.

This definition of an internalized social object corresponds to the action theory aspect of the definition of a need-disposition. Need-dispositions, when seen within an action programme, are internalized social objects. This explains why within FSI, which is largely within action theory, Parsons uses the two terms interchangeably. In opposition to the programme of psychology, which takes as its basic referent point the individual, Parsons is offering a programme of sociological psychology. Personality psychology has tended to have an image of man apart from society and explains his activity in terms of personality units that are defined in relation to the individual. If one accepts this view of man, then the Hobbesian problem of a war of all against all is difficult to avoid. On the other hand, by giving as basic building blocks of personality, units that are seen as social, Parsons is able to transcend the Hobbesian problem. In a discussion of Freud's theory of object-relations, he says that had Freud lived, he would (1965, p.107)

> have had to become, in part a sociologist, for the structure of these object-systems is - not merely is influenced by - the structure of society itself.

Parsons characterizes the internalized social objects or need-dispositions in terms of PVs. In this way he has not only a theory of how a child learns but also of what a child learns. Initially the child learns that he is social (mother-child identity). Then he learns to act specifically or diffusely, followed by affectively-neutrally; universalistically-particularistically; and qualitively-performanily (if such a word is possible), in this order. (8)

The child starts with a number of drives (e.g. hunger) that provide the initial set of ends. The baby's mother (or other agents of socialization) are the means to satisfying these ends, and over the course of about a year the baby comes to cathect the mother not as a means to satisfying these ends but as a part of a social relational end. The baby sees himself as responding to mother and, as such, socially. The first point to note is that this process is one of an organism becoming social. Second, that organic drives are essential to start the learning process as they provide the initial set of gratifying ends. Finally, that while many of the learning processes involve a differentiation of ends, the replacement of one end (satisfaction of organic needs) by another end (a social relational one of being responsive to mother) is possible. It is interesting to speculate instead that a differentiation does occur. The child develops a social and non-social self. The non-social self might be seen as similar to Freud's id (though Parsons argues that Freud should see the id as social; WP, ch.1). The non-social self would be the source of the 'unsocialized impulses' in man which keep him from ever completely accepting his social role. This position can provide a baseline from which to respond to Wrong's (1961) objection that Parsons has an 'oversocialized' image of man.

Parsons' analysis of becoming social finds support in one theory of autistic children. This theory says that autistic children are fundamentally non-social. This, it is argued, is a result of a 'clockwork regularity' with which their mother interacted with them (e.g. strict schedule feeding). No possibility of responsiveness was allowed for or reacted to in the child, with the result that he never became social. Complete lack of regularity in the responses of the agents of socialization would also produce this, and Pye's (1963) discussion of Burmese child-rearing practices suggests this is possible, though the case he examines is less extreme. By this line of analysis, how social or non-social an individual is is socially determined.

After the child has become social, he learns the attitudinal PVs before the object categorization ones. Parsons says that (FSI, p.138)

> attitudinal structure has priority, because motivational stability, on the requisite levels, is a precondition of coping with and internalizing a more complex object world. To reverse the order would not be possible for a 'personality' system, because there would be no way of dealing with the differentiated object categories in any motivationally stable way.

Parsons' justification for the priority of universalism-particularism over quality-performance in the learning of the object categorization PVs seems culture bound (FSI, p.51):

> We presume that the (the child) cannot learn to assume primarily achieved roles until he has achieved a meaningful orientation to the 'relation' between familial and extra-familial roles and objects.

There is no obvious reason why one could not have achievement values within a family or kin setting. It would be interesting to see if there is any variability by social structure of the order in which these distinctions are learnt. However, later in this chapter, when discussing Piaget, it will be shown that he gives the same order of acceptance of PVs for lower-class Swiss children.

Learning a PV distinction must be interpreted in a special way. Parsons is aware of the problem, for he says (FSI, p.138):

> This, of course, is in no way to suggest that the differentiation of the situational world formulated in the other pair of pattern variables (object categorization ones), is irrelevant at this stage (Oedipal). The idea that all the pattern variables are involved in four universally relevant dimensions is not disproved by the above analysis.

The problem basically is that Parsons claims that the PVs are dichotomous and that no action has a determinate meaning until a PV from each PV pair has been chosen (TGTA, p.77). Now by this analysis of socialization all the PVs are not 'learnt' until about the age of ten. It is clearly not acceptable to say that a child's actions until he is ten or so lack meaning. Consequently we must ask how the PVs are 'involved' before they are 'learnt'.

Learning here means coming to accept as a way of structuring the world and particularly to find that such a structuring is morally significant. Prior to the 'learning' of a PV pair, the PV choice exists only at the level of action (e.g. universalism is involved in the judging of distances that are involved in a child walking). Those aspects of an action which are characterized by other than the learnt PVs are relevant only as a means in the understanding of that action. For instance, the child recognizing (cognitively) his mother (universalistic criteria are involved) is important only as a means to allowing the child to establish certain attitudinal relations.

A parallel problem to that with the PVs exists with the FDs, for these too in this programme are classifications of patterns of meaning from the subjective point of view. A similar type of solution would appear to be required. Parsons' whole discussion of the FDs in FSI is very confused, as the following examples illustrate. He says, for example (FSI, p.134):

> the first fission, from the one to the two-unit stage can be said to constitute establishment of the discrimination between adaptation and integration with special reference to the attitudinal aspect, namely specificity and diffuseness ...

In terms of one PV, distinction, only two groups of FDs can be distinguished - in this case A and G from I and L. Consequently the child cannot be establishing the discrimination between A and I. Parsons goes on to say that (FSI, p.134) 'it would not be possible to make a good case for the reverse thesis' (i.e. that the child learns to discriminate L and G). I shall not try to solve a problem to which there is too little information by the analysis of the PV-FD relationship given in chapter 5. With one distinction, specificity-diffuseness, it is impossible to separate out two functional meanings, as both A and G are characterized by specificity, while both I and L are characterized by diffuseness.

A similar problem to that found in the anal stage description occurs in the Oedipal. Learning the importance of the difference between affectivity and neutrality is insufficient in itself to distinguish, as Parsons suggests, I and A (FSI, p.84 and p.134). Rather, one must say that, given that he has learned affectivity-neutrality or specificity-diffuseness, the child can in an attitudinal framework distinguish all four functional problem areas.

When discussing the Oedipal stage (learning affectivity-neutrality), Parsons ends up with a personality structure with a G, I and two L components and completely lacking an A component. He says (FSI, p.84):

> In schematic theoretical terms we may say that this differentiation separates the two aspects of the content of the latency cell of our general paradigm, the 'tension management' aspect and the 'pattern-maintenance' aspect.

As there are only four components at this stage and the latency cell is subdivided, Parsons must miss something out - and it is the adaptive cell. His diagram on p.82 of FSI contains all the correct boxes. However, the A and L boxes need to be reversed for the diagram to be correct. Reality testing characterizes an adaptive box while esteem characterizes a latency box.

PARSONS AND PIAGET

In this section I wish to discuss the relationship between Parsons and Piaget to show how each partially confirms the other, how Parsons can be used to help explain some of Piaget's work, and how some of Piaget's work is needed to supplement Parsons. The relationship between their theories has been obscured by the fact that Parsons takes as his starting point the series of social systems in which the child is, while Piaget's focus is the individual child. I presented Parsons' theory of socialization from the point of view of the child in order to facilitate comparing their theories.

Parsons claims for the originality of his approach (FSI, pp.55-6):

> The conception of the internalization of social objects is of course not new ... It is, however, new to think in terms of the internalization of a 'system' of objects and identify that with integrated participation in a specifically and technically delimited system of

> social interaction, and further, of course, to arrange these social systems in a continuously articulated series.

When it is remembered that social objects are patterns of meaning, and that a system of such objects, as the subjective point of view is being taken, is a world view - an interrelated way of responding to the world; and that the series of social systems refers to the empirical sources of the inputs which the child finds meaningful, then Parsons can be seen to be quite similar to Piaget. Both see a series of qualitatively different approaches to reality. Parsons perhaps has gone a step beyond Piaget in characterizing these in PV terms. Neither sees the problem of a child's growing up in terms of co-ordinating a set of separate drives. Rather, each sees the child as having a set of ways of approaching reality that are undergoing processes of fission in response to the pressure of the social environment. Parsons calls the process differentiation, Piaget dissociation. Parsons, like Piaget, accepts that while a child may use the words of a language, he can mean something quite different by them from adults (FSI, p.78).

Piaget accepts that a child's conception of the material world cannot come solely from interaction with it. He says (1967, pp.384-5):

> No direct experience can prove to a mind inclined towards animism that the sun and clouds are neither alive nor conscious.

The main theme of one of Piaget's books is that the way a child views physical causality is initially an extension of his understanding of social relationships. He does not separate physical causality from social compulsion or moral necessity (1970). Given Piaget's acceptance of the social base of conceptions of reality, and that they cannot be refuted by observation, it does not seem unfair to characterize one focus of his concerns as how a child acquires programmes, which I have argued is a central concern of Parsons.

Parsons' and Piaget's work can be shown to fit together both in the stages they see a child going through and in the various mechanisms they see involved. The fit with the discussion of what children learn is important, as Piaget based 'The Moral Judgment of the Child' largely on lower-class Swiss children (1968, p.37), while Parsons has been thinking in relation to middle-class American children. In addition, if the relationship between Piaget's and Parsons' theories can be clarified, then all the work that Piaget and his followers have done can be related to Parsons' theory and used to develop it.

Piaget describes the child's view of physical reality as being an extension of the social-moral world. He describes (1967, p.220, my emphasis in quotation marks)(9)

> the child's belief in animism and in an animism that is not very theoretical (its object is not to explain natural phenomena), but 'affective'. The sun and moon take an interest in us.

This appears to fit with Parsons' view that the attitudinal PVs are learned before the object characterization ones, as the meaning of the world is seen in 'affective' terms.

Parsons sees a fit between his ideas and Piaget's with regard to Piaget's distinction between the type of morality that characterizes this stage and the next (FSI, p.123):

> Perhaps it is legitimate to interpret Piaget's distinction between cooperation and moral realism in this context. In the case of moral realism an obligation of obedience is attached to the source of authority as such. In that of cooperation, the rules of the game are subject to revision in the light of the interaction of the players, defined as peers. The age-range of these phenomena as Piaget reports them fit with this interpretation.

It is possible to go further in the similarities among the stages. Piaget divides the relations of co-operation into two (1968, p.284):

> mere equalitarianism makes way for a more subtle conception of justice which we may call 'equity', and which consists in never defining equality without taking account of the way in which each individual is situated ... In the domain of distributive justice, equity consists in taking account of age, of previous services rendered, etc., in short, in establishing shades of equality.

Equalitarianism appears to be based on universalism. The emphasis is on all participants in a process being judged by one set of rules that applies to all participants in the same way. The next stage, equity, involves seeing as significant the relative position of each child (e.g. letting younger children shoot their marbles at a target from a closer position). This involves the child's acceptance of the achievement-quality distinction as significant. As was mentioned earlier, this fit provides a good deal of support for the PV order being correct, as Piaget was dealing with lower-class Swiss children.

Parsons can be used to strengthen Piaget's theoretical account of the origins of morality. Piaget accepts Bovet's account of the origin of morality, but adds to it that there are two types of respect - 'rules due to unilateral respect, and rules due to mutual respect' (1968, p.79). He interprets Bovet's position thus (1968,pp.100-1):

> How, asks M. Bovet, does the sense of duty appear? Two conditions, he says, are necessary, and their conjunction sufficient. 1. The individual must receive a command from another individual; the obligatory rule is therefore psychologically different from the individual habit or from what we have called the motor rule. 2. The individual receiving the command must accept it, i.e. must respect the person from whom it came ... The appearance of the sense of duty in a child thus admits of the simplest explanation, namely that he receives commands from older children (in play) and from adults (in life), and that he respects older children and parents.

Both Parsons and Piaget agree upon the first condition that moral rules come out of social, not individual, processes. Piaget's second condition is, however, not an answer to the origin of morality but a shifting of its focus from rules to persons. Respect, if the conditions given are to be sufficient, must involve a moral aspect. If respect does not involve a moral aspect then an additional condition or some explanation is required to move from 'acceptance' (the other term used) to something moral. Consequently, Piaget fails to explain the origin of duty, which is for him the first type of morality, but rather says that duty initially involves people and not rules. As an explanation of the origin of morality, Piaget's position is circular or missing a step. The change Piaget wishes to make in Bovet's position is to distinguish two different types of respect - unilateral and mutual. He simply asserts that (1968, p.102) 'as the child grows in years the nature of his respect changes.'

Parsons' account of socialization and becoming moral avoids this problem, for he starts with the child pursuing the gratification of basic drives like hunger. The child's pursuit of gratification also provides a mechanism to explain how the two types of respect arise. Initially the bulk of a child's gratification is controlled by his parents and, given their power and knowledge, he is forced to give unilateral respect. After the age of five or so, however, the child mixes increasingly with his peers. He is forced to obtain gratification from them. His relationship with them will tend to be of a more equalitarian nature and he will be able to focus on the rules.

Scattered throughout Piaget's work are various remarks that fit with Parsons' account of how learning occurs. Piaget's distinction between the level of action and the level of thought appears to fit with Parsons' account of learning in two ways. Piaget says that various principles come into play at the level of action first. He also says that a child sees various moral principles (e.g. considering intentions) as applicable to himself before he applies them to others. This can be interpreted as saying that a child learns particular actions before he learns the meaning of a general class. In addition, it can be seen as showing how PVs or FDs can be involved before they are learnt. Piaget also seems to accept something like Parsons' tendency to generalize, for he says (1968, p.406):

> To ensure that the functional search for organization exhibited by the initial sensori-motor and affective activity give rise to rules of organization properly so called, it is sufficient that the mind should become conscious of this search and of the laws governing it, thus translating into structure what till then had been function and nothing more.

The basic difference between Parsons and Piaget comes from Piaget seeing the process as child development while Parsons sees it as a child learning. Learning, as we have seen, involves seeing the child as basically responding to external pressure. Development, on the other hand, lays stress upon the child's own activity in determining the end result. The child is seen as engaging in cognitive activity for its own sake as well as to obtain goals. Parsons, though, sees thinking as a response to frustration. Piaget's position denies the possibility of the stable state that Parsons starts with. Piaget has principles that accept a child's tendency to seek moderate novelty. The child searches for gratification instead of being forced to seek it. Instead of seeing a child develop a cathexis on the means as Parsons does, Piaget sees a child as bored with the familiar and seeking out the new. The problem in Parsons' position that Piaget points to is one that will be central to the next chapter. Parsons does not allow for human creativity. Sometimes failure and frustration may not be imposed from the outside and people create it instead for themselves. And sometimes they overcome it themselves. Perhaps the best way of summarizing the relationship between Parsons and Piaget is to say that Piaget forgets that a child sometimes cries, while Parsons forgets that a child actively thinks.

7 Social order: a problem solved too well

In chapter 2 I argued that the central focus of 'The Structure of Social Action' was the utilitarian dilemma, not positivism and idealism. Starting from the Hobbesian problem of avoiding a war of all against all, Parsons goes as far as to define sociology in relation to it (SSA, p.768):

> If this property (common-value integration) is designated the sociological, sociology may be defined as the 'science which attempts to develop an analytic theory of social action systems in so far as these systems can be understood in terms of the property of common-value integration.'

In the last four chapters I have traced how Parsons in his action programme locks man more and more firmly into the pattern of a society. Social control is seen as an aspect of all activity. Following this perspective through, Parsons says that the continuance of a pattern 'is to be treated as not problematical' (SS, p.204). In this chapter I shall argue that Parsons has engaged in theoretical 'overkill' on the problem of order. He has solved the problem too well. Parsons runs into problems when he tackles activities that go against the maintenance of a fully integrated, stable, consensual society - conflict, social change, and deviance. Despite problems in treating these subjects that come from relying on external sources of 'disturbance', his central theoretical problem, I shall argue, is creativity.

Parsons argues that any adequate theory of stability can also account for change. The same factors that explain stable processes also explain change. No special theory of change is required (SS, pp.230-3; pp.481-90; SECP, p.21). With this approach, and the view that the maintenance of the status quo is unproblematic, there are two basic ways of seeing conflict, social change and deviance. The first is to analyse them as departures from the polar type of a fully integrated society. The second is to see them as externally induced. Parsons uses both lines of attack on the problem.

That Parsons has difficulties in accounting for change is not a novel criticism. In fact, it has been the focus of the bulk of the secondary criticism of Parsons. The merit of this critique, if merit it has, is that it roots his account of social change and conflict in his general action theory, rather than simply attacking Parsons for having a consensus assumption.

CONFLICT

Parsons' core case which was set out in chapter 4 involves a consensus and a pattern of integrated institutionalized roles. The view of social activity as involving an integrated set of common ends is of theoretical importance, not a usual state of affairs, Parsons claims in SSA (p.263). 'Every society', he says (EST, p.267), 'has important elements of conflict.' He handles these elements, which do not conform to the theoretical core case, as extensions of the core case. Thus conflict is seen as the absence or breakdown of consensus.

Parsons points out that the more a pattern is institutionalized the more a pattern of 'self-interest in conformity with it develops' (EST, p.139). Conflict in a society is seen as an attack on vested interests. Of these, he says (EST, p.241):

> It is inherent in the nature of an institutional system that it should create, and is in part supported by, a complex system of vested interests ... Among 'interests' in general those that may be called 'vested' are distinguished by the fact that they are oriented to the maintenance of objects of interest which have already become established.

One major form of conflict is an attack on vested interests. Those with the vested interests will react emotionally and defensively against those in conflict with them. Their reaction will be based upon both the interests and the feeling that their concerns are legitimate. Those attacking these vested interests will either attack them weakly, as they feel somewhat guilty about attacking legitimate interests, or will repress their guilt and attack the vested interests fanatically (EST, pp.238-74). This type of description assumes that those in conflict with the vested interests at one point were a part of the consensus and thus feel ambivalent about attacking the interests.

Parsons identifies two principles that generate tension, strain, conflict and social change in his core case. The first is that the social system can never be perfectly integrated with the personality and cultural systems (SS, pp.16-17). For instance, values (a part of the cultural system) tend toward internal consistency, and Parsons claims that (TGTA, p.175):

> no fully integrated internally consistent system of value-orientation can be adequate to the functional needs of any concrete system of action. Given the inevitability of strain, there must therefore be adaptive value-integrations in the sectors in which the dominant value-integration is least adequate and which compensate for these inadequacies.

This citation also indicates the other main internal source of strain. Given some differentiation of the social system, the value system institutionalized will be more appropriate to one sector than another. An early example Parsons gives of this is tension in the United States, which has stressed achievement and universalistic values between the occupational system (where these are appropriate) and the kinship system (where they are not). This tension he sees as leading to compromises such as hiring people of one's own ethnic group (TGTA, p.174). In his later work he characterizes the sectors in FD terms and thus has criteria to determine 'appropriate' values (see chapter 5 for a discussion of the PV-FD linkages).

This passage illustrates another feature of Parsons' thinking about conflict and strain. A strain calls up solutions to the strain. If there is to be strain, and 'bearable strain' as opposed to conflict, then something must occur that reduces the strain. Parsons tends to assume that a problem needs a solution and often sees it 'calling up' a solution. While a problem will generate efforts to alleviate it, Parsons at times (e.g. when discussing McCarthyism in the US (SPMS, pp.226-47)) slips into a teleological position in which the successful solution of the problem is assumed.

In order to illustrate these points I shall briefly outline his account of Nazi Germany (EST, pp.104-41), which is, in my opinion, his best analysis of conflict. (1) He starts by posing a problem for the Marxist (2) analysis of the rise of fascism. This has seen fascism as an expression of petty bourgeois distress that was able to consolidate its hold on power as the bourgeoisie and finance capital felt they could use the Nazis to suppress a threatened proletarian revolution. This, he argues, is inadequate, for it does not indicate what the significant differences are between Germany and the US or Britain, which explain the failure of fascism to arise in these countries. What must also be included in the analysis is an ideology which he calls (EST, p.109) 'Prussian conservatism', which he sees as centrally involved in the German state. This was supported particularly by feudal-militaristic Junkers and a civil service that was oriented to a highly formal legalism. These values were of considerable importance as the late date of German industrialization had given the government bureaucracy a larger degree of control of the economy than in Britain or the US. This value complex was further strengthened by a general emphasis on formal status and strong sex role differences.

Parsons sees the rapid industrialization and urbanization of Germany as having created two groups in Germany, each with substantial feelings of insecurity. One group compulsively debunked all the traditional values just discussed, while the other reacted in a fundamentalist direction. The Nazi hatred of the Jew, capitalism, Bolshevism, secularism and the emancipation of women is seen as an expression of this fundamentalism. This was then channelled into a direction compatible with the fundamentalism-nationalism and the romanticised military group which allowed strong sex role differentiation. The conflict that led to the rise of the Nazis is seen as a breakdown of integration (3) leading to ambivalence which is then channelled in a direction compatible with one side of the ambivalence.

The basic problem with this type of approach is that conflict is seen negatively - the absence of integration. As Parsons argues throughout SSA, residual concepts hide unexplored problems. In the Nazi example, it is the strength of the Nazis - regardless of what they were expressing; how did they have the power base to get and consolidate their hold on power?

I want to explore theoretically the problem of the residual category here a little more to clarify what is needed for a social action programme analysis of conflict. This line of analysis is easiest to understand if we start from a frequent objection to Parsons. The objection, to state it succinctly, is that social systems simply are not characterized by a consensus. In fact this has been the focus of so much disagreement, particularly with Parsons, but also with much mainstream American sociology, that sociologists are frequently divided into consensus and conflict schools. The basic response to this objection is that where there is not a consensus, there is not a social system as Parsons defines it. If somebody says, 'South Africa is riddled with conflict between blacks and whites: it is ridiculous to call it one social system', then the only answer is: 'Of course it is. South Africa contains at least two distinct social systems if not a great many more. Any adequate analysis of South Africa will have to involve an analysis of the relations between a great many social systems.'

I suspect that Parsons is wrong in many cases about how much of a consensus exists. He calls many interaction patterns social systems that should not be called such. However, the fault is not as large as some of his critics have suggested, for they tend to neglect the backdrop of everyday life that we take for granted (such as the almost universal acceptance of money). It would not be worth the trouble to prove either that Parsons is empirically wrong in a number of cases where he thinks a consensus assumption holds or that his critics have pushed the point too far, for this would get me into too detailed a discussion of some particular example. Anybody who disagrees with this view will reject any particular case I might establish as atypical, and to do it for a large enough number of cases to be convincing would involve writing several books. The basic point is that unless a consensus exists, for Parsons no social system exists. How widespread consensus is is a matter for empirical investigation. The less widespread and the less extensive is consensus in the population of people being analysed, the more it will be necessary to analyse them in terms of various social systems. The practical complexity of some pieces of research may be immense, though for certain purposes it may be possible to ignore conflicts and disagreements.

This reply, that a social system does not exist unless a consensus exists, basically merely serves to shift and not to solve a problem. The new problem becomes how one analyses relations, conflictual or otherwise, among social systems. To this question Parsons does not supply an answer on the theoretical level. Instead, he falls into a trap that many 'conflict theorists' are in. He sees conflict as the obverse of consensus (SS, p.39):

> The polar antithesis of full institutionalization is, however, 'anomie', the absence of structured complementarity of the interaction process or, what is the same thing, the complete breakdown of normative order in both senses ... Just as there are degrees of institutionalization so are there degrees of anomie. The one is the obverse of the other.

In other words, conflict is the Hobbesian war of all against all. Conflict is the result of each individual or each separate social system pursuing different and incompatible specific ends that are either individual ends or those specific to a particular social system. This is the type of approach to conflict that underlies most of games theory work on conflict. (4) However, if Parsons' analysis of consensual action holds, then this type of analysis of conflict is unsatisfactory. (5) Parsons' solution to the utilitarian dilemma, as was seen in chapter 4, involved accepting a social image of man. Thus if an analysis of conflict is to fit with his analysis of consensus, people in conflict must be seen socially and not individualistically. If men can agree about social ends, then they can also disagree about them, and misunderstand each other about them. Parsons' actual analysis of conflict, as has been seen, does view men as social. He does this, however, by seeing conflict as a breakdown of consensus, and not by building up from the anomic situation.

SOCIAL CHANGE

Parsons initially saw social change as a result of overcoming vested interests. While not completely abandoning this, after the development of his analysis of patterning in terms of the FDs, he came to analyse social change as functional differentiation. The meaning of this in action theory was clarified in chapter 5. What remains to be discussed is the process through which Parsons sees functional differentiation as occurring.

The easiest way of setting out Parsons' view of how this process occurs is to parallel it with the analysis of socialization given in the previous chapter. Parsons' analysis of functional differentiation in Some Considerations on the Theory of Social Change (1961) starts from the assumption of a stable situation. He next assumes that for some reason or other there is a deficit in G. In other words, an external factor prevents people from obtaining goals to the extent they feel they have a right to expect, and they become frustrated. Next, there must be opportunities to engage in activities that lead more effectively to the goal(s). Some people try these new means (A). This then raises a problem of legitimation. The particular activities must come to be seen as an acceptable way of doing things (L). These types of activities then come to be accepted (I). This can be represented diagrammatically as in Figure 7.

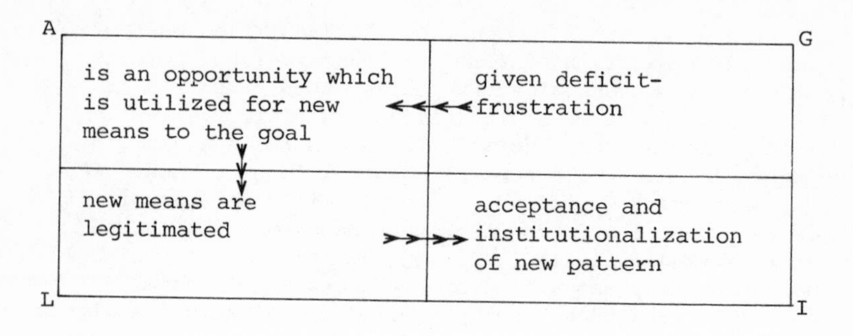

FIGURE 7

This model is the same as the socialization model, except that it is on a more macroscopic scale. The seven-step model that Parsons gives in ES can also be paralleled to the socialization model, as follows:

Socialization	Social change
G Goal attainment deficit produced by agents of socialization	1 Goal attainment deficit a given
feeling of frustration	2 'Unjustified disturbances' (6)
A Learning specific new means	3 Mobilizing resources for new attempts to realize the value pattern
L The child realizes the particular means are part of a general class	4 Supportive tolerance of new ideas
	5 Positive attempts to increase specification of the new ideas
I Development of a cathexis on the new pattern	6 Attempts to implement
	7 Acceptance if successful (7)

Not only does the social change model involve the same sequence of FD phase movements as the socialization model, but the structure of explanation is parallel. Each starts with a stable system and a process of change or socialization is started off by a given external source of disturbance that creates a problem. The response is a passive one of developing new means that eventually are accepted as morally legitimate patterns that cope with the disturbance. At first sight there appears to be a difference between the two theories, as Parsons does not see the social change model as determinate. That is to say the society may not go through the sequence of phase movements. Despite the possibility of using new means to attain various goals more efficiently, the society may stick to its old ways. The reason that the social change model is not determinate, while the socialization model is, as was discussed in chapter 6, is that the term 'socialization' presupposes the outcome. Parsons does not deal with 'failed' socialization. If the 'socialization' model is seen as an analysis of a mother-child interaction, and it is not assumed that the mother will successfully use her power to ensure socialization, then the socialization model is also indeterminate. As Parsons' theory of social change is his theory of socialization 'writ large', the problems with it are identical to those of the socialization theory. As these have already been discussed, I will simply note them. They are an assumption that change comes from the outside and is not internally generated, and the absence of an account of creative responses to the problems or opportunities. To say that there is 'supportive tolerance' for new ways does not explain how somebody comes up with a new way.

One possible way out of the reliance in the theory on external sources of change (8) is to go back to the two internal sources of strain that were discussed in relation to Parsons' analysis of conflict. These are that no social system can be perfectly integrated with its cultural system and the personality systems of its members, and that the value system institutionalized in a social system will be somewhat inappropriate to some functional sectors of that social system. If these two principles were developed, then an analysis of society seeing inherent in it elements of strain and thus, potential conflict and social change might be possible. This seems the most promising way out of Parsons' 'overkill' on the problem of order.

Parsons' discussion of social change in terms of the FDs is appropriate. As he sees the patterning of a society in terms of the FDs, he should describe social change in terms of them. Just as a Marxist sees a change in class structure as the most important change that can happen in a society and focuses on explaining this, so Parsons sees the key change in societies as functional differentiation. He sees this as a reformulation of Weber's process of rationalization (ES, p.292):

> We would like to reformulate the process of rationalization (as presented by Weber) as the tendency of social systems to develop progressively higher levels of structured differentiation under the pressure of adaptive exigencies.

The adequacy of functional differentiation to account for the social changes that are of most interest to us is difficult to assess at present, as not enough history has been looked at in this way. Some cases that Parsons does look at suggest some utility to the approach. For instance, he argues that the modern economic system could have developed only as a result of activities of social units independent of the state, as political groups tend to be both traditional and oriented to the short run. The family firm is seen as crucial to the development of modern capitalism as it allowed the functional differentiation of the A and G spheres. He also sees the growth of a differentiated legal system (I) as crucial to the growth of modern capitalism. However, economic growth in underdeveloped countries today must be politically led, he argues (SPMS, pp.98-131).

DEVIANCE

Parsons' major treatment of deviance is in SS, and was thus written before his development of the FD classification. In this section, I shall first analyse his treatment of the subject and then reformulate it in terms of the FDs. I shall argue that his analysis of deviance is an analysis of 'failed' socialization.

In chapter 1, I discussed briefly how Parsons has two definitions of deviance, one in action theory, one in systems theory. While they are given in two consecutive sentences as alternative definitions of the same phenomenon, if the reader compares this section with the discussion of deviance in chapter 8, the difference between them will be clear. His action theory definition is (SS, p.250):

> deviance is a motivated tendency for an actor to behave in contravention of one or more institutionalized normative patterns.

Parsons' analysis of deviance is stated in terms of the ego-alter interaction discussed in chapter 4, and provides a good example of the extension of a core case. He starts from the consensus situation reached at the end of the ego-alter interaction (SS, p.252):

> such an interaction system is characterized by the complementarity of expectations, the behavior and

> above all the attitudes of alter conform with the expectations of ego and vice versa.

As has been discussed, such a system has no built-in source of change, and change has to come from the outside. Parsons makes an assumption of a given exogenous source of change (SS, p.252):

> Let us assume that, from whatever source, a disturbance is introduced into the system, of such a character that what alter does leads to frustration, in some important respects of ego's expectation-system vis-à-vis alter.

The next step in the analysis is crucial to the structure of explanation (SS, p.252, my emphasis in double quotation marks):

> This "failure" of the fulfillment of ego's expectations places a 'strain' upon him, that is, it presents him with a problem of 'adjustment' in the terms which we have used.

In addition to the problem of how to cope with the new situation, ego also has an emotional response (SS, p.253):

> Ego must have some reaction to the frustration which alter has imposed upon him, some resentment or hostility. In other words the cathectic orientation acquires an ambivalent character.

Ego is both committed to alter and the normative pattern and not committed to them. If ego maintains his commitment to the pattern and/or alter, he has a conformative need-disposition; if not, he has an alienative need-disposition (SS, pp.263-4). Both of these will be compulsive, so we get compulsive conformity and compulsive alienation. The changed actions of alter produce not only a change in the interaction pattern but also a change in ego's need-disposition system. If the conformative need-dispositions are strongest, then ego will insist more strongly on alter adhering to the normative pattern. He will compulsively demand stricter adherence by alter to the rules that existed prior to the change in alter's behaviour. He will demand that by the old standards alter be not just good but very good. Alter, whose motivational structure has developed similarly to ego's, will find it harder to conform to the previous standards than before his change in activity. Given that he has changed his activity, his probable response is to move even further from the original pattern of interaction. Thus a vicious circle of deviance is established. This is parallel to the ambivalence of those in conflict with vested interests. Three other vicious circles are possible, one based on ego's compulsive conformity to alter and two on ego's compulsive alienation from either the pattern or alter. These aspects of Parsons' analysis of deviance lead to the classification of deviance shown in Figure 8.

	Focus on social objects	Focus on norms
Conformative dominance		
Alienative dominance		

FIGURE 8 Parsons' deviance typology (9)

There are several features to be noticed about this view of deviance. The first is an assumption of a one-to-one relationship between motivation and behaviour. By giving a classification of deviance in which one dichotomy is conformative dominance-alienative dominance, Parsons is assuming that given an alienative need-disposition the person will act in a compulsively alienative way. This does not square with the rest of his theory, for he says that the personality level and the social system level are interdependent but independent. Here he makes a direct transition from one level to the other. While the one-to-one relationship may hold frequently, it fails to hold in all cases, as the rest of Parsons' theory recognizes. For instance a man may be motivated to rob a bank, but not to do so because of a policeman on the corner.

Recognizing this problem allows an interpretation of compulsive conformity by which it is deviant. The problem here is that if a person is conforming, even if he is doing so compulsively, then his actions are not deviant (i.e. are not violating institutionalized expectations). However, from the logic of Parsons' analysis, it is the case that what the 'compulsive conformist' is doing is not living up to the norm compulsively, but rather living up to the cultural ideal of the norm not the institutionalized norm. If this is the case, then the person is violating the institutionalized norm and is deviant even though social control may be difficult to apply in many cases. I suggest that conformative dominance and alienative dominance be reinterpreted as directions of deviance. In the case of conformative dominance, the individual moves away from the institutionalized norm towards the cultural ideal, (10) while alienative dominance involves movement in the opposite direction. Seen this way, this distinction may cover the active-passive dichotomy that Parsons uses to subdivide each of the cells in the typology of deviance given. I say 'may', as Parsons does not explicate extensively this distinction and thus it is uncertain precisely what it means.

Parsons sees the vicious circles of deviance leading to the development of ambivalent motivational structures in each individual. This allows him to say both that a consensus exists in terms of which the act is deviant and that deviance also exists. The deviant is both part of and not part of the consensus. The deviant is seen not as somebody with different values but as somebody who accepts the system's values on one level and rejects them at the same time. A case where this type of ambivalence seems a correct characterization of the actions is a middle-class male committing adultery, although it does not fit some cases of deviant behaviour - i.e. actions which are in violation of the norms of a social system. In such cases, Parsons would argue, the behaviour should not be analysed as deviance but as something else (say conflict between two social systems).

A key feature to note in the structure of the explanation is that Parsons presents the situation in terms of a failure creating a problem. Failure is seen as imposed from outside of the system, and this failure leads ego to seek new means to the end of adjusting. Ego is seen as somebody with a problem to solve. The theory is passive in nature, for ego is given the problem: ego is faced with responding to a new situation not of his own making. Like Merton (1968, pp.175-248), he sees deviance as resulting from failure. He does not consider the possibility that people are deviants not because they cannot get in on the American Dream but because they consider it a nightmare.

Noting this feature of the structure of the explanation provides a base for reformulating Parsons' theory of deviance in terms of the FDs. A change in the external situation causes the level of goal attainment to be lowered. The person becomes frustrated (G) and perceives and adopts new and deviant means to achieve his goal(s) (A). In Matza's (1964) terms, he has drifted into deviance. He is engaging in deviant activity but has not become part of a delinquent subculture. Next in response to the actions of alters, he generalizes the particular actions to be part of general class of actions (L). The deviance theory most applicable here is labelling theory. (11) The last stage is the person coming to accept and act in terms of this label (I). The type of analysis most relevant here is that given by R.A. Scott in his 'The Making of Blind Men' (1969).

The stages and the logic of this analysis are identical to that of the socialization analysis given in the preceding chapter. The only difference is that the means the person seeks out, generalizes and accepts are deviant. Thus he does not become 'socialized' - meaning a part of the consensus. Instead what happens is a 'failure' of socialization.

When Parsons' analysis of deviance is reformulated in FD terms as 'failed socialization', his problem with creativity can be noticed. The person again fits into some general but socially known category of deviant (e.g. juvenile delinquent). Deviance is a response to frustration. He responds to problems instead of creating opportunities for deviance.

CONCLUSION

Parsons, in describing his own ideology, says that it tends towards a humanistic liberalism. However, he qualifies this by saying that his position (SPMS, p.224)

> differs in not being in the older sense an individualistic liberalism. If the individualistic assumptions are modified in favor of a set which not only admit the necessity but assert the desirability of positive social organization, much of the ideological conflict between the three positions as total 'systems' (liberalism, socialism and capitalism) evaporates.

Accepting a social image of man, Parsons is not a typical liberal. Rather than rooting his social philosophy in an individual seen as independent of society, Parsons sees society as central. He wants a society that creates men who value individualism. However, this individualism is seen as rooted in a type of society, for man is social.

8 Open social systems theory or structural - functionalism

In chapter 2, I argued that SSA was the book of somebody who thought he was reconciling positivism and idealism but whose actual problematic was utilitarianism in general and the classical economists' account of the rise of capitalism in particular. His voluntaristic theory, I argued, was not a reconciliation of positivism and idealism. Another problem for Parsons' voluntaristic theory, which was raised in chapter 2, was his treatment of economic rationality and common values. By seeing them as emergent properties, he does not integrate them theoretically into his unit act framework. The last five chapters have dealt with his action programme which focuses on the subjective meaning of actions and is in the idealist tradition. The core case of this programme is the institutionalized ego-alter interaction which can be seen as developing out of the unit act framework. This chapter focuses on the aspects of Parsons' work that developed from the other sides of these unresolved problems in SSA - positivism and 'emergent' properties.

Believing that he is developing one programme, Parsons never clarifies the basic framework of systems theory separately from action theory. The first part of this chapter will set out the basic essentials of the systems approach and show that Parsons accepts them. The starting point of Parsons' social systems programme is the view that the activities of people can be seen in terms of an open system. Open systems are boundary-maintaining and have 'G' states or equilibrium points. A systems theory analysis focuses on the functions of activities in the system for the system as a whole, and defines system elements in terms of their relationships to be organized whole. In elucidating this perspective, I shall be concerned with showing why it involves a positivistic approach.

Next, I shall argue that Parsons makes some significant contributions to this approach. These contributions are his FDs, which are a classification of the types of consequences an activity can have on a system as a whole, and his analysis of differentiation in terms of them. The other main claim of the next sections is that his application of systems theory is inadequate.

OPEN SYSTEMS

Parsons is concerned with a particular type of system, namely an open system. Open systems exist in environments and receive energy from outside of themselves. On the other hand, closed systems are ones that are isolated from all outside forces. No materials, energy or anything else can enter or leave a closed system. If one conceives of a social system as closed, then no new ideas can affect it. In a closed system, final conditions are determined by initial conditions. If one sees a social system as a closed system, then once it is stable it remains stable, for nothing can upset it. In an open system, on the other hand, initial conditions do not completely determine the conditions of the system at some later point, as what goes on in the environment also affects the open system. If a social system is seen as open, then it can be affected by outside forces (e.g. new ideas, other societies), and if stable at some point can become unstable at a later point. (1) An open system is boundary-maintaining. Parsons explains why (TS, p.36):

> a boundary means simply that a theoretically and empirically significant difference between structures and processes internal to the system and those external to it exists and tends to be maintained. In so far as boundaries in this sense do not exist, it is not possible to identify a set of interdependent phenomena as a system, it is merged in some other, more extensive system.

In other words, only if phenomena are more interconnected with each other than with other phenomena from the point of view under consideration (e.g. mechanical, chemical or social), does it make sense to call the phenomena in question a system. If there is no way in which the phenomena are boundary-maintaining, then they must be analysed as part of a larger system. One is saying that what has been called a system is in fact merged with some portion of its environment, and it plus this portion of the environment can be treated as a system. (2) This programme also sees open systems as having equilibria or

'G' states. For a system to be open and boundary-maintaining, it is necessary that processes internal to the system result in some features that serve to separate the system from its environment. Such features are 'G' states or equilibria of the system. As these terms, and particularly 'equilibrium', have been used in a wide variety of ways, it is necessary to specify precisely what is meant here. Henderson, who Parsons says was the main source of his idea of the importance of system (SS, p.vii), defines an equilibrium as (1935, p.47)

> a state such that if a small modification different from that which will otherwise occur is imposed upon a system a reaction will at once appear, tending toward the conditions that would have existed if the modification had not been imposed.

This definition of equilibrium fits with Nagel's definition of an equilibrium point (1964) and Rudner's definition of a 'G' state (1966, ch.5). A 'G' state is any set of values of variables or a value of a variable towards which a system tends. To assert that a 'G' state or equilibrium exists is to say not just that a feature of a system is there, but also that there are forces that tend to recreate the equilibrium if it is disturbed. (3) One of the laws of interactive processes that Parsons gives shows that he accepts this point (WP, p.100; cf. ES, p.256):

> once a disturbance has been introduced into an equilibrated system there will tend to be a reaction to this disturbance, which tends to restore the system to equilibrium.

A 'G' state or equilibrium can have many forms and be maintained in many ways. For instance a 'G' state can be a state of conflict. A recent anthropological analysis of conflict approaching it from the systems theory perspective is Rappaport's (1970) analysis of the relationships among the pig, gardening and warfare cycles in the New Guinea Highlands. Equilibria can also be maintained by conflict. A classical example of this from biology is the number of different species that can exist in a given area. Here one of the principle mechanisms maintaining the 'G' state (so many of each different species) is bigger eating smaller (Lotka, 1956, pp.161-84). In sociology, Boulding (1957) has shown that the Malthusian model can be reformulated in systems theory terms. The mechanisms of maintaining the equilibrium are 'famine, pestilence and warfare'. A 'G' state or equilibrium can also be a rate of change. Parsons talks of a 'moving equilibrium' (SS, p.250) which does make sense despite Rex's (1968, p.133) claim that this is 'essentially a contradiction in terms'. It is possible to say, 'This system tends to maintain a certain rate of change of some variable', without contradicting one's self. An unfortunately familiar example is inflation, which can be a stable rate of change in the value of money or an accelerating at some given speed rate of change in the value of money.

Having clarified the concept of equilibrium or 'G' state, it is now possible to define the concept of function in relation to it. If an action has the consequence of tending to maintain the 'G' state, then it is functional. If an action has the consequence of tending to move the system away from its 'G' state, then it is dysfunctional. Saying that 'x is functional' is not necessarily putting a seal of approval on x, though it is true that Parsons sometimes uses the word to do so. To say that x is functional (or dysfunctional) is not go give an explanation of x but rather is part of an explanation of the persistence (or change) of the system's 'G' state. Parsons says that he is using the concept of function in the same way as Cannon, a biologist, does (1964b, p.327). Cannon (1932) talks about a 'homeostatic state' of an organism which is essentially a 'G' state, and discusses how various processes function to maintain this. Parsons sees the key feature of functional analysis as the relating of processes to the maintenance of a system, or to the breakdown of a system (SS, pp.21-2; EST, p.218; TS, p.36).

In Parsonian systems theory, to say that 'x has a function of y' is to say that x has certain consequences for the system as a whole. For instance, to say that an activity has an adaptive function is to say that it produces facilities which, from the point of view of the system as a whole, enable the system to adapt. This approach to functionalism is different from that of Merton, who lacks a conception of the whole. When Merton (1968, pp.73-138) says that 'x has a function y', he means that 'x has certain consequences for y'. This approach loses one of the main advantages of systems theory, which is to see things in their overall context. Merton's functionalism sees things in a piecemeal way, one item is related to one another. K. Davis (1967) carries this to its logical and absurd extreme and sees being a functionalist as simply thinking in cause and effect terms.

With this clarification of the nature of the open systems programme it is possible to understand the limitations of Malinowski's (1922) analysis of the Trobriand Islands. This case has been an influential core case for sociology and for Parsons (1970, p.826). As an anthropologist, concerned with providing an alternative to the diffusionist and evolutionary schools of the late nineteenth and early twentieth century, Malinowski stressed that Trobriand society had to be seen in terms of itself. He looked at various institutions such as the Kula (4) and showed how they fitted into various other institutions (e.g. the prestige system and trading between the islands). Each institution is presented as supporting each other institution. The result is a completely static picture of a totally integrated society.

In terms of the open-closed distinction, Malinowski saw the Trobriands and the other islands participating in the Kula as a closed system. For instance, he takes no account of the introduction of new ideas into the system, though Roman Catholic missionaries were on the island at the time. (5) Even if it is accepted that Trobriand society was fully integrated, had he seen the society as open, he would have been forced to consider the mechanisms that handled new inputs from the environment. Recognizing that Malinowski was treating the Trobriands as a closed society, and that modern sociology sees societies as open, should enable us to use Malinowski as a core case while at the same time realizing its limitations. Its basic limitations are the assumptions that the equilibrium is static and consensual.

Having clarified the concepts of 'equilibrium' and 'function', it is now possible to argue that for Parsons the equilibrium of a social system and the structure of a social system must be one and the same thing. This is to say that, without realizing it, Parsons has defined these two concepts in an equivalent manner. He says about structure (TS, p.36):

> The concept of structure focuses on those elements of the patterning of the system which may be regarded as independent of the lower-amplitude and shorter time-range fluctuations in the relation of the system to its external situation. It thus designates the features of the system which can, in certain strategic respects, be treated as constants over certain ranges of variation in the behaviour of other significant elements of the theoretical problem.

Parsons goes on to relate the concept of 'function' to that of 'structure' (TS, p.36):

> functional considerations relate to the problems of 'mediation' between two fundamental sets of exigencies: those imposed by the relative constancy of 'givenness' of a structure, and those imposed by the givenness of the environing situation external to the system. Since only in a theoretically limiting case can these two be assumed to stand in a constant relation to each other, there will necessarily exist a system of dynamic processes and mechanisms. (6)

If these two quotes are looked at together, it can be seen that a structure of a system is composed of those features of a system that are relatively stable and for which there are mechanisms that maintain that stability. This is the definition of an 'equilibrium' which Parsons accepts. The extent of Parsons' confusion about systems theory is revealed in the fact that he uses both these words in his major works without realizing that they have the same meaning.

Parsons sees the structure of a social system being composed of values, norms, collectivities and roles. This is by the above analysis a theory of what is most stable in a social system. In other words, he is claiming that other features of a social system are more changeable than these. He arrives at this view of structures from his combination of action and systems theory.

This transference of the action theory conception of structure into systems theory seems inadequate. For instance, that the population size of a social system will be a 'G' state under certain circumstances can be argued on the basis of Malthus. It seems best to say that value, norms, collectivities and roles are 'G' states of a social system, but that there can be others. One can then make the argument that these are features of all social systems and thus an analysis in terms of these will prove the most fruitful for sociology. However, one must remain aware of the possibility of other 'G' states, a possibility which Parsons never discusses.

SYSTEMS THEORY AND POSITIVISM

Parsons says (EST, p. 229):

> But the structure of social systems cannot be derived directly from the actor-situation frame of reference. It requires functional analysis of the complications introduced by the interaction of a plurality of actors.

This position follows from the view presented in SSA that social activity could not be understood purely in a unit act framework, but that social systems had various emergent properties. To cope with these Parsons recommends structural-functionalism. This, he says, is a 'second best type of theory' (SS, p.20). The ideal type of theory for Parsons is one that allows one to trace out all the effects of one set of activities on all other activities. In sociology, however, he argues, knowledge of how one set of human activity affects other activities is so limited that another approach must be used. While sociologists cannot trace out all the particular effects of an activity, they can grasp the overall effect of an activity on society as a whole. Activities must be seen in terms of their place in a system and examined in terms of their effects on the structure of that system (i.e. their functions). I prefer the term systems theory for this type of programme rather than structural-functionalism, for, as I have argued, Parsons equates structure and equilibrium and the term function has a use in both action theory (see chapter 5) and systems theory.

Having discussed open systems, their structure and functions, it can now be argued that this is not an alternative way of getting at the same things as action theory does. Instead it is fundamentally different type of programme to action theory and involves a positivistic-behaviouristic definition of concepts. Action theory focuses on the individual actor and the meanings he attaches to his actions and builds up an analysis of society from this starting point. Systems theory starts from a different point. Everything is described in terms of relationship to the system of which it is a part, and the analysis focuses on the consequences of an activity for the system. One starts with the system as a given, and analyses the consequences of various actions on the system as a whole. The focus is not on what the actor means to do, but on the actual consequences of what he does. In other words, what man does is described not in terms of what he intends to do, but in terms of the real effects of his activities. A systems theorist 'looks down' on particular activities from the vantage point of the whole. He can be compared to an airline pilot flying over a city. The pilot does not see the way from A to B in the city; he sees a whole pattern of roads. He would see some as thoroughfares and others as ancillary roads feeding these.

Looking at activities from the point of view of the whole as opposed to the point of view of the individual actor leads to a positivistic approach to defining action. Unlike action theorists who use 'verstehen', system theorists take the point of view of a detached neutral 'scientific' observer. From the point of view of the whole, what the actor thinks he is doing is not relevant; what is relevant is what he does. And what he does will be seen not from his point of view, but from the system's point of view. As was discussed in chapter 4, Parsons has both action theory and systems theory definitions of roles. His action theory one is in terms of expectations, while his systems theory one is (SS, p.25)

> what the actor does in his relations with others seen in the context of its functional significance for the social system. It is this which we shall call his 'role'.

By this definition, a person's role is his place in the overall organization of things. It is what the actual consequences of his activity are. Activities are grouped together by the consequences they have for the system, not the actor's expectations. Role integration in this approach means that the roles fit together in such a way that they tend to produce a certain type of consequence. For instance the roles of executive, foreman and factory worker are integrated if these activities interrelate in such a way to have the consequence of producing goods. No claim is being made that there is any feeling of solidarity. (7) Role conflict, on the other hand, exists when the consequences of different roles do not mesh together.

If one wishes to look at a particular role, one must define it behaviourally. One is concerned with isolating a certain set of behaviour that has a certain consequence. It is irrelevant whether the individual who performs the role uses it as a unified set of actions or sees it as part of several roles (by the action theory definition). This implies that saying a person has a role means that under certain sets of circumstances the person will behave in certain ways. As an example, I shall examine what is meant in systems theory by the role of voter. First of all, a person can be said to vote only on account of the existence of a relationship between the behaviour of putting an X on a piece of paper and a consequence - namely the determination of some government or law. Second, what the person intends to do (e.g. please his wife) is irrelevant. What matters is that he performs a specific piece of behaviour - putting an X on a piece of paper. If one says that somebody is a voter, this means that under specified circumstances (e.g. election day), he will behave in a specified way (placing an X on a ballot paper), and that this has a specified type of consequence for the system (determination of government or law).

In his personality theory, Parsons defines a mechanism in such a way that it is clearly positivistic - if the word 'mechanism' did not give this fact away in itself (TGTA, p.125):

> When the processes of learning and performance are classified on the basis of the way they serve to meet the requirements of the system, they are termed mechanisms. That is, a process is a mechanism, insofar as it is viewed in terms of its relevance to the problems of the system.

Other concepts in systems theory have to be defined in the same positivist way. In chapter 6, I discussed Parsons' concept of a need-disposition. It can now be seen why the dispositional aspect of this concept lies within systems theory.

It sounds strange, I realize, to say that Parsons, who throughout his work insists on the subjective point of view, has a programme running through is work that involves defining its basic units in a positivistic way. However, for what it is worth (and in isolation it is only an indication) he does at one point see no contradiction between behaviourism and action theory (TGTA, p.234):

> Logically the scheme (the theory of action) is founded on certain categories of behavior psychology. These contain by implication the main categories of the frame of reference of the theory of action.

As Parsons does not continue to say: 'Therefore I repudiate SSA', it seems fair to say that he does not realize the implications of this statement.

In order to illustrate some of the points made so far in this chapter and show how muddled Parsons is, I want to look at his discussion of deviance. His action theory definition of deviance is a 'motivated violation of institutionalized expectations' which focuses on the meaning of the action to an actor and through the consensus assumption society. His systems theory definition is (SS, p.250):

> deviance is the tendency on the part of one or more of the component actors to behave in such a way as to disturb the equilibrium of the interactive process (whether a static or moving equilibrium).

Whether something disturbs the equilibrium or not is a matter of the consequences of an action. Conformative action will disturb the equilibrium in some cases, while deviant action (defined in action theory terms) may maintain it. What people intend to do and what the actual consequences of an action are need not be the same thing. This systems theory definition of deviance also illustrates how confused Parsons is about the nature of systems theory. His definition of deviance and of dysfunctional activity are one and the same. As was discussed earlier in this chapter, an activity is dysfunctional if it tends to move the system away from its equilibrium point. It is of course possible to define deviant activity as dysfunctional activity in systems theory. However, if one does so, then it is necessary to be clear that one is stipulating a definition. Having stipulated this definition, one should then make clear the implication that a theory of deviance so defined is a theory of social change.

THE FUNCTIONAL DIMENSIONS

The FDs in systems theory are a classification of types of consequences an action can have on the system as a whole. To say an action is in a particular FD is to say that it has primarily (8) a particular type of consequence for the system. Parsons here is filling in a major gap in sociological theory. Marx showed that different actions (e.g. profit-making), independently of the intentions of the actor, have an effect on the social structure (e.g. revolution). Parsons goes a stage further by attempting to provide an exhaustive classification of the types of consequences an action can have on the system. Instead of just being able to say an action is functional or dysfunctional, one can say 'how' an action is functional or dysfunctional.

Some of the groundwork for this conception of the functional dimensions is laid in WP, but its more completely worked-out form is to be found in 'The Point of View of the Author' and in 'The American University'. Parsons attempts to show that the FDs are an exhaustive classification of types of consequences by obtaining them by crossing two 'axes of differentiation'. This is illustrated in Figure 9.

	instrumental	consummatory	(Parsons' terms)
	production of facilities	channelling of facilities	(my interpretation)
external	A	G	
internal	L	I	

FIGURE 9

The external-internal axis follows from the open system programme. There will be some aspects of the interactions that affect the relationship of the system to its environment (external), and some aspects that concern the irrelationships among the system units themselves (internal). Parsons defines this axis (1964b, p.328):

> When we have a system composed of two or more interacting actors in an environment, however, two further exigencies have to be taken into account ... These are (1) internally, exigencies of stable interrelation of the action units vis-a-vis each other, and (2) the meeting of the exigencies of generalized relation

> between its system and the external situation conceived as a set of facilities and conditions of operation of the system.

The environment of the social system is the rest of the human action system. (9) Parsons sees the human action system as made up of the behavioural organism, the personality system, the social system and the cultural system. The environment of the social system is the organism (and the material world through the organism), the personality system, other social systems and the cultural system. An external consequence is one which affects the relationship of the social system under consideration to one or more of these environments. An internal consequence is one that affects the relationships between system parts by either maintaining or changing their relationships.

The second axis of differentiation Parsons calls instrumental-consummatory. This distinction is unacceptable in systems theory for it deals with the subjective meaning of an action to an actor. The purpose of the distinction, Parsons says, is to deal with the process of implementation in time (1964b, p.333). He says (Amer U, p.12):

> It is a distinction between processes which build up resources for future utilization and those which actually put them to use, thereby destroying them through consumption.

This is not a definition of instrumental-consummatory, for whether a process 'builds up resources for future utilization' is a matter of what its effects are, not a matter of what it means to actors. The citation does, however, provide a system consequences type of distinction that can be used as an axis of differentiation. I have called this axis production of facilities - channelling of facilities. The facilities are for the maintenance (or change) of the 'G' state or equilibrium. Production of facilities refers to processes that can be utilized by the system in a number of different ways. Facilities are generalized in that they can be channelled in a number of different ways to maintain or change a 'G' state. On the other hand, 'channelling of facilities' refers to the processes by which the 'G' state is directly changed or maintained. The main justification for interpreting this axis in this way is that when crossed with the external-internal axis it generates four categories that fit the labels which Parsons gives to his FD categories.

Crossing these axes of differentiation produces internal and external production of facilities boxes and internal and external channelling of facilities boxes. In other words, the system is seen as having processes that are directly involved in internal and external 'G' states and processes that produce facilities that maintain or change these 'G' states. I shall now examine each FD in turn.

External channelling of facilities means acts which have the direct consequence of maintaining (or changing) the relationship of the system to its environment. This relationship is one way of interpreting goal-attainment (G). At one point, when discussing goal attainment, Parsons says that (TS, p.39) 'A goal is therefore defined in terms of equilibrium.'

External production of facilities means acts which have the consequence of producing (or not producing) facilities that can maintain (or change) the relationship of the system to its environment. This seems a reasonable conception of adaptation. Internal channelling of facilities means acts which have the direct consequence of maintaining (or changing) the relationships between the system parts. The focus of integration is not on feelings of solidarity, but on the fit among system parts (e.g. roles). Latency is internal adaptation. Pattern-maintenance and tension-management is being interpreted to mean the production of that which can be used to maintain the internal structure.

The FDs are a classification of activities in terms of consequences, and this raises an important question. What time span is involved in consequences? The answer would appear to be that the shorter the more useful this classification of consequences is, as the following example makes clear. Suppose a group of hippies has a 'happening' during which they cover all the walls of the house with paint, and which clarifies how their roles intermesh. Several years later an art dealer sees the walls and offers to buy 'the art' for a large sum of money. Classifying the consequence as integrative seems more fruitful than classifying it as adaptive. Immediate consequences is a contradiction in terms, so some time scale, no matter how small must be involved. The shorter the time span involved, the more closely the open system approximates to a closed system, and the less the interaction of the activity with inputs from the environment needs to be considered.

One basic merit of defining the FDs in terms of external-internal and production of facilities-channelling of facilities or production of facilities-utilization of facilities in maintaining (or changing) a 'G' state is that this roots the FDs in the fundamentals of open systems theory. (10) The FDs provide by this analysis an exhaustive classification at a certain level of the types of consequences an activity can have on the system. Distinguishing clearly those processes that affect the relationship of the system to its environment from those that affect the relationship between system components makes possible greater clarity in thinking about some problems. It warns one that one cannot assume that processes maintaining the internal state of a system will maintain the relationship of the system to its environment. The internal state of a social system may prevent certain relationships of the system to the environment. For instance, the role relations within a task-oriented group which serve to maintain the authority of the leader may prevent it coming up with answers to the problem at hand, as this may require paying attention to a low-status member. Discussion of this possibility is ignored in Bales' book and in chapter 4 of WP. Parsons, in discussing Bales' results, does not attempt to remedy this omission. The omission in the context of small group analysis is strange in light of the numerous studies of authoritarian versus democratic small groups.

It is also possible on the basis of this analysis to point to a fault in the definition of structure that Parsons gives and that was discussed in a previous section. This is that he sees the elements of permanency being maintained only vis-à-vis the environment. In other words, he is, in this definition of structure, considering the system to have only an external 'G' state and not an internal one. This results, I suspect, from his confusion of action theory and systems theory. In action theory, as was discussed in chapter 7, a consensus exists that is liable to disturbance only from an external source. Transferring this tendency of thought into systems thinking leads to seeing the equilibrium of a system as being maintained only vis-à-vis the environment. (11)

As one is talking about the effects of an activity in 'classifying' it in a particular FD, to do so is to make a claim about the type of consequences of that activity. One is not stating what type of meaning it has. Consequently, the systems programme classification of an activity in an FD and the action programme one need not agree. There is no a priori reason to believe that when an actor does an action with an adaptive meaning to him (and through the consensus assumption, the rest of the social system), the action is in fact adaptive. Only if we assume correct knowledge does this relationship hold. A one-to-one relationship between the meaning interpretation of the functional dimensions and the consequences interpretation holds only if there is a consensus (necessary for the meaning interpretation), and the actors have total knowledge and act in terms of it. In other words, the relationship holds only for a group of 'super-sociologists' in full agreement with each other.

One interesting use of the FDs is to classify theories in terms of them. This can lead to greater clarity about the differences among them. For instance, one can bring some order into the consideration of various theories of social stratification by classifying these theories in terms of the FDs. Various theories of stratification can be classified as in Figure 10.

A	G
Davis and Moore and many replied to	Marcuse
Anarchists	Marx Parsons
L	I

FIGURE 10 A classification of theories of stratification by their claims about the consequences of stratification

Davis and Moore (1966) argue that stratification has the consequence of allocating and motivating people to fulfil roles in a manner that enables society to achieve its major objectives. Stratification ensures that there are people doing adequately what needs to be done for the society's continued existence. In terms of the FDs, they are claiming that stratification is adaptive - it provides facilities that are used to maintain an external 'G' state. The interesting thing about a number of their critics (e.g. Tumin, 1966) is not that they disagree with the level of efficiency that Davis and Moore claim for the stratification system in doing this, but that they accept that this is the basic type of consequence of stratification. Classifying Davis and Moore's stratification theory as adaptive allows one to see clearly what the alternatives to their position area. This lays the groundwork for a systematic set of alternatives to their position, and forces one to consider their position against these.

Marcuse's (1968) analysis of the stratification system sees its primary effects as being on the personalities of people in making them 'one dimensional'. In terms of the FD framework, he is claiming that stratification is a 'G' state of the social system maintained directly against pressure from personality systems. The anarchist view of the administrator, if they admit the need for one, tends to reveal a view of stratification as a means to internal 'G' states. The administrator has no prestige as an administrator, and his sole function is to enable activities to be co-ordinated when for some technological reason this is required. (12) Both Parsons and Marx see the stratification system as integrative. Marx argues that the basic consequence of stratification system for a society is class conflict which he sees as internally generated (i.e. as an internal 'G' state). Parsons sees the stratification system as holding a society together and promoting stability rather than change (TS, p.59). Both agree, however, in seeing stratification as being in the integrative box. While Marx sees it as dysfunctional, Parsons sees it as functional. Parsons specifically relates stratification to class conflict (TS, pp.59-60):

> The major function of the institutionalization of class status is to minimize class conflict, but often it is not very successful.

Tausky's (1965) analysis of Parsons' theory of stratification sees this theory as being basically similar to Davis and Moore's. How he comes to this conclusion, after discussing for most of the article how the value system relates to the prestige system and is rewarding to actors, is a mystery to me. Either he fails to understand the significance of what he is saying about Parsons, or he fails to understand Davis and Moore, but I would not like to guess which.

The Fds also provide a set of functional prerequisites for any social system. Social systems must have processes occurring in them, if they are to persist, that maintain external and internal 'G' states and which provide resources to maintain these 'G' states. As the FDs are rooted in the fundamentals of open systems theory, one knows that on their level of generality they provide an exhaustive classification. The FDs by their level of generality - they apply to any social system, not just societies - allow one to classify other sets of functional prerequisites. For instance, the list of functional prerequisites given by Aberle et al. (1967) can be seen as particular instances of those of Parsons, as Table 2 shows.

TABLE 2 A schematic comparison of Parsons' functional prerequisites with those of Aberle et al. (1967, p.322)

Parsons	Aberle, Cohen, Davis, Levy and Sutton
A	Biological extinction or dispersion of the members
G	Apathy of the members
I	War of all against all
L	Absorption of the society into another

PARSONS' APPLICATION OF THE FUNCTIONAL DIMENSIONS

Parsons' basic application of the FDs is summed up in Figure 11.

A	G
economy	polity
religious ritual socialization	stratification legal system
L	I

FIGURE 11

To claim that a particular type of activity (e.g. economic) has primarily a particular type of consequence (e.g. adaptive) is to make a major claim about it. As was seen when various theories of stratification were classified in terms of the FDs, there are, at least for stratification, alternatives to Parsons' view. To decide among the alternatives in this or any other case would involve a detailed assessment of the alternative theories of various institutions and the evidence for each theory. Consequently, I shall restrict myself to showing that Parsons has not on the whole discussed the types of considerations required to show an activity is in a particular FD. Despite this, at times, the categories do lead Parsons to important insights into the types of consequences activities have for society, though he fails to recognize the significance of some of his claims. The basic tendency behind his own placing of activities is, I shall argue, a utopian view of society. Essentially, I shall argue that seeing activities in relation to the FDs has the potential for generating significant insights. While Parsons at times has these, on the whole, his analysis of society in terms of the FDs reveals a utopian view of society. (13)

What Parsons includes in G is interesting (ES, p.81):

> the large-scale self-financing of expansion by business firms means that these firms have undertaken considerable political functions.

He is saying here that resource allocation is by its nature a political decision. How resources are allocated is a direct channelling of facilities with regard to the environment of the social system. Resource allocation is a 'G' state of a society. Resource allocation has a direct effect on the material environment through the organism. By using his categories, Parsons is able to cut through the normal political scientists' conception of the political process as well as a lot of ideological distortion. American business says that the government should stick to its own sphere and leave the economy (adaptive box) to 'free enterprise'. Parsons' theory leads one to recognize that corporate self-financing involves, by its very nature, political decisions. Parsons is squarely in accord with Marx with regard to the power of the bourgeoisie. While the ideology of capitalist society may not lead people to see corporate self-financing as political, this is its real nature. This position is in fundamental opposition to the position he takes about US society when reviewing C.W. Mills' 'The Power Elite' (SPMS, pp.199-225). In fact, the position taken in ES should lead Parsons to accept much of Mills, even though they have a different conception of power, and also to criticize Mills for not realizing the political strength of the business elite.

Parsons places ritual in latency on the basis of Durkheim's analysis of it (TS, p.39). He could just as easily have based the claim on Marx, who sees religion as the opiate of the masses. The argument in this perspective essentially is, that ritual is an internal generalized facility on account of the support it gives to the stratification system.

Parsons places the economy in the adaptive box on the basis that it provides facilities that enable a society to maintain itself against the environment. The view is probably correct for a number of societies. However, it is arguable that, for some societies, it is in G. For instance, in some underdeveloped countries the international economic and stratification system may force the country's economy to remain at a particular level. The imperialism hypothesis argues that underdeveloped countries must specialize in the production of raw materials (mineral or agricultural) for the developed countries. The political system must act to support this economic structure. In other words, political processes become facilities for maintaining a particular economic structure. Alternatively, for many societies, it can be argued that the vested interests in the economy are so strong that the political sphere adjusts to the economic instead of the other way round.

The basic criticism of Parsons here is that he does not consider this possibility and how to cope with it. There is one interesting answer. This is that, in a case like this, an analysis of the economy by standard economic techniques will fail. Such an economy is not really an economy but something much more like a political sphere. Only an analysis of it as a polity will produce an adequate understanding of it. One could give as evidence in support of this view, the difficulty that economists have in trying to come to grips with underdeveloped countries.

If one considers Parsons' view of the economy in conjunction with his view of the other sub-systems, one can see a utopian streak coming through in his analysis of society. He sees the polity as being concerned with the attainment of 'collective goals' (STMS, p.308). While it is possible that the society has as its external 'G' state, one that represents an enactment of its collective goals, it is also possible that its external 'G' state has little or anything to do with the goals most of the population hold for the society. For instance, it has been known to be the case that the political process has allocated resources not on the basis of the needs of society, as most of its population see them, but into the politicians' own pockets. Parsons also sees society with a stratification system and legal system (I) that is supported by parents socializing their children into accepting it. Parsons does not talk of any incompatibility between the external and the internal 'G' states. Parsons' basic image of a society is one where the economy provides resources for the polity to attain collective goals. Children are socialized into accepting the stratification system. As the collective goals of the society are being achieved, it is not surprising that there is not friction between the external and internal 'G' states. In other words, he has a utopian vision of society in which the social system is completely under man's control. Society functions harmoniously to achieve the goals that men wish it to. The hopes and dreams of men are implemented without any systematic frustration of their efforts.

Aside from a conservative political bias in his thought, Parsons probably arrives at this utopian position on account of his accepting that he has one theoretical position. Action theory, as has been discussed, focuses on the meaning of actions and thus does not include latent consequences. In addition, it was seen to involve a consensus assumption. These two features of action theory, if transferred into systems theory, can generate a utopian view of society.

FUNCTIONAL DIFFERENTIATION

Parsons sees social systems as tending to form sub-systems (14) specialized in each of the FDs (ES, p.47):

> total societies 'tend' to differentiate into sub-systems (social structures) which are specialized in each of the four primary functions.

In other words, he sees the processes that produce a particular type of consequence (e.g. integrative) as tending to form systems within the larger system. To say an integrative sub-system exists is to say that the processes in the integrative box are more closely tied to each other than to processes in other boxes. It will not be as fruitful for the understanding of an integrative activity to see it in relation to non-integrative activity as to see it in relation to other integrative activity. (15) Parsons sees the same tendency towards functional differentiation at work within each of the four sub-systems. For instance the integrative sub-system tends to develop its own specialized processes of adaptation etc. The tendency to functionally differentiate is at work within each sub-system of a sub-system and so on. However in one's analysis one has to take account of the process only as far as it has gone, so one is not faced with an infinite number of sub-systems.

This claim that societies tend to differentiate into sub-systems focused around each of the FDs is a sweeping, bold claim that applies to the interrelations of every role etc. in society. Classifications do not exist in a void. On examination they are found to underlie major assertions about reality. The use of the FDs in Parsons' analysis of functional differentiation illustrates how it is possible to see theories rather than classifications in Parsons, as was claimed in chapter 1. Some of the things that Parsons groups together using this approach are interesting. For instance, central banks and parts of insurance companies (ES, p.60) are in G and not A. Rather than see insurance companies as a business like any other business, Parsons sees them as political. One will be able to make more sense of aspects of insurance companies if one analyses them as political institutions rather than economic ones. The basis for this is the claim that some activities of insurance companies are more closely tied to political activities than economic activities. For instance, insurance pension schemes are often closely related to government ones.

A critic might say that, yes, it does group some things together in an interesting way, but there are some cases where it is wrong. For instance, how about science? Science affects man's ability to manipulate the environment and thus is adaptive. However, it also affects our fundamental understanding of the meaning of reality (L). Thus if you try to analyse science as within the adaptive system by pointing to the links between scientific research and economic considerations about what research to fund, this critic might say, I shall point to the links between science and our basic beliefs. Thus not everything in the adaptive box forms a system. The reply to this must be that the critic has a built-in assumption in his argument - science itself forms a system. Just because our everyday language breaks reality up in a certain way is not a reason for sociologists to do so also. Is it not possible that applied science and parts of experimental science are most closely tied to the adaptive box (i.e. form part of the adaptive system), while theoretical science forms part of the latency system? Science is not the unified (causally) activity that language suggests it to be. An adequate analysis will break it into two parts that are each more closely tied to other things than to each other. Other examples of 'contrary cases' might be handled differently. For instance, Parsons by implication sees the family and arms purchases as part of the latency system. Arms expenditures are in L, as he sees them being consumed by society as a whole (ES, p.55). Instinctively it seems better to place arms purchases in G and relate them to political changes. The basis for this would be that their basic consequence is to affect relationships with other societies. These examples are intended to show some of the ways one might go about developing this programme. To one who disagrees with it and produces a 'contrary' instance, one can say: let me analyse it for a while; there may be some linkage between this and other things 'not dreamt of in your philosophy'. To assess this programme will require a considerable effort at its development. But on a tentative basis, one can at least say that it is interesting and worth pursuing further.

Parsons extends this programme by saying (ES, p.83):

> In general our functional sub-system categories correspond more closely to organizationally differentiated sectors of the social structure as the society approaches greater 'structural' differentiation.

His application of this, however, seems faulty. He sees the US as having reached the highest level of functional differentiation of any society (ES, p.288) and calls it the 'new lead society' (SMS, ch.6). A laissez-faire economic structure where there are numerous small firms securing bank loans is more differentiated than a situation where oligopolies control their own financing. The first of these would characterize the US non-agricultural economy in the mid-nineteenth century, while the second characterizes the US economy now. Parsons, as was discussed in the section on his application of the FDs, accepts resource allocation to be a political function. What he fails to recognize is that this means that the US economy now is less differentiated than it was in 1850. Parsons also applies this idea about functional differentiation to the USSR (ES, p.83):

> modern totalitarian societies such as Soviet Russia bring most of the economy under exceedingly stringent governmental (hence in our sense primarily political) control ... How stable, beyond the period of 'forced draft' development, such a fusion may be is a crucial question about such societies; will certain 'natural' tendencies for the economy to differentiate from the polity appear or will they be inhibited?

Precisely the same line of reasoning would seem to apply to corporations' self-financing. In view of the fact that most major investment decisions in the USSR are taken by the State Planning Organization (Gosplan) and not the productive unit (i.e. factory), it appears that in this respect the USSR economy is more differentiated from the polity in this respect than the US economy. By Parsons' reasoning, the USSR economy should be relatively stable, and a crucial question about the US would be whether 'certain natural tendencies for the economy to differentiate from the polity' will appear. My inclination is to accept that the theory is correct and Parsons' application is inadequate.

So far I have been dealing with what might be called the analytic approach to functional differentiation. In this, one starts with the four FDs and sees activities as becoming increasingly specialized in each. The concrete approach to sub-system analysis involves focusing on particular complexes and seeing them as becoming increasingly specialized in one particular functional dimension as functional differentiation occurs. For instance, taking this approach, the economy is one of possibly several systems which have come to have a primarily adaptive function. This is to say that the economy's consequence for the social system is the provision of facilities.

Other systems which are relatively independent of the economic system may also have the consequence of providing facilities for the social system. This is not as powerful a variant of the programme as the analytic approach as it does not claim that everything in a functional box forms a system. However, when I look at Parsons' discussion of economic theory and his input-output analysis, this concrete approach will be seen to be implicit. The names he gives to various categories will be seen to imply a concrete approach, though at no place does he spell it out explicitly. Yet, as will be seen when his input-output analysis is discussed, there are some problems with using this approach.

The functional differentiation approach lends itself easily to incorporation within an evolutionary perspective. Some things that can be done easily are also brilliant and this is one of them. Parsons argues that significant increases in the generalized adaptive capacity of a society result from increased functional differentiation. By an increase in generalized adaptive capacity, Parsons means (SMS, ch.2) that the society can cope with a wider range of inputs from its environment. Successful coping occurs when the social system can handle these inputs without its equilibrium being upset. For instance, one society has a larger generalized adaptive capacity than another if it can cope with a wider range of personality types among its members.

The logic behind functional differentiation having the effect of increasing generalized adaptive capacity is that differentiation produces more specialized structures. For differentiation to produce an increase in generalized adaptive capacity, the new differentiated structure must be included or integrated into the society (SMS, pp.10-12). Doing this will involve generalizing values. (16) The logic here is that a value that had previously led to one type of behaviour must now lead to a wider range of types of behaviour.

In SECP and SMS, Parsons presents an evolutionary view of human history in functional differentiation terms. He also includes the idea of evolutionary universals. These he defines (STMS, p.493):

> An evolutionary universal, then, is a complex of structures and associated processes the development of which so increases the long-run adaptive capacity of living systems in a given class that only systems that develop the complex can attain certain higher levels of general adaptive capacity.

Parsons sees four evolutionary universals as required for the emergence of human society (STMS, p.495) - religion, communication with language, kinship and technology. The next two evolutionary universals (STMS, p.496) are 'social stratification' and 'a system of explicit cultural legitimation of differentiated societal functions, preeminently the political function independent of kinship'. Finally, the evolutionary universals required for modern society are (STMA, pp.503-19) bureaucracy, money and economic markets, generalized universalistic norms (a legal system that is based on formal rationality) and democratic association. The idea behind the notion of an evolutionary universal seems sound, and so does seeing historical evolution in terms of functional differentiation. I lack the detailed knowledge of history necessary to assess Parsons' attempts in these areas. If these are unsatisfactory, other attempts to implement the programme should be made.

INPUT-OUTPUT ANALYSIS

While societies tend to functionally differentiate, and this means that an activity is more interconnected with those in the same FD and form a sub-system, this is not to say that activities do not have effects on those in other FDs. Parsons describes these in terms of inputs and outputs. To say one particular box (e.g. the A box of the A sub-system) has an output to another (e.g. the A box of the G sub-system) is to say that it affects this box. To say one particular box (e.g. the A box of the A sub-system) receives an input from another box (e.g. the A box of the G sub-system) is to say it is affected by the activities in that box. Perhaps the best known examples in social science of this type of approach are the political systems models of Easton (1965) and the input-output analyses of economics.

Parsons does not see the inputs and outputs among the boxes as being random, but rather that some interchanges are more important than others. Smelser says (1970, p.17) (17) that in ES, chs. 2 and 4, it

> proved fruitful to assume that each sub-system interchanges with every other sub-system primarily at 'one' boundary only (though secondarily at others), yielding a total of six primary boundary-interchanges ...

These interchanges can be represented for the whole society in Figure 12. It is possible to set any one of these exchanges out in more detail. Figure 13 shows Parsons' presentation of the interchange between the adaptive and latency sub-systems.

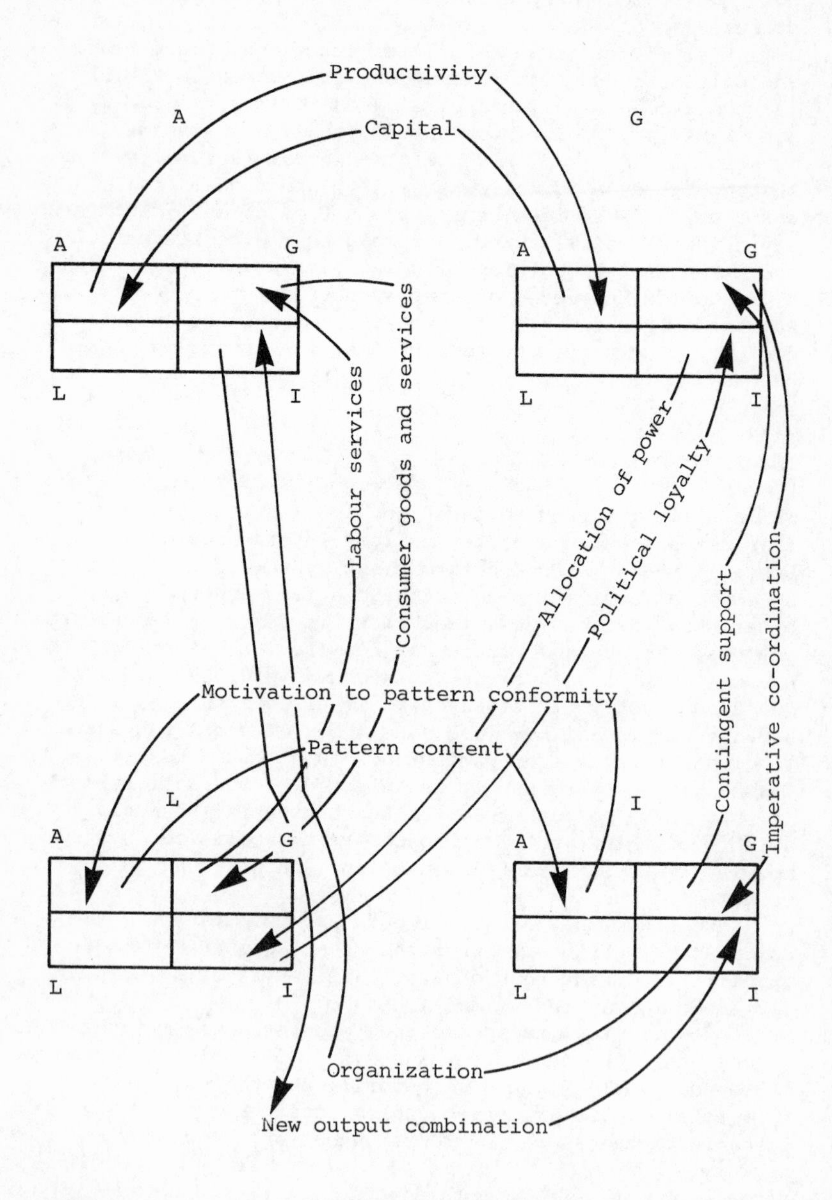

FIGURE 12 Boundary interchange between the primary subsystems of a society (ES, p.68)

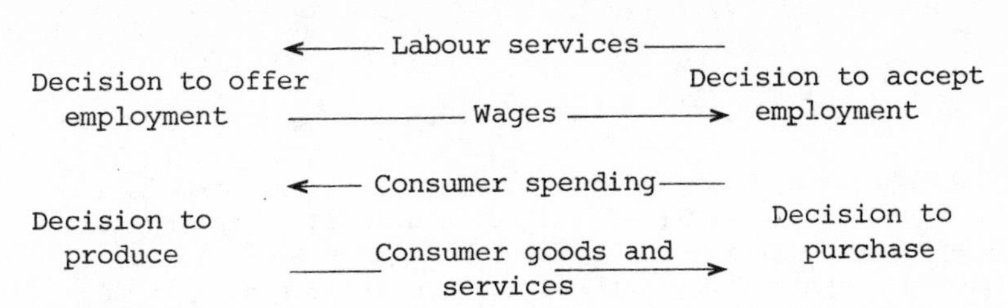

FIGURE 13 The double interchange between the economy and the pattern-maintenance sub-system (ES, p.71)

Parsons in Figures 12 and 13 is making an important claim. To single out one particular interchange out of nine possible ones is to make a definite commitment about how activities are interdependent. He is claiming that the most important interactions between system parts in different FDs are those represented by his arrows. In other words, an arrow showing one box has an output to another box is a shorthand way of saying that the activities in the first box have a larger effect on the activities in the second box than they do on any other box except those in the same sub-system in which they are.

Before assessing his input-output analysis, several general features of it must be commented upon. The first is that Parsons claims to deal with the interdependence between the adaptive sub-system and the latency sub-system. He is taking the analytic, not the concrete, approach to functional differentiation. However, the names he gives to the categories suggest he is implicitly taking a concrete approach. For instance, he identifies the adaptive sub-system with the economy. Now if one says that Parsons is dealing with an adaptive sub-system (i.e. one of several adaptive sub-systems) in interdependence with a latency sub-system, several possible interpretations are opened up. The first is that all adaptive sub-systems are interdependent with all latency sub-systems. The second, and this appears more plausible, is that the adaptive sub-system is interdependent with primarily one latency sub-system (e.g. the economy with the family). Parsons, as he sets out his theory using the analytic approach, never gets into this problem.

A second feature of his theory, which will be seen to be important when his applications are looked at, is that he labels a number of things in an action theory way (e.g. decision to accept employment) as opposed to behaviourally. The third feature is that all inputs and outputs are double interchanges. In other words, what has an output to one activity also has an input from that activity.

PARSONS' APPLICATION OF INPUT-OUTPUT ANALYSIS

Parsons makes an input-output analysis of the interchanges among the sub-systems of society and in ES, treating the adaptive sub-system as itself composed of sub-systems, does an input-output analysis of the interchanges among these. To assess each interchange would be to assess the total range of interdependency of social activity. Some of the interchanges he mentions are fields of specialization in themselves. For instance, the interchange of the I box of the L sub-system and the I box of the G sub-system (political loyalty - allocation of power) is the focus of the analysis of revolutions for some theorists. While I will not discuss any particular interdependence in depth, I will specify the basic method that underlies Parsons' statement of interdependencies. In doing this I am going to make a big assumption. This is that how Parsons labels his boxes is satisfactory for considering the analytic approach. Alternatively, my discussion can be seen as a discussion of the concrete approach where the interdependence is between the particular systems his category labels fit.

Essentially Parsons' method for determining the input and output is to state the obvious. And what is obvious is the common sense embodied in our everyday culture/ ideology. If our everyday culture does not provide an answer, then Parsons takes the banal in accepted academic theories. Furthermore, he interconnects things in such a way that one has a picture of a 'trouble-free' perfectly integrated whole. The picture is made to look even more stable by having double interchanges. If two boxes are directly interdependent, as opposed to interdependent through a series of other boxes, then things look more stable as there are fewer places where one can see problems. Typical of the range of interdependencies Parsons sees is that between the G box of the A sub-system and the G box of the L sub-system. He sees this as an exchange of wages for labour services and wages for consumer goods (ES, p.71) or, to simplify, labour for goods. Now, clearly, this is correct. If people in society do not work, no goods are produced. This can hardly be described, though, as a new insight into society. It should be stressed that the level of analysis is the system level. There are individuals who receive goods and do not work, while there are also workers who may receive no goods and starve. However, on the system level, for an ongoing system, people work to produce goods.

Parsons sees the interchanges between the I box of the A sub-system and the I box of the I sub-system as entrepreneurial service for profit and demand for new produce combinations for new output combinations (ES, p.79). The first of these interdependencies is the standard economic factor of production and its return analysis. I should perhaps have written, 'standard forty years ago'. Now many economists would accept that the bulk of profit in the US economy comes from the oligopoly or monopoly position of firms. The other interchange involves the acceptance of the free market ideology. Demand for new products is met by new output combinations. No mention of the role of advertising. In addition, it is not clear that the effect of the new output combinations is primarily on the I box of the I sub-system. Consider the case of television or printing. Surely these new output combinations have had more effect on the A box of the L sub-system (external facilities for socialization). The effect of new output combinations also can be very disruptive to a society. Consider the introduction of iron or gunpowder.

It would be possible to go on and give more examples, but these two seem sufficient to establish that what Parsons has done in his input-output analysis is to state common sense in fancy words. The plausibility of it comes from the statement of the widely agreed, and the action theory framework. If the interchanges are looked at in a means-ends way and the words he uses to describe the boxes fit action as opposed to systems theory, then they appear plausible. Labour is a means to getting wages and wages are a means to getting goods. Perhaps this type of analysis might be called ordinary language systems theory. One takes what one's language and everyday experiences tells one about the world and slots it into the appropriate boxes. The world is causally interconnected in just the way our language would lead us to believe. Sociologists are unnecessary.

While Parsons' application of input-output analysis boils down to 'ordinary language systems theory', there is a worth-while enterprise to be undertaken. However, it is a very complex one, and probably one has to specify the type of system one is dealing with before one can give the inputs and outputs. Nevertheless, the interdependencies between the sub-systems of a society must be analysed before one can claim to have a satisfactory analysis of that society.

Parsons' ordinary language systems theory seen less as

an analysis of society and more as a codification of our standard knowledge as represented in our culture and current academic theories is extremely worth while. By systematization of these views, or at least a large proportion of them, Parsons makes it possible to go about giving a consistent critique of them. Instead of being restricted to purely isolated criticisms of items of our common understanding, a codification of this understanding makes possible a thoroughgoing criticism. Implications of any criticism become easier to trace.

CONCLUSION

Parsons has made some interesting and worth-while contributions to social systems theory. Sometimes, and I am inclined to say, in spite of himself, he realizes the potential of his theoretical concepts in his applications. By and large, he manages to state only the trivial in his applications. By separating systems theory from Parsons' application of it, I have arrived at a more favourable assessment of Parsons than C.W. Mills. There are, however, similarities between my view and Mills' assessment (1970, p.59):

> I began this chapter with a question: Is grand theory, as represented in 'The Social System', merely verbiage or is it also profound? My answer to this question is: It is only about 50 per cent verbiage; 40 per cent is well-known text book sociology. The other 10 per cent, as Parsons might say, I am willing to leave open for your own empirical investigations. My own investigations suggest that the remaining 10 per cent is of possible - although rather vague - ideological use.

9 Some analyses using both the action and systems programmes

Parsons is confused. His action programme is mixed up with his systems or structural-functional programme throughout his work. In the previous six chapters I have separated these programmes of Parsons from each other and presented each separately as coherent overall approaches to theorizing. The reader can by comparing the sources cited in chapters 3 to 8 see the extent to which these are intermingled in Parsons. It would have been possible to write six chapters of the form: Parsons is inconsistent here, and here, and here, and here. However, I felt it was better to go behind his muddle to the two types of programmes that run through his work.

What I want to do now however is illustrate how completely Parsons runs the two approaches together. In order to do this I have copied out pp.31-2 from his article Some Problems of General Theory (1971). Those sections that are in the action programme appear in italics and those sections in the systems programme appear in ordinary type. Those passages that make sense in both appear in capital letters. I have eliminated his footnotes and replaced them with my own where I think that the status - action theory or systems theory - of a remark requires clarification. The purpose of this analysis is to show how one can go about separating Parsons' two programmes and to illustrate how muddled he is.

> There is a fundamental basis of differentiation along the range of temporal sequence which consists in the fact that there is not a simple one-to-one relation between conditions necessary for the attainment of a given goal-state and its attainment. The same conditional state of affairs (THE ESTABLISHMENT OF WHICH MAY ITSELF CONSTITUTE A GOAL) (1) can often be a condition of the attainment of a plurality of different goal-states, some of which are alternatives to each

other in that, given a set of conditions, only one of a pair of goal-states is realistically attainable. Therefore the processes involved with establishing conditions of future goal-states, and the more ultimate or 'CONSUMMATORY' processes of approaching such goal-states, tend to become differentiated in living systems. *At the action level this is very much involved with the means-end relationship. Activities concerned with the procurement of means not only may be logically distinguishable from those concerned with goal-attainment, but are in many cases realistically different.*

This distinction has become increasingly prominent in the course of evolution because adaptive capacity has become increasingly generalized and goal-attainment capacity increasingly flexible. This is one of the bases of the 'activism' which is far more prominent in the sphere of behavior than in that of metabolic or vegetative functions. Here it has become established usage - after much controversy - to speak of an organism as engaged in goal-seeking behavior. (2) *This may be defined as behavior which has the 'meaning' (or possibly the intention)* of altering the otherwise obtaining organism-environment relationship in a direction more favorable than otherwise to the maintenance of the pattern of the organism. THIS MIGHT BE MANIFESTED, FOR EXAMPLE, IN FOOD-GETTING ACTIVITIES, WHERE THE PROCUREMENT OF FOOD WOULD CONSTITUTE THE ATTAINMENT OF A GOAL.

A similar distinction holds for the processes of internal mediation, namely between processes which preserve and protect the system's potential for actualization of its pattern, and those which 'mortgage the future' *in some kind of consummatory interest. We may thus take this axis of differentiation, of the establishment of general conditions for the attainment of system ends on the one hand, and action on the basis of such conditions on the other, as the second basic axis of differentiation of living systems, cross-cutting the first.*

In a sense, both the system-environment AND THE TEMPORAL PATTERN MAINTENANCE-GOAL ATTAINMENT AXES ARE FOCI OF CONTINUOUS VARIATION. The case for dichotomizing is more immediately clear in the former context. The differential between internal system states and those of the environment in general is not continuous but involves boundaries. In higher organisms, potential food in the environment is not the same as digested nutritional material in the blood stream; the former, among other things, is much more diverse. *In the temporal axis, there is, however, a parallel in the*

> *'turn' from a system's 'interest' in the 'stock' of instrumentally utilizable facilities, and of their consummatory utilization for specific ends. There are, then, boundaries of the meaning of temporal selection - on the action level 'choice '* - which in certain respects correspond to the boundary between system and environment. IN BOTH CASES THEY CONSTITUTE SOMETHING AKIN TO 'WATERSHEDS'. On one side of the boundary, processes work to produce one kind of result; on the other side, quite another kind. It is a qualitative distinction, not a question of position along an unbroken continuum. It should be made clear, however, that the distinctions being drawn do not imply that a structure in a living system cannot be involved in processes on both sides of either of the two 'boundaries'.
>
> THE LOGICAL OUTCOME OF DICHOTOMIZING ON BOTH OF THE TWO PRIMARY CROSS-CUTTING AXES OF DIFFERENTIATION IS A FOUR-FOLD CLASSIFICATION OF FUNCTION. IN TERMS OF PREVIOUSLY ESTABLISHED USAGE, THE FOUR FUNCTIONS ARE REFERRED TO AS PATTERN-MAINTENANCE (*internal*-means), INTEGRATION (*internal*-ends), GOAL ATTAINMENT (*external*-ends), AND ADAPTATION (*external*-means).
>
> AMONG THE FOUR, PATTERN MAINTENANCE OCCUPIES A SPECIAL PLACE IN THAT IT IS THE FOCUS OF STABILITY IN BOTH OF THE TWO MAIN RESPECTS. It is internal rather than external, in the sense of being insulated from the more fluctuating processes of the environment, and it is associated with the long run and insulated from the continuing adjustments which the adaptive and GOAL-ORIENTED PROCESSES on the part of plural units bring about in the internal subsystems. The distinctive features of this greater stability are formulated as constituting a pattern which is distinctive of this system or type of system, and which may be presumed to be, or to have a tendency to be maintained in the face of fluctuations in the relevant environmental conditions and over time.

The preceding illustrates the extent of Parsons' confusion. It would not, however, be profitable to continue the chapter in this manner. Instead I want to look at several topics Parsons covers - economic theory, power, and universities in the United States. In the latter two cases I will show how his confusion prevents an adequate analysis. Yet at the same time, I shall argue that the way he tackles each of these topics contains some good ideas that should not be overlooked.

THE REDUCTION OF ECONOMICS: A WORTH-WHILE PROJECT POORLY EXECUTED

Parsons gives the following as his basic conclusion about the relationship between economic theory and his own theory (ES, p.295):

> Our central proposition is that economic theory is a special case of the general theory of social systems, which is in turn one of the main branches of the developing general theory of action.

Parsons claims to have a theory about social activity. As this encompasses the economic sphere, he has to come to grips with economic theory. To do this, he must do a reduction of the type discussed in chapter 1. As was discussed there, he must show that economic theory can either be deduced from his position or reduced to his position or some mixture of these. If he cannot, then economic theory is independent, and he must give up his claim to have a general theory of social activity. Parsons claims to do a deduction (ES, p.8) but, as will be seen from the following discussion, a mixture of deduction and reduction is actually involved. Parsons sees himself as integrating economic theory with sociological theory. For instance, in chapter 4 of ES, where he discusses how sociological theory could help determine the value of a number of economic variables, he is accepting an under-labourer role for sociology that accepts the bulk of economic theory. He fails to recognize that, to reduce economic theory to sociological theory, it may be necessary to reject a significant portion of the claims and analyses of economists.

On several grounds considerable disagreement can be expected between economic and sociological theories. Economists choose and evaluate their programme in terms of its fruitfulness for understanding only the economic universe. What economists call their boundary assumptions will tend to be determined by how they intend to analyse economic activity, rather than by a consideration of the factors (many non-economic) that a sociologist would consider relevant. The tendency of sociologists and economists to disagree is one of the major reasons why making an attempt to reduce and deduce economic theory is worth while. Simply because economics is now a separate area in the academic division of labour is no reasons why it must always remain so. These areas, instead of being unrelated, will be forced into a conflict. If sociologists claim to understand man's activities, and economic activity is an activity of man, then sociologists should try to show that by a mixture of deduction and reduction, they can come to grips with economic theory. Academics have been too inclined to see different areas instead of competing theories.

This type of deduction-reduction project can be carried out in other areas. For instance, sociology is in the same relationship to political theory as economic theory. The advantages of theoretical unification are so well known that it is clear that such deduction-reduction projects should be undertaken. If sociologists claim to have an analysis of human activity in society, then they should be sociological imperialists. Sociologists who are unwilling to be imperialists should offer an explanation of why man suddenly becomes a different type of animal governed by different laws when he engages in economic or political activity.

Some of Parsons' arguments in ES are relevant to a deductive-reductive enterprise in his action programme, while others fit his systems programme. Without sorting these two types of arguments out, I shall list several criticisms of economics that Parsons gives:

1 it becomes inappropriate even to refer to utility at this level in terms of individual preference lists or indifference curves (ES, p.22).
2 This (seeing capital provision as a political decision) is obviously a radical departure from traditional economic analysis, which has tended to treat the supply of capital funds as directly dependent, in one sense or another, on some money payment, usually interest (ES, p.75).
3 The usual view of the accelerator tends to reduce it to an intra-firm engineering problem, which assumes either that the production sub-system saves enough to finance any required investment or that no irregularities develop between firm and investor on the one hand and between investor and supplier of funds on the other. In a highly differentiated economy, these assumptions seem unrealistic, even for constructing a restricted model of the business cycle (ES, p.220).
4 Finally, only through the analysis of institutional structure and its relation to the processes of the economy can economic theory be incorporated into the general theory of social motivation, and hence be relieved of the necessity of resting on 'ad hoc' hypotheses about 'human nature' which are psychologically and sociologically dubious, if not downright untenable (ES, p.184).

In the course of his book, as the preceding citations show, Parsons makes major criticisms of economics. He rejects indifference curve analysis, available capital as being a function of the interest rate, and the accelerator, and feels that economics is based on 'dubious, if not downright untenable' 'hypotheses about human nature'. His conclusion, which I have already cited, is that economics is a special case of sociological theory. Now at this point Parsons should continue by saying: 'Therefore sociological theory is inadequate and rests on a 'dubious, if not downright untenable' 'set of assumptions'. If he does not wish to draw this conclusion, he must accept that expanding sociological theory to cover economic activities will not leave economic theory unchanged. One cannot integrate economic theory, as it stands now, into sociology. However, sociological imperialism and the resultant conflict with economists should produce a better analysis of social activity - economic and non-economic.

POWER

Parsons' definition of power straddles his action and system programmes. This allows him to claim he has resolved certain problems which in fact he has not. Nevertheless the elements of his definition in each programme do contain useful insights into the nature of power. His basic definition is (STMS, p.308):

> Power then is generalized capacity to secure the performance of binding obligations by units in a system of collective organization when the obligations are legitimized with reference to their bearing on collective goals and where in the case of recalcitrance there is a presumption of enforcement by negative situational sanctions - whatever the actual agency of that enforcement.

Seeing power as a capacity is to see it in positivistic system theory terms. As Giddens says, seeing power as a feature of a system (1968, p.265)

> allows him to shift the entire weight of his analysis away from power as expressing a relation between individuals or groups, towards seeing power solely as a 'system property.'

It is from this perspective that Parsons makes a claim about power that Foss (1963) objects to strongly. Parsons says: 'Whether there is opposition or not is empirically very important but theoretically secondary matter' (STMS, p.225). The problem for Parsons is that good theories should focus on what is 'empirically very important'. Power is, among other things, a relationship between individuals or groups. Nevertheless, there is, as Parsons points out, a major advantage in seeing power as a system capacity. One does not have to see power in a zero-sum way (STMS, pp.332-45). The power of a system can increase or decrease. This type of view of power is attractive to Parsons, as he is looking at society in relation to a long run perspective. A modern functionally differentiated society does have more power than a less differentiated one. In looking at social change throughout history there has been a growth in power and this is both theoretically and empirically important. In this perspective, the opposition to power is not only theoretically but also empirically unimportant.

Parsons' action programme conception of power sees it as a form of communication. This communication has two major characteristics. What is communicated is legitimate in relationship to the group's goals. Second, the individual or collectivity to whom the message is addressed expects that if they are seen not to conform with the instructions, then they will be penalized. It is important to be clear about the limits of Parsons' conception of power in action theory. A robber pointing a gun at me and saying, 'Hand over your money', does not have power over me. This is not to say I will not hand over my money. I will hand over my money as he has threatened force. However, all force is not power. A communication is an exercise of power only where it is legitimate. Only those with authority can exercise power. Authority Parsons defines as (STMS, p.320)

> the aspect of a status in a system of social organization, namely its collective aspect, by virtue of which the incumbent is put in a position legitimately to make decisions which are binding, not only on himself but on the collectivity ...

Power depends for its existence on a consensus, as its use must be legitimate. Parsons develops a view of power that stresses that it can be used to achieve 'what both sides in a power relationship desire' (Giddens, 1968, p.263). The view that Parsons takes of voting fits with this perspective. There are so many uncertainties in the political sphere that one cannot usually rationally decide who to vote for. Thus voting is usually nonrational and based on 'the principal solidarity groups in which the voter is involved' (STMS, p.235).

Parsons stresses that power is symbolic (STMS, pp.308-9) and parallel in nature to money; spending money, he stresses, is a form of communication (Amer U, p.24). Force has the same relationship to power as gold does to paper money. It is an ultimate back up, but if everybody wants gold for their money, it cannot be provided. Similarly, if all exercises of power have to be backed up by the use of force, the authority structure will collapse.

Power inflation and deflation are possible. The view that power can be used to do things that most people want and that it cannot in a complex society be backed up each time by force provides a useful corrective to many conflict theorists. Power is not inherently exploitative. However Parsons' problem is that he has pushed the view too far. There are no clear demarcation lines among power being supported, accepted, lived with and acquiesced to. Pushed to its extreme, Parsons' view can imply that the hanged man wills his own death.

UNIVERSITIES IN THE UNITED STATES

Parsons' most recent book, 'The American University', written with Gerald Platt, is a good example of how confusing action theory and systems theory leads to an analysis that makes sense only if it is assumed the participants are all super-sociologists in complete agreement with each other. Parsons says (Amer U, p.158):

> What has been presented in the present chapter is an 'ideal type' in the Weberian sense of that term. Such a type has both normative and explanatory significance, which derive from the assumption that values and norms formulated as part of it may influence the concrete action of participants in the system being analyzed ... Another question is how far the ideal type used for analytical purposes in fact describes the actual behavior within the system of reference and in what principal respects is deviant from it.

From the action programme side of his ideas, Parsons has described the university system in terms of the norms of its participants. From this normative description he then proceeds to interconnect the activities so described in the way the participants see them as connected. These interconnected activities are placed in his systems theory input-output analysis boxes and thereby given explanatory significance. The result is the ordinary language systems theory described in chapter 8. Thus Parsons gets an 'ideal type' that has 'both normative and explanatory significance'. Because of his confusion of action theory and systems theory he fails to see why his analysis at points might be problematic. It is not surprising, in view of his theoretical confusion, that several reviewers (e.g. Gusfield, 1974, p.293; Sexton, 1974, p.296) attack him for his failure to deal with material that disagrees with his own point of view.

One interesting idea in the book, and one well worth developing, is that the latency sector or sub-system of a society has its own special mode of organization. Partially Parsons characterizes it negatively by saying it is not a market, bureaucratic or democratic mode of organization. In a more positive way, he characterizes it as a (Amer U, p.129) 'stratified collegial association' with the institution of tenure being important. What is needed (which Parsons largely lacks), is an analysis of this mode of organization of a similar type to the one Weber gives of bureaucracy. It seems worth while trying to formulate an ideal type of latency organization. Parsons does provide a base, but more detail is needed.

10 Conclusion

Parsons' work flows from the analysis he gives of some of the major problems confronting sociology in SSA. What this means is that at the centre of his work lies a fundamental confusion. His voluntarism is too eclectic to reconcile positivism and idealism. Running throughout his work are two different programmes - a social action one in the idealist tradition and a social system one in the positivist tradition. The action programme focuses on the meaning of an action to an actor, while his social systems programme focuses on the consequences of an activity for a system of activity. Parsons does not have an action system, as he claims, but only a behavioural system and a separate action theory.

People who attempt new and major projects are often muddled. However, we keep returning to their work because they lacked a tradition that defined their problems neatly. Thus they are forced to deal with most of the complexities of the issues with which they are concerned. They cannot hide behind a tradition that gives them 'pat' answers to their problems. Their confusion is often worth exploring in detail. This, at least, has been my experience with Parsons.

When one separates his action programme out from his work, he can be seen to have made substantial contributions to this type of approach. Normally, theories in the idealist tradition focus on unique clusters. While still accepting the subjective point of view and the use of 'verstehen', Parsons sees the orientations of actors as being of a limited range of types which he classifies in terms of the PVs. By a consensus assumption, he is able to talk about the social meaning of actions and he classifies these in terms of the FDs. What makes the PV and FD classifications particularly significant is that Parsons relates them to each other. This relationship and his analysis of the differentiation of meaning provide the foundations to an analysis of the patterning of meaning in a society. He provides action theory laws.

When one separates his social systems programme out of his writings, one can see that in this approach also he has made substantial contributions. The FDs provide a classification, rooted in the fundamentals of open systems theory, of the types of consequences an activity can have on a system. In terms of the FDs, Parsons goes on to develop an analysis of the differentiation of societies into sub-systems. His input-output analysis is a way of stating the interdependencies among the sub-systems. In his application of social systems theory, he betrays a highly utopian view of society. He does what I have called ordinary language systems theory.

This type of systems theory facilitates his running of action and systems theory together. Parsons sees men doing what they intend to do together. For the intentions of men and the consequences of their activities on the social whole to be the same, one must assume perfect knowledge and a consensus. For an action programme and systems programme analysis to give the same results, one must assume a society of 'super-sociologists' in complete agreement.

The objective of combining the meaning of an action to an actor and its consequences is, however, a natural one for sociologists to have. The meaning of an action allows one to comprehend the reasons of an actor for his action. When one thinks about one's own actions, one's reasons are what subjectively seem important to why one did something. On the other hand, sociologists are also interested in the real consequences of the interactions of a plurality of actors.

Many have criticized the level of abstraction of grand theory. Suffering from myopia and unable to look beyond the survey data of the last thirty years, they miss seeing grandeur and fascination of general theory. It is the attempt to understand the nature of man as it manifests itself throughout history and in social relationships varying from a couple in love to nations at war. Parsons' answer to what the nature of man is, is that man is social.

Notes

1 THE FRAMEWORK FOR ANALYSING PARSONS

1 Gouldner does more than this as well.
2 See for instance J. Hospers (1965), a standard text-book in the area.
3 A definition by this approach is analytic for the definition is seen as a spelling out of what is being defined. For instance, in 'Man is a featherless biped', 'featherless biped' is seen as something contained (though covertly) in the concept 'man'. On the other hand, if one says 'This pen is red', then what is contained in the predicate (red) cannot be in any way deduced from the subject (pen). The influence of Aristotle can be seen in the subject-predicate formulations of the definitions.
4 'A priori' means 'logically prior to looking at the world' while 'a posteriori' means 'logically after looking at the world'.
5 The 'must' of logical necessity.
6 Probably because he was so impressed with Newton's theories and their success that he was concerned primarily with underpinning these.
7 By satisfactory is meant satisfactory in the terms of the framework. For instance in science an order would be unsatisfactory if it violated the laws of logic.
8 For instance Kant (p.12) gives as an instance of a synthetic 'a priori', 'that in all changes of the material world the quantity of matter remains un-changed', which contradicts Einstein's theory of the relationship between energy and mass.
9 M. Schlick was a member of the Vienna Circle and a logical positivist.

10 While there seems no satisfactory definition of empirical within this framework, empirical is thought of as characterized by positive attributes. For a discussion of the problem of defining empirical see A. Pap (1966, ch.5).

11 For falsificationalists only the truth value false can be assigned. We can know some beliefs are false but not establish any beliefs as true. In addition there are existential statements (There is an X) which can be confirmed but not falsified. These are held to have no legitimate role in science. See J.W.N. Watkins (1957).

12 These definitions may be seen as implicit rather than explicit, e.g. E. Nagel (1961).

13 He also allows analytic propositions as definitions.

14 I shall examine closed and open concepts in the next section in detail, so will not give a precise definition of these terms now. For the present argument the following difference is sufficient: if a concept is closed what is included under it is clearly specified, while if it is open then it is not. If force is a closed concept we can state in advance precisely what will count as a force, while if force is open we cannot.

15 A limited amount of dynamism is introduced into the position by saying 'in principle specifiable'. This modification does not change the basic nature of the position.

16 For an historical account of how the motion of force has changed in meaning see M. Jammer (1957).

17 A few key references in this dispute are P.W. Bridgman (1936), and C.G. Hempel (1965, pp.101-33).

18 See A. Einstein and L. Infeld (1961, pp.69-122) for such an account.

19 While this section is based heavily on Wittgenstein's analysis of words, to make use of this analysis it is not necessary to accept his theory of meaning which is encapsulated in the quotation.

20 A core application is a central example of the term. It is often one which is likely to be used in giving a 'demonstrative definition' of the term.

21 What follows is not strictly an historical account of how the definition of the word changed. Rather it is an analysis of the implications of various extensions in application of the word as some theorists have developed it.

22 Alternatively they could keep changing their definition. However by the positivist account this process would have been arbitrary.

23 Range here does not mean that a new instance of the core application may be found in the sense that we have applied the word 'blackbird' to 200 birds and now apply it to the 201st. Rather, range means the type of bird to which the word is applied.

24 Or uses. To simplify matters I shall deal with the case of the single core use first and deal with the problems of core uses later.

25 For an account of this position see P. Duhem (1954).

26 One definition of empirical is: 'a proposition whose truth value can be ascertained only by experience' (Pap, 1966, p.98). The analysis of programmatic assertions thus specifically excludes the possibility of their being empirical by one common definition of empirical.

27 Beyond a certain point of change in the core usage, the programme is abandoned as will be discussed. However, some change of the core usage is compatible with holding the same programme as the discussion of definitions will show.

28 How we choose between programmes will be discussed in the section on programme development.

29 An assertion could be necessary as our minds could not think any other way. This would not make it necessarily true. On the other hand an idea could be necessarily true and we be able to think its contrary.

30 Not even the certainty that falsificationists have that certain theories are false.

31 This account of the nature of definitions creates a number of problems since logic tends to assume concepts with 'sharp edges'. For instance, this account of definitions precludes the use of Venn diagrams to represent logic. For a discussion of Venn diagrams see W.V.O. Quine (1960, pp.69-72).

32 By this approach there is one more category open and operationalized. This appears to be a sub-class of programmatic assertions, though an analysis of it would involve a more detailed analysis of operationalization in order to clarify the differences between it and closed. An example of an open and operationalized concept might be the 'n Achievement' of D. McClelland (1967). Perhaps this is how 'model accomplishments' should be considered in relation to paradigms by Kuhn (1966).

33 See E. Durkheim (1966, ch.3) for a discussion of the normality of crime.

34 See ch.7.

35 See ch.8.

36 A large number of experimentalists accept a positivist ideal of science - the facts determine the results. This means that the extension is often disguised by saying things like 'in order to cope with data limitations'.

37 This is one of the reasons they draw such a sharp line between the context of discovery and the context of validation. The first, in the approach taken in this chapter, is where concepts are most open and the breakdown of the analytic-synthetic (= empirical) distinction most apparent. In the context of confirmation, which is where concepts are closed, the analytic-synthetic (= empirical) distinction appears to hold.

38 This approach highlights more strongly the danger of dogmatism than does that of the holders of the analytic-synthetic distinction, as this approach recognizes that faith does play a role in what theories men accept. This advocacy of being aware of several theories, has similarities to the position taken by P. Feyeraband (1968, pp.12-39). We also say when discussing how to avoid a criticism of linguistic philosophy, made by Gellner that to discuss whether free will and determinism were compatible one had to look at different theories that made these assertions.

39 Parsons uses the word 'reduced' to mean 'derived' (e.g. SSA, p.70; SS, p.6). This is not the meaning intended here.

40 Can 'X is good' be reduced to any criteria of good. The label 'naturalistic fallacy' comes from G.E. Moore (1903, chs. 1, 2). For a general collection of readings on the subject see W.D. Hudson (1969).

41 The key modern reference in this is G. Ryle (1965).

42 'Deduced' is used in its strict sense.

43 The reverse is also possibly the case but for simplicity this possibility will be ignored.

44 Reduction is concept variant, while deduction is concept invariant.

45 This option is like the extreme of the second, except that economics is shown to be worthless. In the extreme of the second case, economics is independent of social systems theory, but this independence has been shown to be based on a misconception of what economic activity is.

46 The process of 'undermining' concepts is similar to processes philosophers use in their analyses of words. This suggests that philosophers have a legitimate role to play in science. It seems no accident that many of the fundamental breakthroughs in science have

been made by men with a deep awareness of philosophical problems.

47 In the economics and sociology example, there is no disagreement over prices and quantities of goods bought and sold.

48 This underlies G.E. Moore's analysis of the 'naturalistic fallacy'. Basically one commits a category mistake by misidentifying the type of entity one is dealing with - placing it in a wrong category. For instance it is frequently claimed that describing mental events in physical terms (e.g. as nerve impulses) involves a category mistake, for mental events in principle cannot be so described.

49 Whether it is adequate for the body-mind question to which he wishes to apply it is outside the scope of this book.

50 Whether his analysis applies to this case again is outside the scope of this book. The basic objection here is that whether witches exist or not is or may be a factual question. This type of objection is not applicable to the economics and social systems theory example as the existence of prices, quantities, etc. is not being disputed.

51 G.C. Homans (1968, p.10) says:

> Much modern sociological theory seems to me to possess every virtue except that of explaining anything. Part of the trouble is that much of it consists of categories or pigeonholes, into which the theorist fits different aspects of social behaviour. No science can proceed without its system of categories, or conceptual scheme, but that in itself is not enough to give it explanatory power. A conceptual scheme is not a theory. (I am thinking particularly of the work of my colleague and friend Talcott Parsons.)

52 In saying this, I am not saying that Mulkay denies other levels of analysis. Ogles (1961) in a short article on how it is legitimate to criticize a theory makes a similar point. He also talks about 'programmatic theory' but does not spell the term out, so I do not know how close his ideas are to my idea of a programme.

2 PARSONS' VOLUNTARISTIC THEORY

1 I would like, however, to draw the reader's attention to the excellent criticisms of Parsons on Durkheim by Giddens (1972, pp.38-48) and Pope (1973).

2 Or more accurately economically instrumental. Whether an action is instrumental depends on the state of mind of the actor. Whether an instrumental action is rational depends on whether it leads to the desired result.
3 See E. Nagel (1961, p.369) for a similar definition of emergence. This argument on emergence is heavily indebted to Nagel. The problem is more complex than presented here as the two conceptions of economic activity exist within different programmes (see ch.9 for a further discussion of the economic case). They do not cover identical cases and the decision as to which one to accept involves questions of programme choice. The second definition of economic action given is, however, consistent with the subjective framework of the unit act. One must thus argue that a satisfactory reduction of the first conception of economic rationality can be accomplished (see ch.1 for a discussion of reduction).
4 Whether there are any emergent properties that are emergent because of the nature of the property, I do not know (a possible candidate is mental events from the molecules of the brain). What I am willing to say is that what Parsons labels as emergent properties in SSA are later integrated into his theory and thus these are dependent on his theoretical approach, not the nature of the property itself.
5 In addition to presenting this as a conclusion, at other points he sets himself the task of attacking all variants of positivism, including behaviourism (e.g. SSA, p.125).
6 L. Althusser (1969, p.66) defines problematic as 'the constitutive unity of the effective thoughts that make up the domain of the existing ideological field which a particular author must settle accounts in his own thought.'
7 In doing literary criticism of an age, one often looks at the second-rate writers of a period rather than the greats. The great writers transcend their age; the 'hacks' reveal it. For similar reasons, it is often helpful to read the early work of a thinker. Being cruder than his later work, it reveals the thinker's concerns more clearly.
8 In the Preface to SSA, p.vi, Parsons says the four writers he is concerned with were all involved in the problem of interpreting capitalism and economic individualism.
9 One interesting bit of support for this is that Homans has argued the thesis the reverse way - i.e. that

utilitarianism is implicit in the basic premises of behaviourism. By utilitarianism is meant here that men act to maximize their happiness and are from this point of view rational. He calls it 'the so-called theory of rational behavior' (1969, p.13).

10 According to Kolakowski (1972, p.216), Husserl sees nineteenth-century positivism as reduceable to biology.

11 B. Barry (1970, pp.76-85) argues that the utilitarians did not have random ends but had the beginnings of a behavioural learning theory about ends (see esp. p.82). If we accept this, it makes no difference to Parsons' main line of analysis, as he argues that utilitarianism leads to behaviourism (SSA, p.86). The implications of Barry's remarks on Mill is that he went further to realizing the implications of the utilitarian position than Parsons saw him as doing.

12 Parsons had arrived at this earlier (1935, p.295).

13 As his analysis of how they accept values and how ends are socially formed deepens, he moves to a fully social image of man (see chs. 3 and 4 of this book).

14 If one wished to relate Lukacs to the convergence claim, one could claim he was a confirmatory instance. However, if one did so, one would have to see Sartre as a refutation.

15 Essentially he sees Parsons as shifting from a view of man as creator to man as the puppet of external forces.

16 Mulkay also sees a break, and says (1971, p.41): 'Parsons superimposes structural-functionalism on the emergent theory of social action to attain his own theoretical ends.' If by 'superimposes' Mulkay means that Parsons has both types of theory in his subsequent work, then I agree with him. However, one of the major weaknesses of Mulkay's analysis is that he does not follow this comment through.

3 TYING MAN TO SOCIETY: THE PARTIALLY SOCIAL IMAGE OF MAN

1 Utilitarian philosophies set out what men should do in this framework. Whether they are satisfactory moral philosophies is dependent among other things upon the adequacy of this framework for describing all actions. By challenging the descriptive adequacy of utilitarian frameworks, I am arguing that all utilitarian moralities are inadequate at least. However instead of tackling their account of justice as many philosophers who wish to attack the position do, I am tackling their account of things like love and hatred.

2 In chapters 4 and 6, how they grow out of his inter-

action will be discussed. Parsons' analysis of this leads him out of the utilitarian framework.

3 Though in so far as they are ends-in-themselves as well, they cannot be explained in this way.

4 The marginal return is the difference in return that results from the last unit of input into the process. For a discussion of marginal concepts see P. Samuelson (1961, pp.411-689).

5 M. Olson (1971) argues the case through in terms of public goods (goods that are available by their nature to some public), and shows that only under exceptional circumstances will it be in an individual's interest to contribute toward attaining these. For any reader familiar with elementary public finance theory, I recommend Olson's proof. To be fair to Olson, I would like to point out that he recognizes that he is dealing with only some public goods, not all. He excludes goods that represent the enactment of major values.

6 I am concerned with assessing Parsons in the light of present understanding. Thus while Barry's and Olson's analyses were written after Parsons developed his social utilitarian theory, their arguments are considered. That they do not see Parsons as having an answer to this problem is largely a reflection on the lack of clarity of Parsons' writings.

7 Olson (1971, pp.60-5) discusses social ends but his conception of them is individualized, and not as social relational ends.

8 Freud is often seen as accentuating the non-rational in man. Thus my suggestion that he has extended the analysis of man's actions in a means-end framework and thus in some way sees action as rational may sound ludicrous. This I suggest is because Freud's results seem subjectively to be strange and thus we feel he is glorifying the non-rational. However the structure of his explanation can be seen as one that extends the means-end framework.

9 Based on SS, pp.69-88; especially the diagrams on p.73 and p.79. The meaning of the terms in the left hand column is clear if one thinks of them in relation to economic activity which is the core case of instrumental activity for Parsons.

10 Jarvie, as is characteristic of people holding this position, focuses on attacking the irrational and ends up ignoring the non-rational. For instance he accepts that 'cargo cults' are purely means of getting cargo and ignores other aspects of them (e.g. assertion of the worth of the indigenous people; the sexual freedom that is sometimes part of cargo cults).

11 The other person they should read is E. Berne (1968).
12 For a detailed analysis of this problem see A. Bitz (1972).
13 He sees Merton as primarily applicable to societies where achievement values are central, while he sees his own classification as fitting this type of society and ones where ascriptive values are central (SS, p.258).
14 This conception of a profession excludes the clergy, a point which Parsons should raise but does not. It would be wrong to characterize the clergyman's role the way this description of a professional role does. In addition the clergy are often more concerned with the word of God than applying science in society.
15 He here also notes specifically that this conception of the economy minimizes the importance of property rights in the economy.
16 Bershady (1973, p.122) is unhappy and reasonably so with Parsons' claim to derive the PVs and argues that he generates them 'by formal analogy'. This points to a problem but does not solve it. Two questions must be asked now - 'What is the analogy to?' and 'How satisfactory is the analogy?' It seems simpler to see Parsons doing a faulty derivation.
17 In TGTA and SS, Parsons has a fifth PV - self-orientation - collectivity-orientation. As he later drops this as a PV and relates it to the FDs, it will be discussed in relation to the FDs subsequently.
18 On Parsons' whole derivation, see also SS (pp.58-67).
19 An interesting parallel exists between this cathexis of the pattern and Freud's secondary narcissism (1962, pp.36, 53-6).

4 THE SOCIAL IMAGE OF MAN

1 The concept of gratification as releasing motivational tension fits with Freud's pleasure principle. S. Freud (1961, p.1) defines the pleasure principle as follows: 'The course of those (mental) events is invariably set in motion by an unpleasurable tension and that it takes a direction such that its final outcome coincides with a lowering of that tension - that is, with an avoidance of unpleasure or a production of pleasure,' Also see S. Freud (1962, p.12).
2 A hermit is often seen as a non-social individual, yet to understand him apart from the society which led him to this way of life is impossible. Perhaps the better candidate for being non-social is the manipulator who treats everybody as means to his own ends.

3 As Black (1964, pp.272-3) points out, Parsons gives a number of different characterizations of cathexis. It seems basically to mean to want as it gratifies.
4 Parsons says that the cognitive and cathectic aspects are the 'two most primary or elementary aspects' of 'the "need disposition" system of the individual actor' (SS, p.7).
5 WP (p.35) says that if it were not, 'the types of meaning problem we have in mind could never arise.'
6 Where he does see them as a means to attaining gratification (e.g. SS (p.11), where he says 'a conditional standard comes to be set up'), he is back into a social utilitarian programme.
7 An unfriendly response is also possible. The key point here is that whatever ego does is interpreted in terms of friendly-unfriendly not, for example, businesslike-unbusinesslike.
8 Parsons' definition of institutionalization quoted earlier contains implicitly a perfect knowledge assumption - alter cannot make a mistake in interpreting ego's action.
9 For an interesting discussion of a particular social meaning, see Balchin (1966).
10 H. Marcuse (1969, p.44) defines surplus repression as 'the restrictions necessitated by social domination'.
11 This analysis is the basis of my disagreement with Black's attempt to present Parsons' position in terms of eight basic premises. He assumes that Parsons sees all action as directed towards goals (1964b, p.272), without recognizing that Parsons also includes expressive action. In effect, what Black tries to do is generate Parsons' social action programme from his social utilitarian one. As these two programmes involve different conceptions of the basic nature of man, this enterprise is not feasible. However, given the confusion in Parsons, it is not surprising either.
12 He does this even within one page. There are both systems theory and social action theory definitions of a role on p.25 of SS.
13 'Can be', as his definitions of structure are usually within systems theory.

5 THE PATTERNING OF MEANING: PATTERN VARIABLES AND FUNCTIONAL DIMENSIONS

1 For instance, Blain (1970, p.167) says: 'Parsons' four function paradigm has become the best known, with the possible exception of the pattern variables of his contributions to sociological theory.'

2 See Murphy (1971, p.57) for a parallel criticism to Whyte's.
3 The second order derivative of action is symbolism.
4 In SSA (p.601), Parsons accepts that there are a limited range of value-patterns. The PVs developed later can be seen as an attempt to classify them.
5 See chapter 6 for a discussion of need-dispositions.
6 It would be helpful in this respect if more sociologists were science fiction addicts. The merit of some recent SF (not the monsters-in-outer-space adventure type) is that by creating bizarre worlds it makes one aware of many things one takes for granted in our world. Consider for instance B. Aldiss (1967), where in effect the implications of a perfect knowledge assumption with regard to the feelings of affection of anybody to anybody else is made. He then traces out the implications of this for how people relate to each other.
7 If he reifies himself, then one would be concerned with his orientations to himself.
8 Perhaps another approach would be to place phenomenological brackets around an experience and see if its components were describably in PV terms.
9 This comment on Gouldner (1971) sums up my general view of his 'The Coming Crisis of Western Sociology'. This book contains not an analysis of Parsons but an attack on a very crude and uncritical interpretation of him. This comment can be generalized. Most people seem to find Gouldner interesting except on theories they are sympathetic to and have worked with. Of whatever theory to which one is sympathetic, one finds Gouldner to have given a caricature. In fact he caricatures all positions. This is by no means a worthless enterprise. It warns us of the crude ways positions can be taken.
10 'Comes from' both in the sense of generated by and related to. WP (p.74) gives a table showing the relation between Bales' categories and the FDs. Bales' categories can be seen as operationalization of the FDs for small task-oriented groups.
11 For another general discussion of the generation of the FDs see Amer U, pp.10-12.
12 Protestants tend to emphasize good works, Catholics faith (i.e. a state of being).
13 Religion, as all the religious wars of history prove, may also have a lot to do with why societies are not cohesive.
14 He is clearly muddled. The only question is the possible directions in which the muddle can be cleared up.

15 How such an argument might be made will be discussed later in this chapter when the relationship between the PVs and FDs is discussed.
16 Functionalists on the other hand tend to be supporters of a social order and lack moral objections to such assertions.
17 This is not to say that Marxists are necessarily uninterested in the question. It is simply to say that the theory does not confuse them.
18 For a discussion of the experimental set-up see R. Bales (1950) and WP (ch.4).
19 For a full account see R. Bales and F. Strodtbeck (1951).
20 Some complexities would arise from the fact that Bales assumes, as has been noted, a consensus, and scores the action on this basis. This assumption of a consensus would have to be checked.
21 See WP (p.74) for the relationship between these and the FDs.
22 Parsons' statement that Durkheim's analysis of ritual puts it in L (TS, p.39) is within systems theory.
23 He also sees some appropriate PV combinations as having 'strains' in them. On the whole he seems to see these as stable though with problems, while the others he sees as unstable and likely to change unless very special circumstances exist.
24 The subculture of violence hypothesis is also relevant to these.

6 SOCIALIZATION

1 In addition, in his diagram on p.168, he labels the A and L boxes as instrumental and the G and I boxes as expressive. However, he says in the text on the same page that the A and G boxes are instrumental.
2 In some ways, so long as the belief that it would undermine morality exists, his position does not require him to say whether it would actually do so.
3 Parsons at one point accepts this position (1935, p.290). J.F. Scott (1963, p.722) justifiably points to the implications of this for any sociological theory.
4 J. Ladd (1957) is concerned with 'descriptive ethics'. His concern is with an accurate description of an ethical code, not with explaining why people hold moral beliefs. This argument would not apply to descriptive ethics.
5 See H. Dretzel (1973) for a collection of such studies.

6 Based on a diagram in FSI (p.198). The following discussion of the phases is primarily based on FSI, pp.193-224.
7 This is the crux of my disagreement with Atkinson's (1971) interpretation of Parsons.
8 This paragraph is based on FIS, p.134 and p.149. This I am taking as representative of Parsons' basic theoretical position.
9 See also Piaget (1971, p.140), where he says that ego-centrism is the denial of the objective attitude, and consequently of logical analysis. It therefore gives rise to subjective synthesis.

7 SOCIAL ORDER: A PROBLEM SOLVED TOO WELL

1 This is not an accident, in my opinion. Having done his doctorate in Germany, he has some empathy with Germans yet was distanced from the situation by his dislike of the Nazis.
2 I would be inclined to say Stalinist.
3 Empirically the assumption of a previous consensus is dubious. As Bismarck said, Germany would be united by 'blood and iron'.
4 For an introduction to the mathematical essentials of this type of approach see J. Kemeny, J. Small and G. Thompson (1966, pp.335-83).
5 D. Atkinson (1971, ch.2) also finds fault here, but from a very different theoretical perspective from my own.
6 These 'unjustified disturbances' can be reinterpreted in a value-neutral way by seeing them as one side of the ambivalence reaction to vested interests that was discussed in the previous section.
7 Based on ES, pp.246-74.
8 Parsons frequently says that change can be internally generated. The problem is that he does not explain how.
9 Based on a diagram in SS, p.259. The diagram in the text includes another variable, active-passive, which has not been included for reasons that will soon be apparent.
10 A. Bitz (1972) argues that this is one of the major causes of creativity.
11 I am referring to the type of theory Schur (1971) discusses, not some of the early work of the National Deviancy Conference which has sometimes been called labelling theory.

8 OPEN SOCIAL SYSTEMS THEORY OR STRUCTURAL-FUNCTIONALISM

1. I am concerned with elucidating the distinction open-closed as it applies to social systems. The key difference in natural science between an open and closed system is that a closed system obeys the second law of thermodynamics which is the law of entropy, while an open system does not. This law states that the trend of affairs is towards disorder or chaos, and the levelling down of differences. For instance higher forms of energy like light get broken down into lower forms like heat. Nobody in sociology to my knowledge has applied this to a social system seen as closed. Consequently, it seems better to see a closed social system as stable rather than as tending to 'run down'.
2. The only reason this line of reasoning does not apply to a closed system is that there is no environment; it makes no sense to talk of a boundary.
3. G. Sommerhoff (1950) takes a similar approach to some open systems by defining 'goal-seeking behaviour' as 'directive correlation'. Sommerhoff sees directive correlation in terms of a system being able to respond to a range of possible variations in the environment in such a way that the system attains a focal condition. To say that a cat is directively correlated with regard to a mouse is to say that the cat can respond to the range of ways a mouse may try to escape in such a way as to catch the mouse.
4. An exchange of a shell necklace for shell armbands that takes place in the Trobriands and some of the neighbouring islands.
5. When doing economic research in the Trobriands for the Australian National University New Guinea Research Unit in June 1967, I was told by the Catholic mission that they had been on the island for over seventy years.
6. Later in this chapter, I shall criticize Parsons for seeing structure only in relationship to the external environment of the system, for there are also internal processes that affect the structure.
7. D. Lockwood (1964) distinguishes the action theory and systems theory conceptions of integration. In terms of the analysis given here, it is possible to see the difference in the two concepts of integration as symptomatic of a larger confusion.
8. An activity can have more than one type of consequence. Parsons' functional differentiation hypothesis, to be discussed later in the chapter, sees activities as increasingly coming to have one type of consequence.

9 See SECP (ch. 2) for a discussion of the human action system.
10 Even before Parsons had developed the axes of differentiation he claimed that the four FDs were involved in the frame of reference provided by a boundary maintaining system (see WP, p.165). His analysis of why (WP, pp.91-9), is more 'ad hoc' than the analysis given which is based on the axes of differentiation given in 1964b and Amer U.
11 In giving this explanation of why Parsons overlooks the internal 'G' in his definition of structure, I am working at a particular level - namely the level of the structure of his programmes. Undoubtedly, this overlooking of the problem of maintaining an internal 'G' also results from his political orientation which is conservative in tendency.
12 For an interesting science fiction account of a society with this type of stratification system see C.M. Kornbluth (1971).
13 ES, p.81. For empirical support for this claim see J. Galbraith (1967, ch.4). On p.46, he gives saving by individuals as $25 billion and by business firms as $83 billion for 1965. For an analysis of the US economy that makes this central see P. Baran and P. Sweezy (1966).
14 Where no sub-systems exist, he sees activities as tending to have increasingly one type of consequence.
15 If an analysis of an integrative activity in relationship to other integrative activity is already known, an analysis of the activity in relationship to non-integrative activity may bring new insights. This may lead the person to feel that the second analysis is more fruitful. However, the first actually gives more understanding.
16 For a discussion of how values can be seen positivistically - as dispositions - see Homans (1968, pp.30-50).
17 Smelser (1970) is an application of the ideas Smelser and Parsons put forth in ES to the English Industrial Revolution.

9 SOME ANALYSES USING BOTH THE ACTION AND SYSTEMS PROGRAMME

1 Goals as future states of affairs the actor intends to achieve. Sometimes, however, if one is clear about how it is used, as for instance G. Sommerhoff (1950), is, it can be used in systems theory.
2 On the assumption that he is referring to Sommerhoff (1950).

Bibliography

Note All books and articles by Parsons or Parsons and associates are arranged by date of first publication.

ABERLE, D., COHEN, A., LEVY, M. and SUTTON, F. (1967), The functional prerequisites of a society, in N. Demarath and R. Peterson (eds), 'System, Change and Conflict: A Reader on Contemporary Sociological Theory and the Debate over Functionalism', N.Y.: Free Press, pp.317-31.

ALDISS, B. (1967), 'The Primal Urge', London: Sphere Books.

ALMOND, S. (1965), A developmental approach to political systems, 'World Politics', 17(2), pp.183-214.

ALTHUSSER, L. (1969), 'For Marx' (trans. B. Brewster), Harmondsworth: Penguin.

ATKINSON, D. (1971), 'Orthodox Consensus and Radical Alternative: A Study in Sociological Theory', London: Heinemann.

BALCHIN, N. (1966), 'The Anatomy of Villainy', London: Mayflower-Dell.

BALDWIN, A.L. (1964), The Parsonian theory of personality, in M. Black (ed.), 'The Social Theories of Talcott Parsons: A Critical Examination', Englewood Cliffs, N.J.: Prentice-Hall, pp.153-90.

BALES, R. and STRODTBECK, F. (1951), Phases in group problem solving, 'Journal of Abnormal and Social Psychology', 46 (Oct.), pp.485-95.

BALES, R.F. (1950), 'Interaction Process Analysis', Cambridge, Mass.: Wesley Press.

BARAN, P. and SWEEZY, P. (1966), 'Capitalism: An Essay on the American Economic and Social Order', Harmondsworth: Penguin.

BARRY, B. (1970), 'Sociologists, Economists and Democracy', London: Macmillan.

BECKER, H. (1966), Becoming a marihuana user, in J.A. O'Donnell and J.C. Ball (eds), 'Narcotic Addiction', N.Y.: Harper & Row, pp.109-22.

BERNE, E. (1968), 'Games People Play: The Psychology of Human Relationships', Harmondsworth: Penguin.
BERSHADY, H.J. (1973), 'Ideology and Social Knowledge', Oxford: Blackwell.
BITZ, A. (1972), Conformity and Creativity: An Application of Theory to Some Problems in the Sociology of Science, unpublished PhD thesis, London School of Economics.
BLACK, M. (1964), Some questions about Parsons' theories, in M. Black (ed.), 'The Social Theories of Talcott Parsons: A Critical Examination', Englewood Cliffs, N.J.: Prentice-Hall, p.268.
BLAIN, R.B. (1970), A critique of Parsons' four function paradigm, 'Sociological Quarterly', 2, pp.157-68.
BOULDING, K.E. (1957), The Malthusian model as a general system, 'General Systems: Yearbook of the Society for the Advancement of General Systems Theory', 2, pp.102-7.
BRIDGMAN, P.W. (1936), 'The Nature of Physical Theory', N.Y.: Dover Publications.
BUNGE, M. (1963), 'Causality: The Place of the Causal Principle in Modern Science', N.Y.: World Publishing.
CANNON, W.B. (1932), 'The Wisdom of the Body', London: Kegan Paul, Trench Trubner.
CHOMSKY, N. (1959), Review of B.F. Skinner, 'Verbal Behavior', 'Language', 35, pp.26-58.
CICOUREL, A.V. (1968), 'The Social Organization of Juvenile Justice', N.Y.: John Wiley.
DAHRENDORF, R. (1966), 'Class and Class Conflict in Industrial Society', Stanford: Stanford University Press.
DAVIS, K. (n.d.), 'Human Society', N.Y.: Macmillan.
DAVIS, K. (1967), The myth of functional analysis as a special method, in N. Demerath and R. Peterson (eds), 'System, Change and Conflict: A Reader on Contemporary Sociological Theory and the Debate over Functionalism', N.Y.: Free Press, pp.379-402.
DAVIS, K. and MOORE, W. (1966), Some principles of stratification, in R. Bendix and S. Lipset (eds), 'Class, Status and Power: Social Stratification in Comparative Perspective', 2nd ed., N.Y.: Free Press, pp.47-53.
DRETZEL, H. (ed.) (1973), 'Childhood and Socialization', N.Y.: Macmillan.
DUHEM, P. (1954), 'The Aim and Structure of Physical Theory' (trans. P. Weiner), Princeton: Princeton University Press.
DURKHEIM, E. (1966), 'The Rules of Sociological Method' (trans. S. Schrag and J. Mueller), 8th ed., N.Y.: Free Press.
EASTON, D. (1965), 'A Framework for Political Analysis', Englewood Cliffs, N.J.: Prentice-Hall.

EINSTEIN, A. (1960), Introduction to M. Jammer, 'Concepts of Space: The History of Theories of Space in Physics', N.Y.: Harper.
EINSTEIN, A. and INFELD, L. (1961), 'The Evolution of Physics: The Growth of Ideas from Early Concepts to Relativity and Quanta', N.Y.: Simon & Schuster.
FARBEROW, N. and SHEIDMAN, E. (1961), 'The Cry for Help', London: McGraw-Hill.
FARIS, E. (1953), Review of 'The Social System', 'American Sociological Review', 18(1), pp.103-6.
FEYERABAND, P. (1968), How to be a good empiricist - a plea for tolerance in matters epistemological, in P.H. Nidditch (ed.), 'The Philosophy of Science', London: Oxford University Press, pp.12-39.
FIRTH, R. (1961), Suicide and risk-taking in Tikopian society, 'Psychiatry', 24 (Feb.), pp.1-17.
FOSS, D. (1963), The world view of Talcott Parsons, in M. Stein and A. Vidich (eds), 'Sociology on Trial', Englewood Cliffs, N.J.: Prentice-Hall, pp.96-126.
FREUD, S. (1961), 'Beyond the Pleasure Principle' (trans. J. Strachey), London: Hogarth Press and the Institute for Psycho-Analysis.
FREUD, S. (1962), 'The Ego and the Id' (trans. J. Riviere, ed. J. Strachey), London: Hogarth Press and the Institute for Psycho-Analysis.
FREUD, S. (1963), 'Civilization and its Discontents' (trans. J. Riviere), London: Hogarth Press and the Institute for Psycho-Analysis.
FREUD, S. (n.d.), The psychopathology of everyday life, in A. Brill (ed. and trans.), 'The Basic Writings of Sigmund Freud', N.Y.: Random House, pp.35-178.
GALBRAITH, J. (1967), 'The New Industrial State', Harmondsworth: Penguin.
GARFINKEL, H. (1967), 'Studies in Ethnomethodology', Englewood Cliffs, N.J.: Prentice-Hall.
GELLNER, E. (1968), 'Words and Things', Harmondsworth: Penguin.
GIDDENS, A. (1968), 'Power' in the recent writings of Talcott Parsons, Sociology, 2, pp.257-272.
GIDDENS, A. (1972), Introduction to E. Durkheim, 'Selected Writings' (ed. and trans. A. Giddens), Cambridge: Cambridge University Press.
GOULDNER, A. (1971), 'The Coming Crisis of Western Sociology', London: Heinemann.
GUSFIELD, J. (1974), Review of Parsons' and Platt's 'The American University', 'Contemporary Sociology', 3(4), pp.291-5.
HEMPEL, C.G. (1959), The logic of functional analysis, in L. Gross (ed.), 'Symposium on Sociological Theory', N.Y.: Harper & Row, pp.271-307.

HEMPEL, C.G. (1965), 'Aspects of Scientific Explanation and other Essays in the Philosophy of Science', N.Y.: Free Press.
HENDERSON, L.J. (1935), 'Pareto's General Sociology: A Physiologist's Interpretation', Cambridge, Mass.: Harvard University Press.
HOMANS, G.C. (1968), 'Social Behaviour: its Elementary Forms', London: Routledge & Kegan Paul.
HOMANS, G.C. (1969), The sociological relevance of behaviorism, in R. Burgess P. Bushnell (eds), 'Behavioral Sociology: The Experimental Analysis of Social Process', N.Y.: Columbia University Press.
HOSPERS, J. (1965), 'An Introduction to Philosophical Analysis', Englewood Cliffs, N.J.: Prentice-Hall.
HUDSON, W.D. (ed.), (1969), 'The Is/Ought Question: A Collection of Papers on the Central Problem in Moral Philosophy', London: Macmillan.
ISAJIW, W.W. (1968), 'Causation and Functionalism in Sociology', London: Routledge & Kegan Paul.
JAMMER, M. (1957), 'The Concept of Force', Cambridge, Mass.: Harvard University Press.
JAMMER, M. (1960), see EINSTEIN, A. (1960).
JARVIE, I.C. (1964), 'Revolution in Anthropology', London: Routledge & Kegan Paul.
JEFFREYS, M. (1952), Samsonic suicide or suicide of revenge among Africans, 'African Studies', 2(3), pp.118-22.
KANT, I. (1966), 'Critique of Pure Reason' (trans. F.M. Muller), N.Y.: Doubleday Anchor.
KEMENY, J., SMALL, J. and THOMPSON, G. (1966), 'Introduction to Finite Mathematics', 2nd ed., Englewood Cliffs, N.J.: Prentice-Hall.
KOLAKOWSKI, L. (1972), 'Positivist Philosophy: From Hume to the Vienna Circle', Harmondsworth: Penguin.
KORNBLUTH, C.M. (1971), 'The Syndic', London: Sphere.
KUHN, T.S. (1966), 'The Structure of Scientific Revolutions', Chicago: University of Chicago Press.
LADD, J. (1957), 'The Structure of a Moral Code: A Philosophical Analysis of Ethical Discourse Applied to the Ethics of the Navaho Indians', Cambridge, Mass.: Harvard University Press.
LAING, R.D. and ESTERSON, A. (1970), 'Sanity, Madness and the Family: Families of Schizophrenics', Harmondsworth: Penguin.
LOCKWOOD, D. (1964), Social integration and system integrating, in G. Zollschan and W. Hirsch (eds), 'Explorations in Social Change', London: Routledge & Kegan Paul, pp.244-57.
LOGAN, M. (1953), Toward a definition of a profession, 'Harvard Educational Review', 23, Winter, pp.33-50.

LOTKA, A. (1956), 'Elements of Mathematical Biology', N.Y.: Dover.
LUKACS, G. (1972), 'History and Class Consciousness: Studies in Marxist Dialectics' (trans. R. Livingstone), Cambridge, Mass.: MIT Press.
McCLELLAND, D. (1967), 'The Achieving Society', N.Y.: Free Press.
MALINOWSKI, B. (1922), 'Argonauts of the Western Pacific: An Account of Native Enterprise and Adventure in the Archipelagoes of Melanesian New Guinea', London: Routledge.
MALINOWSKI, B. (1948), 'Magic, Science and Religion and Other Essays', Chicago: Free Press.
MARCUSE, H. (1968), 'One-Dimensional Man', London: Sphere.
MARCUSE, H. (1969), 'Eros and Civilization', London: Sphere.
MATZA, D. (1964), 'Delinquency and Drift', N.Y.: John Wiley.
MERTON, R.K. (1968), 'Social Theory and Social Structure', 2nd ed., N.Y.: Free Press.
MILLS, C.W. (1970), 'The Sociological Imagination', Harmondsworth: Penguin.
MITCHELL, W. (1967), 'Sociological Analysis and Politics: The Theories of Talcott Parsons', Englewood Cliffs, N.J.: Prentice-Hall.
MOORE, G.E. (1903), 'Principia Ethica', Cambridge: Cambridge University Press.
MULKAY, M.J. (1971), 'Functionalism, Exchange and Theoretical Strategy', London: Routledge & Kegan Paul.
MURPHY, R.F. (1971), 'The Dialectics of Social Life: Alarms and Excursions in Anthropological Theory', N.Y.: Basic Books.
NAGEL, E. (1961), 'The Structure of Science: Problems in the Logic of Scientific Explanation', N.Y.: Harcourt Brace & World.
NAGEL, E. (1967), A formalization of functionalism with special reference to its application in the social sciences, in N. Demareth and R. Peterson (eds), 'System, Change and Conflict: A Reader in Contemporary Sociological Theory and the Debate over Functionalism', N.Y.: Free Press, pp.47-53.
OGLES, R. (1961), Programmatic theory and the critics of Talcott Parsons, 'Pacific Sociological Review', pp.53-6.
OLSON, M. (1971), 'The Logic of Collective Action: Public Goods and the Theory of Groups' (rev. ed.), N.Y.: Schocken Books.
PAP, A. (1966), 'Semantics and Necessary Truth: An Inquiry into the Foundations of Analytic Philosophy', New Haven: Yale University Press.

PARSONS, T. (1931), Wants and activities in Marshall, 'Quarterly Journal of Economics', 46(1), p.130.
PARSONS, T. (1932), Economics and sociology: Marshall in relation to the thought of his time, 'Quarterly Journal of Economics', 46(2), pp.316-47.
PARSONS, T. (1935), The place of ultimate values in sociological theory, 'International Journal of Ethics', 45.
PARSONS, T. (1949), 'The Structure of Social Action: A Study in Social Theory with Special Reference to a Group of Recent European Writers', N.Y.: Free Press, first published 1937.
PARSONS, T. (1962), 'Toward a General Theory of Action', N.Y.: Harper & Row, first published 1951.
PARSONS, T. (1964), 'The Social System', N.Y.: Free Press; London: Routledge & Kegan Paul, first published 1951.
PARSONS, T., BALES, R.F. and SHILS, E.A. (1953), 'Working Papers in the Theory of Action', N.Y.: Free Press.
PARSONS, T. (1964), 'Essays in Sociological Theory' (rev. ed.), N.Y.: Free Press, first published 1954.
PARSONS, T. and BALES, R.F. (1964), 'Family, Socialization and Interaction Process', N.Y.: Free Press; London: Routledge & Kegan Paul, first published 1955.
PARSONS, T. and SMELSER, N.J. (1972), 'Economy and Society: A Study in the Integration of Economic and Social Theory', London: Routledge & Kegan Paul, first published 1956.
PARSONS, T. (1965), 'Structure and Process in Modern Societies', London: Frank Cass, first published 1960.
PARSONS, T., SHILS, E., NAEGELE, K.D. and PITTS, J.R. (1965), 'Theories of Society: Foundations of Modern Sociological Theory', N.Y.: Free Press, first published 1961.
PARSONS, T. (1961), Some considerations on the theory of social change, 'Rural Sociology', 26(3), (Sept.), pp.219-39.
PARSONS, T. (1964a), Malinowski and the theory of social systems, in R. Firth (ed.), 'Man and Culture: An Evaluation of the Work of Bronislaw Malinowski', N.Y.: Harper & Row, pp.64-79.
PARSONS, T. (1964b), The point of view of the author, in M. Black (ed.), 'The Social Theories of Talcott Parsons: A Critical Examination', Englewood Cliffs, N.J.: Prentice-Hall, pp.311-63.
PARSONS, T. (1965), 'Social Structure and Personality', London: Free Press.
PARSONS, T. (1966), 'Societies: Evolutionary and Comparative Perspectives', Englewood Cliffs, N.J.: Prentice-Hall.

PARSONS, T. (1966), Introduction to M. Weber, 'The Theory of Social and Economic Organization' (trans. A. Henderson and T. Parsons), N.Y.: Free Press.
PARSONS, T. (1967), 'Sociological Theory and Modern Society', N.Y.: Free Press.
PARSONS, T. (1970), On building social system theory: a personal history, 'Daedalus', 99, pp.826-75.
PARSONS, T. (1971), 'The System of Modern Societies', Englewood Cliffs, N.J.: Prentice-Hall.
PARSONS, T. (1971), Some problems of general theory, in J. McKinney and E. Tiryakian (eds), 'Theoretical Sociology: Perspectives and Developments', N.Y.: Appleton Century Crofts, pp.27-68.
PARSONS, T. and PLATT, G.M. (1973), 'The American University', Cambridge, Mass: Harvard University Press.
PIAGET, J. (1967), 'The Child's Conception of the World' (trans. J. and A. Tomlinson), London: Routledge & Kegan Paul.
PIAGET, J. (1968), 'The Moral Judgment of the Child' (trans. M. Sabain), London: Routledge & Kegan Paul.
PIAGET, J. (1970), 'The Child's Conception of Physical Causality' (trans. M. Sabain), London: Routledge & Kegan Paul.
PIAGET, J. (1971), 'The Language and Thought of the Child' (trans. M. and R. Sabain), London: Routledge & Kegan Paul.
PINNEY, H. (1940), The structure of social action, 'Ethics', 50, 164-92.
POPE, W. (1973), Classic on classic: Parsons' interpretation of Durkheim, 'American Sociological Review', 38(4), 399-415.
POPPER, K.R. (1960), 'The Poverty of Historicism', 2nd ed., London: Routledge & Kegan Paul.
POPPER, K.R. (1968), 'The Logic of Scientific Discovery', London: Hutchinson.
POPPER, K. (1969), 'Conjectures and Refutations: The Growth of Scientific Knowledge', 3rd ed., London: Routledge & Kegan Paul.
PRICHARD, H. (1968), Does moral philosophy rest on a mistake, in 'Moral Obligation and Duty and Interest: Essays and Lectures' (intro. J. Wimson), London: Oxford University Press.
PYE, L. (1963), 'Politics, Personality and Nation Building: Burma's Search for Identiy', New Haven: Yale University Press.
QUINE, W.v.O. (1960), 'Methods of Logic' (rev. ed.), N.Y.: Henry Holt; London: Routledge & Kegan Paul.
RAPPAPORT, R. (1970), 'Pigs for the Ancestors: Ritual in the Ecology of a New Guinea People', New Haven, Conn.: Yale University Press.

REX, J. (1968), 'Key Problems of Sociological Theory', London: Routledge & Kegan Paul.
RORTY, R. (1966), Mind-body identity, privacy and categories, in S. Hampshire (ed.), 'Philosophy of Mind', N.Y.: Harper.
RUDNER, R. (1966), 'Philosophy of Social Science', Englewood Cliffs, N.J.: Prentice-Hall, ch.5.
RYLE, G. (1965), 'The Concept of Mind', N.Y.: Barnes & Noble.
SAMUELSON, P. (1961), 'Economics: An Introduction Analysis', 5th ed., N.Y.: McGraw-Hill.
SCHLESINGER, G. (1968), The terms and sentences of empirical science, in P.H. Nidditch (ed.), 'The Philosophy of Science', London: Oxford University Press, p.50.
SCHLICK, M. (1949), Is there a factual a priori? in H. Feigl and W. Sellars (eds), 'Readings in Philosophical Analysis', N.Y.: Appleton Century Crofts, p.281.
SCHUR, E. (1971), 'Labelling Deviant Behavior: Its Sociological Implications', N.Y.: Harper & Row.
SCHUTZ, A. (1962), 'Collected Papers', vol.1: 'The Problems of Social Reality' (ed. and intro. M. Natanson), The Hague: Martinus Nijhoff.
SCHUTZ, A. (1962), 'Collected Papers', vol.2: 'Studies in Social Theory', (ed. and intro. A.Brodersen). The Hague: Martinus Nijhoff.
SCOTT, J.F. (1963), The changing foundations of the Parsonian action scheme, 'American Sociological Review', 29(5), 716-35.
SCOTT, R.A. (1969), 'The Making of Blind Men: A Study of Adult Socialization', N.Y.: Russell Sage Foundation.
SEXTON, P. (1974), Review of Parsons' and Platt's 'The American University', 'Contemporary Sociology', 3(4), pp.296-300.
SMELSER, N. (1970), 'Social Change in the Industrial Revolution: An Application of Theory to the Lancaster Cotton Industry 1770-1840', London: Routledge & Kegan Paul.
SOMMERHOFF, G. (1950), 'Analytic Biology', London: Oxford University Press.
SWANSON, G. (1953), The approach to a general theory of action by Parsons and Shils, 'American Sociological Review', 18(2), pp.125-34.
SYDIAHA, D. (1961), Bales' interaction process analysis of personnel selection interview, 'Journal of Applied Psychology', 45(6), pp.393-401.
TAUSKY, C. (1965), Parsonian stratification: an analysis and critique, 'Sociological Quarterly', 6 (spring), pp.128-38.

TUMIN, M. (1966), Some principles of stratification: a critical analysis, in R. Bendix and S. Lipsett (eds), 'Class, Status and Power: Social Stratification in Comparative Perspective', 2nd ed., N.Y.: Free Press, pp.53-8.
WARNOCK, G.J. (1961), Every event has a cause, in A. Flew (ed.), 'Logic and Language', 2nd series, Oxford: Blackwell, pp.97-113.
WATKINS, J.W.N. (1957), Between analytic and empirical, 'Philosophy', 32, pp.112-31.
WHYTE, W. (1964), Parsonian theory applied to organizations, in M. Black (ed.), 'The Social Theories of Talcott Parsons: A Critical Examination', Englewood Cliffs, N.J.: Prentice-Hall, pp.250-67.
WINCH, P. (1958), 'The Idea of a Social Science and its Relation to Philosophy', London: Routledge & Kegan Paul.
WITTGENSTEIN, L. (1967), 'Philosophical Investigations' (trans. G.E.M. Anscombe), 2nd ed., Oxford: Blackwell.
WOLFANG, M. (1966), 'Patterns in Criminal Homicide', N.Y.: John Wiley.
WRONG, D. (1961), The oversocialized conception of man in modern sociology, 'American Sociological Review', 26(2), pp.183-93.

Index

I have used AP for Action Programme and SP for Systems Programme. As the work that Parsons wrote with others has been treated as part of a body of ideas in this book, no entries for Parsons' collaborators, simply for their collaboration will be found in this index. There is no entry for Parsons, or programme, AP or SP.

Routledge Social Science Series

Routledge & Kegan Paul London and Boston

68–74 Carter Lane London EC4V 5EL

9 Park Street Boston Mass 02108

Contents

Authors wishing to submit manuscripts for any series in this catalogue should send them to the Social Science Editor, Routledge & Kegan Paul Ltd, 68–74 Carter Lane, London EC4V 5EL

●*Books so marked are available in paperback*
All books are in Metric Demy 8vo format (216 × 138mm approx.)

International Library of Sociology

General Editor John Rex

GENERAL SOCIOLOGY

Barnsley, J. H. The Social Reality of Ethics. *464 pp.*

Belshaw, Cyril. The Conditions of Social Performance. *An Exploratory Theory. 144 pp.*

Brown, Robert. Explanation in Social Science. *208 pp.*

● Rules and Laws in Sociology. *192 pp.*

Bruford, W. H. Chekhov and His Russia. *A Sociological Study. 244 pp.*

Cain, Maureen E. Society and the Policeman's Role. *326 pp.*

●**Fletcher, Colin.** Beneath the Surface. *An Account of Three Styles of Sociological Research. 221 pp.*

Gibson, Quentin. The Logic of Social Enquiry. *240 pp.*

Glucksmann, M. Structuralist Analysis in Contemporary Social Thought. *212 pp.*

Gurvitch, Georges. Sociology of Law. *Preface by Roscoe Pound. 264 pp.*

Hodge, H. A. Wilhelm Dilthey. *An Introduction. 184 pp.*

Homans, George C. Sentiments and Activities. *336 pp.*

Johnson, Harry M. Sociology: *a Systematic Introduction. Foreword by Robert K. Merton. 710 pp.*

●**Keat, Russell,** and **Urry, John.** Social Theory as Science. *278 pp.*

Mannheim, Karl. Essays on Sociology and Social Psychology. *Edited by Paul Keckskemeti. With Editorial Note by Adolph Lowe. 344 pp.*

Systematic Sociology: *An Introduction to the Study of Society. Edited by J. S. Erös and Professor W. A. C. Stewart. 220 pp.*

Martindale, Don. The Nature and Types of Sociological Theory. *292 pp.*

●**Maus, Heinz.** A Short History of Sociology. *234 pp.*

Mey, Harald. Field-Theory. *A Study of its Application in the Social Sciences. 352 pp.*

Myrdal, Gunnar. Value in Social Theory: *A Collection of Essays on Methodology. Edited by Paul Streeten. 332 pp.*

Ogburn, William F., and **Nimkoff, Meyer F.** A Handbook of Sociology. *Preface by Karl Mannheim. 656 pp. 46 figures. 35 tables.*

Parsons, Talcott, and **Smelser, Neil J.** Economy and Society: *A Study in the Integration of Economic and Social Theory. 362 pp.*

Podgórecki, Adam. Practical Social Sciences. *About 200 pp.*

●**Rex, John.** Key Problems of Sociological Theory. *220 pp.*

Discovering Sociology. *278 pp.*

Sociology and the Demystification of the Modern World. *282 pp.*

●**Rex, John** (Ed.) Approaches to Sociology. *Contributions by Peter Abell, Frank Bechhofer, Basil Bernstein, Ronald Fletcher, David Frisby, Miriam Glucksmann, Peter Lassman, Herminio Martins, John Rex, Roland Robertson, John Westergaard and Jock Young. 302 pp.*

Rigby, A. Alternative Realities. *352 pp.*

Roche, M. Phenomenology, Language and the Social Sciences. *374 pp.*
Sahay, A. Sociological Analysis. *220 pp.*
Strasser, Hermann. The Normative Structure of Sociology. *Conservative and Emancipatory Themes in Social Thought. About 340 pp.*
Urry, John. Reference Groups and the Theory of Revolution. *244 pp.*
Weinberg, E. Development of Sociology in the Soviet Union. *173 pp.*

FOREIGN CLASSICS OF SOCIOLOGY

●**Durkheim, Emile.** Suicide. *A Study in Sociology. Edited and with an Introduction by George Simpson. 404 pp.*
Professional Ethics and Civic Morals. *Translated by Cornelia Brookfield. 288 pp.*
●**Gerth, H. H.,** and **Mills, C. Wright.** From Max Weber: *Essays in Sociology. 502 pp.*
●**Tönnies, Ferdinand.** Community and Association. (*Gemeinschaft und Gesellschaft.*) *Translated and Supplemented by Charles P. Loomis. Foreword by Pitirim A. Sorokin. 334 pp.*

SOCIAL STRUCTURE

Andreski, Stanislav. Military Organization and Society. *Foreword by Professor A. R. Radcliffe-Brown. 226 pp. 1 folder.*
Coontz, Sydney H. Population Theories and the Economic Interpretation. *202 pp.*
Coser, Lewis. The Functions of Social Conflict. *204 pp.*
Dickie-Clark, H. F. Marginal Situation: *A Sociological Study of a Coloured Group. 240 pp. 11 tables.*
Glaser, Barney, and **Strauss, Anselm L.** Status Passage. *A Formal Theory. 208 pp.*
Glass, D. V. (Ed.) Social Mobility in Britain. *Contributions by J. Berent, T. Bottomore, R. C. Chambers, J. Floud, D. V. Glass, J. R. Hall, H. T. Himmelweit, R. K. Kelsall, F. M. Martin, C. A. Moser, R. Mukherjee, and W. Ziegel. 420 pp.*
Jones, Garth N. Planned Organizational Change: *An Exploratory Study Using an Empirical Approach. 268 pp.*
Kelsall, R. K. Higher Civil Servants in Britain: *From 1870 to the Present Day. 268 pp. 31 tables.*
König, René. The Community. *232 pp. Illustrated.*
●**Lawton, Denis.** Social Class, Language and Education. *192 pp.*
McLeish, John. The Theory of Social Change: *Four Views Considered. 128 pp.*
Marsh, David C. The Changing Social Structure of England and Wales, 1871-1961. *288 pp.*
●**Mouzelis, Nicos.** Organization and Bureaucracy. *An Analysis of Modern Theories. 240 pp.*
Mulkay, M. J. Functionalism, Exchange and Theoretical Strategy. *272 pp.*
Ossowski, Stanislaw. Class Structure in the Social Consciousness. *210 pp.*
●**Podgórecki, Adam.** Law and Society. *302 pp.*

SOCIOLOGY AND POLITICS

Acton, T. A. Gypsy Politics and Social Change. *316 pp.*

Clegg, Stuart. Power, Rule and Domination. *A Critical and Empirical Understanding of Power in Sociological Theory and Organisational Life. About 300 pp.*

Hechter, Michael. Internal Colonialism. *The Celtic Fringe in British National Development, 1536–1966. 361 pp.*

Hertz, Frederick. Nationality in History and Politics: *A Psychology and Sociology of National Sentiment and Nationalism. 432 pp.*

Kornhauser, William. The Politics of Mass Society. *272 pp. 20 tables.*

●**Kroes, R.** Soldiers and Students. *A Study of Right- and Left-wing Students. 174 pp.*

Laidler, Harry W. History of Socialism. *Social-Economic Movements: An Historical and Comparative Survey of Socialism, Communism, Co-operation, Utopianism; and other Systems of Reform and Reconstruction. 992 pp.*

Lasswell, H. D. Analysis of Political Behaviour. *324 pp.*

Mannheim, Karl. Freedom, Power and Democratic Planning. *Edited by Hans Gerth and Ernest K. Bramstedt. 424 pp.*

Mansur, Fatma. Process of Independence. *Foreword by A. H. Hanson. 208 pp.*

Martin, David A. Pacifism: *an Historical and Sociological Study. 262 pp.*

Myrdal, Gunnar. The Political Element in the Development of Economic Theory. *Translated from the German by Paul Streeten. 282 pp.*

Wootton, Graham. Workers, Unions and the State. *188 pp.*

FOREIGN AFFAIRS: THEIR SOCIAL, POLITICAL AND ECONOMIC FOUNDATIONS

Mayer, J. P. Political Thought in France from the Revolution to the Fifth Republic. *164 pp.*

CRIMINOLOGY

Ancel, Marc. Social Defence: *A Modern Approach to Criminal Problems. Foreword by Leon Radzinowicz. 240 pp.*

Cain, Maureen E. Society and the Policeman's Role. *326 pp.*

Cloward, Richard A., and **Ohlin, Lloyd E.** Delinquency and Opportunity: *A Theory of Delinquent Gangs. 248 pp.*

Downes, David M. The Delinquent Solution. *A Study in Subcultural Theory. 296 pp.*

Dunlop, A. B., and **McCabe, S.** Young Men in Detention Centres. *192 pp.*

Friedlander, Kate. The Psycho-Analytical Approach to Juvenile Delinquency: *Theory, Case Studies, Treatment. 320 pp.*

Glueck, Sheldon, and **Eleanor.** Family Environment and Delinquency. *With the statistical assistance of Rose W. Kneznek. 340 pp.*

Lopez-Rey, Manuel. Crime. *An Analytical Appraisal. 288 pp.*

Mannheim, Hermann. Comparative Criminology: *a Text Book. Two volumes. 442 pp. and 380 pp.*

Morris, Terence. The Criminal Area: *A Study in Social Ecology. Foreword by Hermann Mannheim. 232 pp. 25 tables. 4 maps.*

Rock, Paul. Making People Pay. *338 pp.*

●**Taylor, Ian, Walton, Paul,** and **Young, Jock.** The New Criminology. *For a Social Theory of Deviance. 325 pp.*

●**Taylor, Ian, Walton, Paul,** and **Young, Jock** (Eds). Critical Criminology. *268 pp.*

SOCIAL PSYCHOLOGY

Bagley, Christopher. The Social Psychology of the Epileptic Child. *320 pp.*

Barbu, Zevedei. Problems of Historical Psychology. *248 pp.*

Blackburn, Julian. Psychology and the Social Pattern. *184 pp.*

●**Brittan, Arthur.** Meanings and Situations. *224 pp.*

Carroll, J. Break-Out from the Crystal Palace. *200 pp.*

●**Fleming, C. M.** Adolescence: Its Social Psychology. *With an Introduction to recent findings from the fields of Anthropology, Physiology, Medicine, Psychometrics and Sociometry. 288 pp.*

● The Social Psychology of Education: *An Introduction and Guide to Its Study. 136 pp.*

●**Homans, George C.** The Human Group. *Foreword by Bernard DeVoto. Introduction by Robert K. Merton. 526 pp.*

● Social Behaviour: *its Elementary Forms. 416 pp.*

●**Klein, Josephine.** The Study of Groups. *226 pp. 31 figures. 5 tables.*

Linton, Ralph. The Cultural Background of Personality. *132 pp.*

●**Mayo, Elton.** The Social Problems of an Industrial Civilization. *With an appendix on the Political Problem. 180 pp.*

Ottaway, A. K. C. Learning Through Group Experience. *176 pp.*

Plummer, Ken. Sexual Stigma. *An Interactionist Account. 254 pp.*

Ridder, J. C. de. The Personality of the Urban African in South Africa. *A Thermatic Apperception Test Study. 196 pp. 12 plates.*

●**Rose, Arnold M.** (Ed.) Human Behaviour and Social Processes: *an Interactionist Approach. Contributions by Arnold M. Rose, Ralph H. Turner, Anselm Strauss, Everett C. Hughes, E. Franklin Frazier, Howard S. Becker, et al. 696 pp.*

Smelser, Neil J. Theory of Collective Behaviour. *448 pp.*

Stephenson, Geoffrey M. The Development of Conscience. *128 pp.*

Young, Kimball. Handbook of Social Psychology. *658 pp. 16 figures. 10 tables.*

SOCIOLOGY OF THE FAMILY

Banks, J. A. Prosperity and Parenthood: *A Study of Family Planning among The Victorian Middle Classes. 262 pp.*

Bell, Colin R. Middle Class Families: *Social and Geographical Mobility. 224 pp.*

Burton, Lindy. Vulnerable Children. *272 pp.*

Gavron, Hannah. The Captive Wife: *Conflicts of Household Mothers. 190 pp.*

George, Victor, and **Wilding, Paul.** Motherless Families. *248 pp.*
Klein, Josephine. Samples from English Cultures.
1. Three Preliminary Studies and Aspects of Adult Life in England. *447 pp.*
2. Child-Rearing Practices and Index. *247 pp.*

Klein, Viola. Britain's Married Women Workers. *180 pp.*
The Feminine Character. *History of an Ideology. 244 pp.*
McWhinnie, Alexina M. Adopted Children. *How They Grow Up. 304 pp.*
● **Morgan, D. H. J.** Social Theory and the Family. *About 320 pp.*
● **Myrdal, Alva,** and **Klein, Viola.** Women's Two Roles: *Home and Work. 238 pp. 27 tables.*
Parsons, Talcott, and **Bales, Robert F.** Family: Socialization and Interaction Process. *In collaboration with James Olds, Morris Zelditch and Philip E. Slater. 456 pp. 50 figures and tables.*

SOCIAL SERVICES

Bastide, Roger. The Sociology of Mental Disorder. *Translated from the French by Jean McNeil. 260 pp.*
Carlebach, Julius. Caring For Children in Trouble. *266 pp.*
George, Victor. Foster Care. *Theory and Practice. 234 pp.*
Social Security: *Beveridge and After. 258 pp.*
George, V., and **Wilding, P.** Motherless Families. *248 pp.*
● **Goetschius, George W.** Working with Community Groups. *256 pp.*
Goetschius, George W., and **Tash, Joan.** Working with Unattached Youth. *416 pp.*
Hall, M. P., and **Howes, I. V.** The Church in Social Work. *A Study of Moral Welfare Work undertaken by the Church of England. 320 pp.*
Heywood, Jean S. Children in Care: *the Development of the Service for the Deprived Child. 264 pp.*
Hoenig, J., and **Hamilton, Marian W.** The De-Segregation of the Mentally Ill. *284 pp.*
Jones, Kathleen. Mental Health and Social Policy, 1845-1959. *264 pp.*
King, Roy D., Raynes, Norma V., and **Tizard, Jack.** Patterns of Residential Care. *356 pp.*
Leigh, John. Young People and Leisure. *256 pp.*
● **Mays, John.** (Ed.) Penelope Hall's Social Services of England and Wales. *About 324 pp.*
Morris, Mary. Voluntary Work and the Welfare State. *300 pp.*
Morris, Pauline. Put Away: *A Sociological Study of Institutions for the Mentally Retarded. 364 pp.*
Nokes, P. L. The Professional Task in Welfare Practice. *152 pp.*
Timms, Noel. Psychiatric Social Work in Great Britain (1939-1962). *280 pp.*
● Social Casework: *Principles and Practice. 256 pp.*
Young, A. F. Social Services in British Industry. *272 pp.*
Young, A. F., and **Ashton, E. T.** British Social Work in the Nineteenth Century. *288 pp.*

SOCIOLOGY OF EDUCATION

Banks, Olive. Parity and Prestige in English Secondary Education: a Study in Educational Sociology. *272 pp.*

Bentwich, Joseph. Education in Israel. *224 pp. 8 pp. plates.*

●**Blyth, W. A. L.** English Primary Education. *A Sociological Description.*
1. Schools. *232 pp.*
2. Background. *168 pp.*

Collier, K. G. The Social Purposes of Education: *Personal and Social Values in Education. 268 pp.*

Dale, R. R., and **Griffith, S.** Down Stream: *Failure in the Grammar School. 108 pp.*

Dore, R. P. Education in Tokugawa Japan. *356 pp. 9 pp. plates.*

Evans, K. M. Sociometry and Education. *158 pp.*

●**Ford, Julienne.** Social Class and the Comprehensive School. *192 pp.*

Foster, P. J. Education and Social Change in Ghana. *336 pp. 3 maps.*

Fraser, W. R. Education and Society in Modern France. *150 pp.*

Grace, Gerald R. Role Conflict and the Teacher. *150 pp.*

Hans, Nicholas. New Trends in Education in the Eighteenth Century. *278 pp. 19 tables.*

● Comparative Education: *A Study of Educational Factors and Traditions. 360 pp.*

●**Hargreaves, David.** Interpersonal Relations and Education. *432 pp.*

● Social Relations in a Secondary School. *240 pp.*

Holmes, Brian. Problems in Education. *A Comparative Approach. 336 pp.*

King, Ronald. Values and Involvement in a Grammar School. *164 pp.*

School Organization and Pupil Involvement. *A Study of Secondary Schools.*

●**Mannheim, Karl,** and **Stewart, W. A. C.** An Introduction to the Sociology of Education. *206 pp.*

Morris, Raymond N. The Sixth Form and College Entrance. *231 pp.*

●**Musgrove, F.** Youth and the Social Order. *176 pp.*

●**Ottaway, A. K. C.** Education and Society: An Introduction to the Sociology of Education. *With an Introduction by W. O. Lester Smith. 212 pp.*

Peers, Robert. Adult Education: *A Comparative Study. 398 pp.*

Pritchard, D. G. Education and the Handicapped: *1760 to 1960. 258 pp.*

Richardson, Helen. Adolescent Girls in Approved Schools. *308 pp.*

Stratta, Erica. The Education of Borstal Boys. *A Study of their Educational Experiences prior to, and during, Borstal Training. 256 pp.*

Taylor, P. H., Reid, W. A., and **Holley, B. J.** The English Sixth Form. *A Case Study in Curriculum Research. 200 pp.*

SOCIOLOGY OF CULTURE

Eppel, E. M., and **M.** Adolescents and Morality: *A Study of some Moral Values and Dilemmas of Working Adolescents in the Context of a changing Climate of Opinion. Foreword by W. J. H. Sprott. 268 pp. 39 tables.*

●**Fromm, Erich.** The Fear of Freedom. *286 pp.*
● The Sane Society. *400 pp.*
Mannheim, Karl. Essays on the Sociology of Culture. *Edited by Ernst Mannheim in co-operation with Paul Kecskemeti. Editorial Note by Adolph Lowe. 280 pp.*
Weber, Alfred. Farewell to European History: *or The Conquest of Nihilism. Translated from the German by R. F. C. Hull. 224 pp.*

SOCIOLOGY OF RELIGION

Argyle, Michael and **Beit-Hallahmi, Benjamin.** The Social Psychology of Religion. *About 256 pp.*
Nelson, G. K. Spiritualism and Society. *313 pp.*
Stark, Werner. The Sociology of Religion. *A Study of Christendom.*
Volume I. *Established Religion. 248 pp.*
Volume II. *Sectarian Religion. 368 pp.*
Volume III. *The Universal Church. 464 pp.*
Volume IV. *Types of Religious Man. 352 pp.*
Volume V. *Types of Religious Culture. 464 pp.*
Turner, B. S. Weber and Islam. *216 pp.*
Watt, W. Montgomery. Islam and the Integration of Society. *320 pp.*

SOCIOLOGY OF ART AND LITERATURE

Jarvie, Ian C. Towards a Sociology of the Cinema. *A Comparative Essay on the Structure and Functioning of a Major Entertainment Industry. 405 pp.*
Rust, Frances S. Dance in Society. *An Analysis of the Relationships between the Social Dance and Society in England from the Middle Ages to the Present Day. 256 pp. 8 pp. of plates.*
Schücking, L. L. The Sociology of Literary Taste. *112 pp.*
Wolff, Janet. Hermeneutic Philosophy and the Sociology of Art. *150 pp.*

SOCIOLOGY OF KNOWLEDGE

Diesing, P. Patterns of Discovery in the Social Sciences. *262 pp.*
●**Douglas, J. D.** (Ed.) Understanding Everyday Life. *370 pp.*
●**Hamilton, P.** Knowledge and Social Structure. *174 pp.*
Jarvie, I. C. Concepts and Society. *232 pp.*
Mannheim, Karl. Essays on the Sociology of Knowledge. *Edited by Paul Kecskemeti. Editorial Note by Adolph Lowe. 353 pp.*
Remmling, Gunter W. The Sociology of Karl Mannheim. *With a Bibliographical Guide to the Sociology of Knowledge, Ideological Analysis, and Social Planning. 255 pp.*

Remmling, Gunter W. (Ed.) Towards the Sociology of Knowledge. *Origin and Development of a Sociological Thought Style. 463 pp.*

Stark, Werner. The Sociology of Knowledge: *An Essay in Aid of a Deeper Understanding of the History of Ideas. 384 pp.*

URBAN SOCIOLOGY

Ashworth, William. The Genesis of Modern British Town Planning: *A Study in Economic and Social History of the Nineteenth and Twentieth Centuries. 288 pp.*

Cullingworth, J. B. Housing Needs and Planning Policy: *A Restatement of the Problems of Housing Need and 'Overspill' in England and Wales. 232 pp. 44 tables. 8 maps.*

Dickinson, Robert E. City and Region: *A Geographical Interpretation 608 pp. 125 figures.*

The West European City: *A Geographical Interpretation. 600 pp. 129 maps. 29 plates.*

● The City Region in Western Europe. *320 pp. Maps.*

Humphreys, Alexander J. New Dubliners: *Urbanization and the Irish Family. Foreword by George C. Homans. 304 pp.*

Jackson, Brian. Working Class Community: *Some General Notions raised by a Series of Studies in Northern England. 192 pp.*

Jennings, Hilda. Societies in the Making: *a Study of Development and Redevelopment within a County Borough. Foreword by D. A. Clark. 286 pp.*

●**Mann, P. H.** An Approach to Urban Sociology. *240 pp.*

Morris, R. N., and **Mogey, J.** The Sociology of Housing. *Studies at Berinsfield. 232 pp. 4 pp. plates.*

Rosser, C., and **Harris, C.** The Family and Social Change. *A Study of Family and Kinship in a South Wales Town. 352 pp. 8 maps.*

●**Stacey, Margaret, Batsone, Eric, Bell, Colin,** and **Thurcott, Anne.** Power, Persistence and Change. *A Second Study of Banbury. 196 pp.*

RURAL SOCIOLOGY

Chambers, R. J. H. Settlement Schemes in Tropical Africa: *A Selective Study. 268 pp.*

Haswell, M. R. The Economics of Development in Village India. *120 pp.*

Littlejohn, James. Westrigg: *the Sociology of a Cheviot Parish. 172 pp. 5 figures.*

Mayer, Adrian C. Peasants in the Pacific. *A Study of Fiji Indian Rural Society. 248 pp. 20 plates.*

Williams, W. M. The Sociology of an English Village: *Gosforth. 272 pp. 12 figures. 13 tables.*

SOCIOLOGY OF INDUSTRY AND DISTRIBUTION

Anderson, Nels. Work and Leisure. *280 pp.*

●**Blau, Peter M.,** and **Scott, W. Richard.** Formal Organizations: *a Comparative approach. Introduction and Additional Bibliography by J. H. Smith. 326 pp.*

Dunkerley, David. The Foreman. *Aspects of Task and Structure. 192 pp.*

Eldridge, J. E. T. Industrial Disputes. *Essays in the Sociology of Industrial Relations. 288 pp.*

Hetzler, Stanley. Applied Measures for Promoting Technological Growth. *352 pp.*

Technological Growth and Social Change. *Achieving Modernization. 269 pp.*

Hollowell, Peter G. The Lorry Driver. *272 pp.*

Jefferys, Margot, *with the assistance of Winifred Moss.* Mobility in the Labour Market: *Employment Changes in Battersea and Dagenham. Preface by Barbara Wootton. 186 pp. 51 tables.*

Millerson, Geoffrey. The Qualifying Associations: *a Study in Professionalization. 320 pp.*

●**Oxaal, I., Barnett, T.,** and **Booth, D.** (Eds). Beyond the Sociology of Development. *Economy and Society in Latin America and Africa. 295 pp.*

Smelser, Neil J. Social Change in the Industrial Revolution: *An Application of Theory to the Lancashire Cotton Industry, 1770–1840. 468 pp. 12 figures. 14 tables.*

Williams, Gertrude. Recruitment to Skilled Trades. *240 pp.*

Young, A. F. Industrial Injuries Insurance: *an Examination of British Policy. 192 pp.*

DOCUMENTARY

Schlesinger, Rudolf (Ed.) Changing Attitudes in Soviet Russia.

2. The Nationalities Problem and Soviet Administration. *Selected Readings on the Development of Soviet Nationalities Policies. Introduced by the editor. Translated by W. W. Gottlieb. 324 pp.*

ANTHROPOLOGY

Ammar, Hamed. Growing up in an Egyptian Village: *Silwa, Province of Aswan. 336 pp.*

Brandel-Syrier, Mia. Reeftown Elite. *A Study of Social Mobility in a Modern African Community on the Reef. 376 pp.*

Crook, David, and **Isabel.** Revolution in a Chinese Village: *Ten Mile Inn. 230 pp. 8 plates. 1 map.*

Dickie-Clark, H. F. The Marginal Situation. *A Sociological Study of a Coloured Group. 236 pp.*

Dube, S. C. Indian Village. *Foreword by Morris Edward Opler. 276 pp. 4 plates.*

India's Changing Villages: *Human Factors in Community Development. 260 pp. 8 plates. 1 map.*

Firth, Raymond. Malay Fishermen. *Their Peasant Economy. 420 pp. 17 pp. plates.*

Firth, R., Hubert, J., and **Forge, A.** Families and their Relatives. *Kinship in a Middle-Class Sector of London: An Anthropological Study. 456 pp.*

Gulliver, P. H. Social Control in an African Society: a Study of the Arusha, Agricultural Masai of Northern Tanganyika. *320 pp. 8 plates. 10 figures.*

Family Herds. *288 pp.*

Ishwaran, K. Shivapur. *A South Indian Village. 216 pp.*

Tradition and Economy in Village India: *An Interactionist Approach. Foreword by Conrad Arensburg. 176 pp.*

Jarvie, Ian C. The Revolution in Anthropology. *268 pp.*

Little, Kenneth L. Mende of Sierra Leone. *308 pp. and folder.*

Negroes in Britain. *With a New Introduction and Contemporary Study by Leonard Bloom. 320 pp.*

Lowie, Robert H. Social Organization. *494 pp.*

Peasants in the Pacific. *A Study of Fiji Indian Rural Society. 248 pp.*

Smith, Raymond T. The Negro Family in British Guiana: *Family Structure and Social Status in the Villages. With a Foreword by Meyer Fortes. 314 pp. 8 plates. 1 figure. 4 maps.*

SOCIOLOGY AND PHILOSOPHY

Barnsley, John H. The Social Reality of Ethics. *A Comparative Analysis of Moral Codes. 448 pp.*

Diesing, Paul. Patterns of Discovery in the Social Sciences. *362 pp.*

●**Douglas, Jack D.** (Ed.) Understanding Everyday Life. *Toward the Reconstruction of Sociological Knowledge. Contributions by Alan F. Blum. Aaron W. Cicourel, Norman K. Denzin, Jack D. Douglas, John Heeren, Peter McHugh, Peter K. Manning, Melvin Power, Matthew Speier, Roy Turner, D. Lawrence Wieder, Thomas P. Wilson and Don H. Zimmerman. 370 pp.*

Jarvie, Ian C. Concepts and Society. *216 pp.*

●**Pelz, Werner.** The Scope of Understanding in Sociology. *Towards a more radical reorientation in the social humanistic sciences. 283 pp.*

Roche, Maurice. Phenomenology, Language and the Social Sciences. *371 pp.*

Sahay, Arun. Sociological Analysis. *212 pp.*

Sklair, Leslie. The Sociology of Progress. *320 pp.*

International Library of Anthropology

General Editor Adam Kuper

Brown, Paula. The Chimbu. *A Study of Change in the New Guinea Highlands. 151 pp.*

Hamnett, Ian. Chieftainship and Legitimacy. *An Anthropological Study of Executive Law in Lesotho. 163 pp.*

Hanson, F. Allan. Meaning in Culture. *127 pp.*

Lloyd, P. C. Power and Independence. *Urban Africans' Perception of Social Inequality. 264 pp.*

Pettigrew, Joyce. Robber Noblemen. *A Study of the Political System of the Sikh Jats. 284 pp.*

Street, Brian V. The Savage in Literature. *Representations of 'Primitive' Society in English Fiction, 1858–1920. 207 pp.*

Van Den Berghe, Pierre L. Power and Privilege at an African University. *278 pp.*

International Library of Social Policy

General Editor Kathleen Jones

Bayley, M. Mental Handicap and Community Care. *426 pp.*

Butler, J. R. Family Doctors and Public Policy. *208 pp.*

Davies, Martin. Prisoners of Society. *Attitudes and Aftercare. 204 pp.*

Holman, Robert. Trading in Children. *A Study of Private Fostering. 355 pp.*

Jones, Kathleen. History of the Mental Health Service. *428 pp.*

Opening the Door. *A Study of New Policies for the Mentally Handicapped. 260 pp.*

Thomas, J. E. The English Prison Officer since 1850: *A Study in Conflict. 258 pp.*

Walton, R. G. Women in Social Work. *303 pp.*

Woodward, J. To Do the Sick No Harm. *A Study of the British Voluntary Hospital System to 1875. 221 pp.*

International Library of Welfare and Philosophy

General Editors Noel Timms and David Watson

● **Plant, Raymond.** Community and Ideology. *104 pp.*

Primary Socialization, Language and Education

General Editor Basil Bernstein

Bernstein, Basil. Class, Codes and Control. *3 volumes.*

1. *Theoretical Studies Towards a Sociology of Language. 254 pp.*
2. *Applied Studies Towards a Sociology of Language. 377 pp.*
3. *Towards a Theory of Educational Transmission. 167 pp.*

Brandis, W., and **Bernstein, B.** Selection and Control. *176 pp.*

Brandis, Walter, and **Henderson, Dorothy.** Social Class, Language and Communication. *288 pp.*

Cook-Gumperz, Jenny. Social Control and Socialization. *A Study of Class Differences in the Language of Maternal Control. 290 pp.*

● **Gahagan, D. M.,** and **G. A.** Talk Reform. *Exploration in Language for Infant School Children. 160 pp.*

Robinson, W. P., and **Rackstraw, Susan D. A.** A Question of Answers. *2 volumes. 192 pp. and 180 pp.*

Turner, Geoffrey J., and **Mohan, Bernard A.** A Linguistic Description and Computer Programme for Children's Speech. *208 pp.*

Reports of the Institute of Community Studies

Cartwright, Ann. Human Relations and Hospital Care. *272 pp.*

● Parents and Family Planning Services. *306 pp.*

Patients and their Doctors. *A Study of General Practice. 304 pp.*

Dench, Geoff. Maltese in London. *A Case-study in the Erosion of Ethnic Consciousness. 302 pp.*

● **Jackson, Brian.** Streaming: *an Education System in Miniature. 168 pp.*

Jackson, Brian, and **Marsden, Dennis.** Education and the Working Class: *Some General Themes raised by a Study of 88 Working-class Children in a Northern Industrial City. 268 pp. 2 folders.*

Marris, Peter. The Experience of Higher Education. *232 pp. 27 tables.*

Loss and Change. *192 pp.*

Marris, Peter, and **Rein, Martin.** Dilemmas of Social Reform. *Poverty and Community Action in the United States. 256 pp.*

Marris, Peter, and **Somerset, Anthony.** African Businessmen. *A Study of Entrepreneurship and Development in Kenya. 256 pp.*

Mills, Richard. Young Outsiders: *a Study in Alternative Communities. 216 pp.*

Runciman, W. G. Relative Deprivation and Social Justice. *A Study of Attitudes to Social Inequality in Twentieth-Century England. 352 pp.*

Willmott, Peter. Adolescent Boys in East London. *230 pp.*

Willmott, Peter, and **Young, Michael.** Family and Class in a London Suburb. *202 pp. 47 tables.*

Young, Michael. Innovation and Research in Education. *192 pp.*

● **Young, Michael,** and **McGeeney, Patrick.** Learning Begins at Home. *A Study of a Junior School and its Parents. 128 pp.*

Young, Michael, and **Willmott, Peter.** Family and Kinship in East London. *Foreword by Richard M. Titmuss. 252 pp. 39 tables.*

The Symmetrical Family. *410 pp.*

Reports of the Institute for Social Studies in Medical Care

Cartwright, Ann, Hockey, Lisbeth, and **Anderson, John L.** Life Before Death. *310 pp.*

Dunnell, Karen, and **Cartwright, Ann.** Medicine Takers, Prescribers and Hoarders. *190 pp.*

Medicine, Illness and Society

General Editor W. M. Williams

Robinson, David. The Process of Becoming Ill. *142 pp.*

Stacey, Margaret, *et al.* Hospitals, Children and Their Families. *The Report of a Pilot Study. 202 pp.*

Stimson, G. V., and **Webb, B.** Going to See the Doctor. *The Consultation Process in General Practice. 155 pp.*

Monographs in Social Theory

General Editor Arthur Brittan

● **Barnes, B.** Scientific Knowledge and Sociological Theory. *192 pp.*

Bauman, Zygmunt. Culture as Praxis. *204 pp.*

● **Dixon, Keith.** Sociological Theory. *Pretence and Possibility. 142 pp.*

Meltzer, B. N., Petras, J. W., and **Reynolds, L. T.** Symbolic Interactionism. *Genesis, Varieties and Criticisms. 144 pp.*

● **Smith, Anthony D.** The Concept of Social Change. *A Critique of the Functionalist Theory of Social Change. 208 pp.*

Routledge Social Science Journals

The British Journal of Sociology. *Managing Editor – Angus Stewart; Associate Editor – Michael Hill. Vol. 1, No. 1 – March 1950 and Quarterly. Roy. 8vo. All back issues available. An international journal publishing original papers in the field of sociology and related areas.*

Community Work. *Edited by David Jones and Marjorie Mayo. 1973. Published annually.*

Economy and Society. *Vol. 1, No. 1. February 1972 and Quarterly. Metric Roy. 8vo. A journal for all social scientists covering sociology, philosophy, anthropology, economics and history. Back numbers available.*

Religion. Journal of Religion and Religions. *Chairman of Editorial Board, Ninian Smart. Vol. 1, No. 1, Spring 1971. A journal with an interdisciplinary approach to the study of the phenomena of religion.*

Year Book of Social Policy in Britain, The. *Edited by Kathleen Jones. 1971. Published annually.*

Printed in Great Britain by Unwin Brothers Limited
The Gresham Press Old Woking Surrey
A member of the Staples Printing Group

June 1975